EDUCATION IN MULTICULTURAL SOCIETIES

Education in Multicultural Societies

Trevor Corner

Published on behalf of
The British Comparative and
International Education Society

CROOM HELM
London & Sydney

© 1984 British Comparative and International Education Society
Croom Helm Ltd, Provident House, Burrel Row,
Beckenham, Kent BR3 1AT
Croom Helm Australia Pty Ltd, First Floor, 139 King St.,
Sydney, NSW 2001, Australia

British Library Cataloguing in Publication Data

Corner, Trevor
    1. Minorities – Education
    2. Intercultural Education
    I. Title
    370 LC3715

ISBN 0-7099-3407-6

Printed and bound in Great Britain

CONTENTS

SECTION III: EDUCATION AND PLURALISM: THE DEVELOPING COUNTRIES

SECTION IV: COMPARATIVE ANALYSIS IN MULTICULTURAL EDUCATION

ACKNOWLEDGEMENTS

The act of bringing this series of papers into one volume has involved the cooperation of many people. Nigel Grant initiated and convened a conference on the theme 'Education in Multicultural Societies' which was held during the summer of 1978 in Edinburgh; his insights at that time formed the framework for the original papers, whilst his continuing enthusiasm and advice have played a major part in this publication. Keith Watson and Colin Brock, current President and Vice-President of the British Comparative and International Education Society respectively, generously agreed to and assiduously encouraged this present publication as part of the the B.C.I.E.S. series on comparative and international issues.

The original papers from the Edinburgh conference appeared in the 13th Annual Proceedings of the British Comparative Education Society. This current volume contains, in various degrees of revision, a selection of the earlier papers; these are the chapters by Nigel Grant, Alan Davies, Colin Brock, Keith Watson, Mark Bray and Charles Hoy. For the considerable work involved in revision to take into account recent changes in events and considerable shifts in thinking towards multicultural education in the countries concerned, I express my sincere thanks. The chapters on Canada and Yugoslavia, the U.S.A., and Australia are, for the most part, new papers to an international readership, as is the chapter looking at recent developments in the British Isles. To these wordsmiths scattered around the globe - Dan Dorotich, Werner Stephan, James Banks, Dudley Hick and James Lynch - I send my deep appreciation for their efforts.

I would like also to offer my thanks to Peter Sowden, of Croom Helm Publishers, for his invaluable guidance in the process of translating rough draft to symmetrical print, and to Mrs. Anne Ward, who carried out the demanding and arduous job of word-processing all the material; both gave generously of their time and skills.

FOREWORD

Multicultural education is still widely regarded as a "problem", as something to do with racial or linguistic minorities (or "immigrants"), no doubt worthy enough but peripheral to the main concerns of the educational system. Even when action is taken, it is more often than not conceived as remedial action, such as teaching more English (or French or German or whatever) to non-native speaking pupils, helping them to fit into the majority society. Some programmes go further than that - mother-tongue teaching, or more positive treatment of cultural norms - but overwhelmingly two assumptions have lain under most multicultural teaching, little challenged until recently: that it has to do with minorities, and that the eventual aim is integration, even assimilation, to the norms of the majority. It is perhaps significant that in countries as far apart as Scotland and Australia statistics are collected on pupils whose mother-tongue is not English, with little attempt to find out what languages they actually do speak; they are defined by what they lack rather than by what they have.

The authors of this book, in their various ways, attempt to take a broader and more positive view. There are case studies of societies whose multicultural composition makes it necessary to seek some way of reconciling unity and diversity in their educational systems. Developed and developing countries alike are examined, not only because they provide contrasts of wealth and the availability of educational services, but because the nature and dimensions of their multicultural composition can vary greatly; many African and Asian countries are as diverse as they are because they have inherited the artificial boundaries of the colonial period, drawn with little regard for the populations of the territories, and many developed countries have become more diverse because their prosperity has attracted immigration and settlement. This is not an absolute contrast, of course; there has been immigration in Nigeria and South-East Asia as well as Australia, Germany and the United States, and there are indigenous minorities in Canada, the Balkans and the British Isles (a fact that is still often overlooked by public authorities.) Before and after the specific case studies, general themes are also explored, including the fundamental question of language, and there are also attempts to discern generally valid patterns through the use of international comparisons and the application of comparative method.

The justification for this approach is the justification for any kind of comparative study - the use of international comparisons to establish generalisable patterns, and their value as a background of contrasts against which we can examine our own policies and practices. It is hoped, therefore, that this book will prove of interest not only to those involved in comparative and international educational studies, but to any who are concerned with one of the greatest educational challenges of our time - how to educate so that the identity and particular needs of diverse groups can be justly met within the framework both of the larger society and the international community of which it forms part. When looked at in this way, multicultural education can no longer be relegated to the periphery, as something of minority interest only; it is as relevant to majority as to minority communities, for in the international context we all belong to minority cultures - if, that is, we are to take the ideas of international understanding, "global literacy", justice and equality as anything more than well-meaning rhetoric. From this standpoint, the diversity of our societies is an asset rather than a handicap, and multicultural education is an opportunity rather than a problem.

Inevitably, in a collection of this size, there are bound to be omissions; important and relevant case-studies alone could fill several such volumes. More seriously, perhaps, there is an unevenness in the data from many countries, and a relatively underdeveloped conceptual analysis of multicultural education and its translation into policy and practice. There is, in short, a great deal of research crying out to be done, from the straight gathering of valid data to the more sophisticated analytical level. This book moves some way in this direction, and it is hoped to go further in a forthcoming volume. Essentially, the main function of this present book is to survey and sample the field, to put multicultural educational issues in their international context, and to raise some basic questions. If it helps stimulate debate and further study, it will have served its purpose.

Nigel Grant

Glasgow, 1983.

INTRODUCTION

This book is essentially about people, their diversity and the ways in which education effects and develops communication between them. It sets out to explore a 'curriculum of culture', for as Lawrence Stenhouse has written:

"Culture,... is a dynamic field within which and through which individuals make contact with one another. It lies, as it were, between people and is shared by them. In a sense man is always alone, but in sharing culture one loneliness calls out to another and is heard and understood, for to live within culture is to be able to understand, albeit in a partial way, the experience of those around us. It is on this basis that sympathy and cooperation are possible." (**Culture and Education,** 1967)

There is a second focus linking the chapters on the various countries under discussion here. Education in its practical forms has to select from the cultural environment and decide what elements of it are to be most valued. The choice, even for a single culture has been found to be an encyclopaedic task:

"The chief problem was to define the word 'culture'. In the end it emerged that virtually all aspects of life, work, play and imagination were included in the definition, which embraced subjects ranging from children's street games to portrait painting, from eating habits to marriage customs, from the Paisley shawl to the Scottish Enlightenment." (David Daiches: **A Companion to Scottish Culture,** 1981)

So much the more of a challenge is multicultural education which is shown here to be a worldwide phenomenon and of infinite complexity and variety. A general trend, discernable from the beginning of the 1970's, has been the expression of the 'neo-culturism of minorities' when a movement (in reality as much in existence before the establishment of state education systems as in present times) began to reassert itself. Perhaps a third contention is that, seen in historical and comparative perspectives, there are practical and theoretical links between the developed and developing countries which can inform the multicultural curriculum.

But if as J.J. Smolicz has written: "...cultural pluralism is to be seen as a solution to the problems of a society composed of a mosaic of ethnic cultures, this concept requires clarification and study. Unfortunately...there is still confusion between the ethnic or cultural group and the political groups within which such groups dwell" (**Culture and Education in a Plural Society,** 1979). Smolicz adds that

ethnicity - the language, culture and tradition of people - is often confused with **citizenship** - the political allegiance to a territorial state. It is perhaps inevitable that education, which reflects both, also shows the tensions within the society it serves.

The first section of the book looks at perceptions and identities across international boundaries. As chapter one indicates, there are very different levels of recognition of multiculturalism in different countries and language in education has acted as both a form of control, and even suppression, by the denial of minority language to be a medium of education. The development of a dominant national language and its encouragement through education has often been inherent in nation building. The impact on minority cultures and the smaller, nations has been in the more extreme cases, their virtual extinction.

For a country with an imperial past, and made up itself of diverse cultural and political elements, Britain has had to come to terms with the notion that dependence, and its corollary independence, developed within as well as outwith national borders. From the accepted norm that monoculture **should** exist and that education had an integral part to play in its establishment, to accepting educational plurality, implies a radical, and rapid rethink in educational policy. Chapter 2 discusses some of the implications and limitations of multicultural developments across the British Isles.

It is noted at several points throughout the book that in the different countries under discussion the importance of language has taken on a new dimension when viewed from a culturally plural standpoint. There is a danger when a person is living within two cultures that the full context inherent in language is ignored. The short and thoughtful chapter three by Alan Davies is a reminder that vital to the several functions of language is communication, in all its direct or subtle, honest or devious, guises.

Inevitably educational policy in the United States has an effect on many other countries within its sphere of influence. It is important to be aware of changes taking place in the 'melting pot' philosophy, which has informed American education, and which is increasingly being challenged. As James Banks points out in chapter four, there has been a continual tension in American education between the 'salad bowl' and 'melting pot' philosophies; the notions of equality that the dominant philosophy has promoted have been found wanting, in addition to which ethnic movements have set themselves the task of promoting multiethnic educational practice. This chapter highlights some of the very practical problems inside American elementary and high schools and the teaching strategies that assist the formation of a multicultural curriculum.

In the comparison of Canadian and Yugoslavian education and societies, Dan Dorotich and Stephan Werner can call on the experience of their personal biographies to illustrate the full cultural mosaic of these countries which have different economic and political backgrounds. The proximity of Canada to the U.S.A. and the central place of Yugoslavia in the maelstrom of languages and cultures of Central Europe makes it the more remarkable that the two countries have developed distinctive approaches to education, one pluralist, the other "multi-national".

Two chapters on Australia needs some justification: the diversity of its population, if only recently fully recognised both inside and outside of the country, demands the exposition of several viewpoints. The two chapters represent the picture as seen by Dudley Hick as a 'settled' Australian and James Lynch as a visitor trying to understand that society. Both point to the inadequacies of the "White Australia" policy and discuss recent developments in education such as the Galbally Report. Australians would probably be the first to admit that multicultural education is in the very early stages of evolution, but they would be anxious to say that some of the recent reforms are very genuine attempts at broadening the perceptions of what Australian society has to offer.

Taking the Caribbean region, or South-East Asia, or even Nigeria alone they would rival the cultural complexity of all the countries discussed previously. One of the true promises of recognising cultural pluralism is the liberation of knowledge from the straightjacket of narrow educational policy and the opening up of previously unrecognised awareness of learning and knowledge. Such a promise is not realised easily and as Colin Brock points out in chapter eight nowhere is the paradox of cultural suppression and the celebration of individual freedom more obvious than in the Caribbean cultures. The impact on the religious, linguistic and traditional lives of the many Caribbean nationalities is examined in chapter eight. This is followed by Keith Watson's detailed look at the ASEAN countries of South-East Asia, again a region which illustrates the attempts of nations to accommodate traditional culture with the inevitable presence of strong economic and political interests of the developed countries. Finally Mark Bray discusses the impact of introducing a western influenced model of education into the most populous African country and some of the consequences for the diverse tribal affiliations and rivalries in Nigeria.

Charles Hoy's comparative analysis of the chapters which precede section four effectively removes the need for any further comment here. It may only be necessary to add that the dictum "things having been described are then understood, by comparison" is very much the purpose of the book taken in whole. Finally, my thanks are given to all the contributors who have made suggestions for further reading and which have been included in the international bibliography.

1 EDUCATION FOR A MULTI-CULTURAL SOCIETY

NIGEL GRANT

It is not merely to ring the changes in wording that this title differs slightly from that of the present volume, but to emphasise a difference of approach to the theme. Other papers in this book deal with education in particular multi-cultural societies, but this one is concerned with looking at the wider scene in an attempt to clarify the context. The intention is to argue that the broader society of our time, developing through the internationalisation of institutions and life-styles, is itself becoming a multi-cultural society, and that this has inescapable implications for pluralism within existing individual societies.

It has long been customary to dismiss the problem of minorities within particular countries as a matter of peripheral concern, or to ignore them completely, or even to try to assimilate them into the majority culture, by force if need be. Perhaps the best-known example of the uniformist approach has been France[1], under governments of both Right and Left, ever since the Revolution. Barrère set the tone by declaring that "fanaticism speaks Basque, hatred of the Republic speaks Breton", and that only French, "the language of reason", could be tolerated. This policy has continued (although the Mitterand government shows signs of moderating it); true, it has been for some time possible to study Basque, Breton, Occitan and the other minority languages for the **baccaluréat** as subjects, but not to study in them as teaching media; the odd surviving notices prohibiting "spitting or speaking Breton" still sum up attitudes in most official quarters quite accurately. But if France is the classical case, it is by no means alone. Across the Pyrenees, the late Generalísimo Franco felt able to dismiss Catalan, the language of Ramon Llull and Ausias March, as the "tongue of dogs"; and during his lifetime it was rigorously excluded from the schools, as was Basque - only Castilian could be used as a medium of instruction. If this policy seemed to relax somewhat before Franco's death, with the growth of the Basque schools (**ikastolas**), this was more due to governmental

Education in a Multicultural Society

inefficiency than to any change of heart - the Spanish
authorities remained hostile to these developments, but were
unable to do much about them. It took a major overhaul of the
apparatus of the Spanish state to allow even moderate
recognition to the minorities.[2]

But there are plenty of examples from the Anglophone world
as well. Teddy Rooseveldt was doubtless echoing the
sentiments of most of his compatriots when he declared that
there was room in America for only one language, namely
English; and in the British Isles the policy of extirpating
the Celtic languages has been pursued for centuries, was still
going on actively in some places within living memory, and
still continues at least covertly in some parts of Great
Britain, especially in Scotland. If there has been some
change of heart, it is uneven at best - quite supportive in
Wales, and varying from official neutrality and effective
foot-dragging in Scotland to strong support in some regions,
clear hostility in others.[3]

Such attitudes are, of course, easier to sustain within
the borders of nation states, especially when contacts with
other cultures are minimal (or one-sided, as in the colonial
relationship.) But the situation has changed. With the
growth of internationalism, and the development of suprana-
tional complexes such as the EEC and Nordic Council, we are
all minorities now, even the English, the French and the
Germans. Unless we care to presuppose the gradual merging of
the various national cultures into some homogeneous super-
culture - a highly dubious proposition - even those who belong
to national majorities will have to get used to forming with
other cultures relationships based not on dominance but on
cooperation and coexistence. If this seems unduly difficult,
it is as well to remember that (as Alan Davies points out
elsewhere in this book) multi-culturalism is the norm, not the
exception[4]. The idea seems to have dawned, in some quarters
at least, hence the large number of educational conferences,
seminars and publications that have been trying to tackle this
particular theme, in its various aspects, over the last few
years.

So familiar is the idea now that it comes as something of
a shock to realise how recent it is. The problems have been
there for a long time, but have generally been ignored (even
by comparativists, thus demonstrating that they are not
necessarily immune to the ethnocentrism of the cultures to
which they belong.) But it is not difficult to see why this
should be so. The forces favouring increasing cultural
homogeneity have been powerful in the past, and remain so - so
powerful that until a few years ago there were few who doubted
that they were quite irresistable[5].

Some of these forces are political, probably the most
obvious and most readily identifiable, which is why

beleaguered minorities have so often asserted their identity through political demands, whether for some kind of limited autonomy or outright independence. But this, important though it may be, is only one factor; political independence (or some modification thereof) may well provide the opportunity and some of the powers needed to sustain cultural integrity, but is no guarantee. Independence has not managed to halt the decline of the Irish language, nor has the battery of measures adopted by governments of the Republic since its inception[6]. In Quebec, similarly, provincial autonomy (including total control of the educational system) within a federal framework did not prevent the continuing erosion of French by English, even though the French-speakers remained a large majority in the Province - hence the attempts by the Parti Québecois government to strengthen the position of French by the controversial Loi 101[7]. Clearly, forces other than the political are at work.

Mobility is probably one of the strongest of these. In the British Isles, for instance, there has long been migration from west to east in Ireland, from the Highland and Islands to the Lowlands in Scotland, from north to south in Wales, and from all of these smaller countries to England (especially the south-east) and further afield. Not only has this shifted the balance of population; it has had a drastic effect on the viability of the minority cultures.

Scottish Gaeldom is a case in point. Like other minority cultures, the Gàidhealtachd has been subjected to political pressures for centuries. These came from independent Scottish governments long before the Union of 1707; James VI and I was particularly zealous in his attempts to wipe out the Gaelic language. An Act of Privy Council of 1616 declared that "the vulgar Inglishe toung sall be universallie plantit, and the Irishe language, which the one of the principall causis of the continewance of barbaritie and incivilite in the Heylandis and Ilandis, be abolisheit and removeit." (Note the use of "Irish" to deny to Gaelic the status of being an indigenous language at all.) The main device to secure this goal was to be the foundation of schools using English only.[8]

This, and similar measures, had little effect at the time, partly because the resources for the establishing of schools were usually lacking. The really severe blows to Gaeldom were the Battle of Culloden and the subsequent repression, which broke the political base of Gaelic society (affecting even the clans which had supported the Government) and the Highland Clearances of the 19th Century - particularly the latter. Before people were cleared off the land to make room for sheep, half the population lived in the Highlands; since then, with continuing economic decline, the proportion has dropped to under 10 per cent. Although the school system has been vigorous since the 19th Century, its very successes have contributed to the decay of the area. As higher education is available only in the major cities, or near them, academic success has usually meant leaving the Highlands. Lack of job opportunities has had the same effect, a constant bleeding away of many of the ablest and most ambitious young people. The school system, most of the time, has assiduously fostered the use of English only[9]. In any case, it has come to be seen as a system of training for emigration, which has led to a devaluation of the language and culture as irrelevant to job-seeking in the Lowlands or further afield. Many parents even came to think of it as a handicap, and acquiesced in having their children's own language taught out of them, and even beaten out of them. Even today, such attitudes, the result of two centuries of brain-washing as well as the lack of local opportunities, can be encountered readily enough.

True, there has in recent years been some reversal of the drift of population away from the Highlands, but there are circumstances in which inward mobility can have just as devastating effect on small and vulnerable cultures. Incomers, especially if they come in force, can swamp the local language and culture by sheer numbers, particularly since they see no need to learn Gaelic - they are representatives of a familiar, majority, uni-lingual culture coming into one which is essentially bilingual. (This lies behind much of the strong opposition to plans to establish a large NATO base in Stornoway; they have seen what this kind of thing can do often enough already, quite apart from the prospect of being turned into a prime target.) Thus, the indigenous language is diluted further, even in its former strongholds. Similar developments have been noted in Wales, in the Irish Gaeltachta, in the Basque country, in Brittany and a host of other places; minority areas like Catalonia, which seem able to absorb immigrants from other parts of Spain and assimilate them, are the exception. There, the population is sufficiently numerous to withstand some incursion without loss of identity - there are about six or seven million Catalan speakers, after all, which is a vastly stronger base than Gaelic-speaking Scotland, where the latest Census returns showed about 80,000 altogether, including the substantial numbers who live outside the Highlands and are therefore even more vulnerable to language erosion[10]. There is possibly a practical point too: Catalan is close enough to Castilian and its variants to make learning it a relatively easy matter, while learning Gaelic is a quite different matter for an English speaker.

Language is such an obvious characteristic of most cultures that it is tempting to concentrate on it, since the effects of change can be clearly observed; but there are other determinants of identity too, also liable to be affected by mobility, or even the prospect of it. In the USA, for example, there is virtually no machinery to ensure conformity at national level in education; indeed, the climate of political opinion, and of course the Constitution itself, would seem to favour decentralisation and variety. The individual States, not the Federal Government, control the educational systems, and most in practice leave the bulk of decision-making - and fund-raising - to local school districts. In spite of this, given the size and variety of the country, the surprising thing is the degree of similarity in the structure, organisation, content and ethos of education from coast to coast. It is a complex phenomenon, and it would be unwise to oversimplify or overstress it; but there are good reasons for supposing that here too mobility is just as powerful as political forces. If the average American family now moves every three of four years, taking its values and expectations with it, and if the school systems are so organised as to respond to parental wishes more than in most countries, the lack of political machinery need not surprise us; it is not necessary.

There are many examples of this mechanism at work, some of which come very close to home (such as the erosion of the generalist currriculum in Scotland by the importation of specialist assumptions into Scotland from England, or the prospect of having to seek further study or employment outside Scotland - as witness recent moves to introduce the 'A' level examinations in certain Edinburgh schools), but one example will serve to illustrate the process in an extreme form. The Isle of Man, in education and in other things (apart from foreign policy and defence), is quite independent of the English system, not being part of the United Kingdom at all; and yet, in spite of the absence of any machinery for enforcing it, the school system is far more like the English system than is the Scottish, which does have such a link. The key to this seeming paradox is the absence of any higher educational provision on Man. Thus, on the one hand, Manx students going on to the higher stage have to seek it in Britain, and usually in England. The schools are thus under pressure to provide qualifications acceptable for English university entrance; and the tendency for examinations to influence the whole curriculum, even of those who will not be proceeding further, is tolerably well known. On the other hand, having no teacher training system of its own, Man has to rely on the English system; and even though those appointed to teaching posts are usually Manx themselves, they have been trained in England and have received their experience and assumptions there. Thus, at two vital and mutually reinforcing points, mobility contrives to bring the Manx system close to the English, probably closer than any political link would accomplish[11].

Publication, and the mass media generally, have also made themselves felt. This is not, of course, a new process. In Britain, the King James Bible, comprehensible enough in Scotland to make a separate Scots edition seem unnecessary, effectively reduced Lowland Scots from a literary and court language to a collection of dialects (which even now use standard English as an external referent, even among those seeking to withdraw from it.)[12] Later, we find Hume, who spoke Scots, writing in English in order to reach a wider readership – a process we still see in the steady acceptance of American terms (once thought odd or inelegant) into normal British usage, even on the BBC. Radio and television have, of course, greatly speeded up the process, and here again the media are no respecters of regional or national boundaries. It is possible to lay much of the responsibility of Welsh and Gaelic at the door of the broadcasting authorities, but this happens in Ireland too, where it is just as easy (in Dublin at least) to tune in to BBC or Ulster TV as to Radio Telefis Eireann. Textbooks, too, can encourage the centralisation of norms (as witness many of the "British" histories used in Scottish and Welsh schools, which present a consistently Anglocentric, and sometimes astonishingly myopic, point of view.)[13] The smaller countries do have their own presses and publishing houses, but the economics of the business (especially nowadays) favours maximisation of the market, hence falling in with the majority and standardising norms. This is not confined to complexes like the British Isles; the need to rely to a great extent on English language material affects Scandinavia as well as the Celtic areas, though less drastically as yet.

Not only are cultures affected thus; even the ways of thinking about education can be influenced, for the media are an important source of information and, perhaps more important, the ideas and associations that go with it. Most people's sources of information are limited; they rely on their own experience of school (or such as they can remember), on their children's experience (or such as their children, or their teachers, choose to tell them), and on the media. It is therefore more than likely that parents in Scotland or even Ireland have more exposure to fictional accounts of English or even American education on TV than to any of their own systems. No wonder that such terms as 'O' level, 11 plus, direct grant, "public" school, and the like, are in common if inaccurate use, even among pupils and teachers. When it is remembered that words can bring their own auras of association with them, it is not surprising that the media can encourage the homogenisation of the educational climate aswell as the culture of a whole cluster of countries. (That such "normalisation" can be based on misconceptions and even ignorance, and that it usually works in a random manner, raises practical and policy problems that make it impossible to shrug the whole thing off as a normal evolutionary process.)

One way in which systems influence each other is in the importation of models. (The media can make these widely available too.) Sometimes models are forced by one culture on another, particularly in imperial relationships; Macauley's recommendation of a British-style system for India, or the French imposing their own system, right down to details of curriculum, on the parts of Africa they ruled, are classic examples of this. (It often went to ludicrous extremes, like teaching children in Guiné or Dahomey that their ancestors had been tall blond men from across the Alps.) But imperial rule is not necessary; many of these models have survived independence, even turning into caricatures of themselves. Political hegemony, no less than direct rule, may encourage the adoption of models. A familiar case of this is the widespread copying of Soviet practice in Eastern Europe after the Second World War - again, often to an absurd extent, far beyond what could be justified by the argument that the USSR was the only country with the experience of trying to translate Marxist-Leninist theory into educational practice[14].

But prestige, academic or merely social, may be enough, and it need not necessarily be part of a general political or cultural deference (though of course it often is.) Sir Walter Scott, for instance, was largely instrumental in founding the Edinburgh Academy, quite deliberately on the model of the English "public" schools; and some of the Scottish universities during the 19th Century, and again during the 20th, have been particularly liable to infatuation with southern models, especially from Oxford and Cambridge - helped, of course, by the presence of a great many academics from these very places, bringing their habits and assumptions with them. It is sometimes tempting to see the influence of the media at work here too; surely, it is more reasonable to attribute the spectacle of Scottish day schools grouping their pupils into "houses" (and even trying to inculcate loyalty to these quite arbitrary entities) to the recollection of school stories than to any policy worked out from first principles.

Usually, the model of the greater influences the lesser, hence the spread of polytechnical education and unified schooling in the Eastern bloc, or élitism and specialisation in the UK. Not always, however: it **can** happen that a major change is contemplated within a majority system which has no appropriate model of its own to work from, and in such cases convenient models may be sought elsewhere, even from nearby minority systems. Thus, the development of the English civic universities in the 19th century relied heavily on Scottish models. More recently, the Keele Foundation Year and the Open University's credit system owed a good deal to Scottish practice, with some American modifications - partly because, doubtless, the first Vice-Chancellors of both institutions were Scots (with American experience), but also because, as before, the English system had little of relevance to offer in these areas. The spread of the Folk High Schools from Denmark to the rest of Scandinavia shows something of the same mechanism at work[15].

Finally, there is what might be termed the mechanism of coordination. Unlike the others mentioned so far, this is a relative newcomer, and is still in the embryonic stage; but it can be discerned when a group of countries deliberately seeks to find points in the individual systems where some cooperation or equivalence can be organised in the interests of the whole group, without seeking to have one system absorb or even dominate the others. One example - tentative as yet - may be found in the workings of the EEC. There is no specific provision in the Treaty of Rome concerning education, but two of its clauses do have educational implications: the provision for free movement of labour within the Community, and the move towards the harmonisation of professional qualifications[16]. The latter, in particular, is bound to have important effects on higher education and, eventually, on the school systems too. The numbers involved are certainly small in relation to the total school and college enrolments, but one can discern the well-known Law of Filtration or Knock-on Effect here: what happens to the most prestigious courses - law, medicine and, on the Continent at least, engineering - is liable to affect other faculties; the tendencey of other institutions of higher education to emulate the universities is a familiar international phenomenon; so is the impact of university and college requirements on school terminal examinations, whether there is a formalised link or not; and even if the pupils concerned with these are in minority courses (or even separate schools), their capacity to set the pace for other schools and courses is also well-known. Thus, intentionally or not, the coordination of higher professional training is likely to make itself felt, eventually, right down through the whole school system. Nor is the EEC the only body with such harmonisation in mind; the Nordic Council has made the first hesitant moves in this direction[17]. The process is in the very earliest stages, and there is evidence of a considerable degree of national resistance or evasion, but this would seem to be a likely development in the future.

Up to the present, these factors have seemed to work unchecked, reinforcing the assumption that there was an inevitable logic favouring the normalisation of all variants to one preferred culture (or what used to be called, with more confidence than we can muster nowadays, "civilisation" - usually defined as one's own particular culture.) Throughout most recorded history, this view has scarcely been challenged - not, at any rate, by those who wrote the histories. The civilisations of Greece and Rome made practically no concessions to the cultures of peoples they overwhelmed or supplanted; the single exception was Roman deference to the militarily vanquished Greeks, but this arose from a feeling of cultural inferiority on their part, not from tolerance. Everyone else was "barbarian", and became acceptable only on so far as they assimilated to Greek and Roman ways.

Likewise, mediaeval Christendom, though technically defining its identity by adherence to religious doctrine, made it clear whenever the occasion arose that this was not separable from other cultural norms. At any rate, it was not just the churches that followed the expansion of Christendom, but languages, dress, building styles, diet, social mores, everything; it is doubtful if the separation of any of these things would have occurred to anyone at the time. The expanding Muslim civilisation with which expanding Christendom clashed took much the same view. Although the Arabs proved ready to accept aspects of other cultures which appealed to them, they absorbed them and made them their own; and although they tolerated Christians and Jews as "people of the Book", that was as far as it went. Otherwise, Islamicisation meant Arabisation, hence the dramatic spread of the Arabic language; culturally, the Qur'ān did not travel alone[18].

But such "normalisation" did not necessarily depend on conquest. It characterised the "Enlightenment" of the 18th Century no less than the Imperialism of the 20th, the spread of the 20th Century "Global Village" no less than the forceful settlement of the New World. Travel, trade, conversion, economic pressure and cultural prestige, all have tended to favour the adoption of dominant cultures, whether accompanied by arms or not. Most articulate commentators have regarded this as inevitable or even desirable; even those being "normalised" tended to accept the process as being in the nature of things.

There have, of course, been some cracks in the pattern, especially in modern times. In Europe, the 19th Century saw increasing restlessness among submerged nationalities, whether they were asserting their identity against the Ottoman Empire or against the culturally much closer empire of the Habsburgs. This century has seen the collapse of the various European Empires, and varying degrees of cultural reassertion by peoples of the Third World[19]. (This has, naturally, taken different forms, from an adaptation of "Western" modes to political radicalism to conservative or obscurantist revivals, like some of the Islamic fundamentalist movements.) But even the more settled European and North American states, long-established and generally stable politically (at least relatively), have been discovering that the recrudesence of national and cultural minorities is not a phenomenon confined to the Balkans, Mitteleuropa or the Third World. In Canada, there are the well-publicised efforts by the Québecois to be "maîtres chez soi", but other groups too, native and immigrant alike, have been expressing their disinclination to be swallowed up by the larger society. In Great Britain, there is the continuing restlessness of the Scots and Welsh (in the former case, both confused and exacerbated by the failure of central government to implement a majority vote for self-government on a limited scale in 1979.)[20] Ireland is a more

15

complex case, involving minorities within minorities, but many of the developments there fit the general patterns. In Spain, the Basques and Catalans have been pressing for the restoration of their former rights, with some measure of success; and so on[21]. The neat uniformity from frontier to frontier looks a good deal less neat now, in spite of the strength of the unifying forces already mentioned.

There are various ways in which a group may express its identity. Language is a common one, as we have seen; it is particularly conspicuous, has deep psychological roots, and can act as a vehicle for a culture on many levels. Few groups differ from their neighbours in language only, but it is an obvious characteristic to emphasise, as it can symbolise so many other things at the same time. (The use of one's language in schools may also be an easier concession to obtain than major political or constitutional change.) Thus, the Catalans in Spain, the Flemings in Belgium, the Macedonians in Yugoslavia, and the Georgians, Armenians and others in the USSR, are among the groups that have fixed on language as the sine qua non of their identity. (In the case of the Soviet nationalities, this is one kind of differentiation recognised by the authorities, whereas others might not be.)

But in other cases the clearest distinguishing feature may be religion, as in Northern Ireland; whichever group we are thinking about there, it must be obvious that religious affiliation is one of a whole cluster of criteria - cultural, historical, social, economic - but it is the most conspicuous and, like language in other cases, touches on so many aspects of life, including the schools. In Yugoslavia, the Bosnians are linguistically indistinguishable from the Serbs, but find it convenient to summarise their historical differences by referring to their religion; indeed, "Muslim" is generally taken in the Census to mean Bosnian, though not all Bosnians are Muslims, and there are Muslims among the other nationalities as well, notably the Albanians.[22]

But it is not always as clear as this. Although language is a prominent issue in Wales, only a minority of the Welsh actually speak it; yet the anglophone majority are emphatic that they are not English. There is not all that much difference in language (or religion) between the Scots and the English, Montenegrins and Serbs, Slovaks or Czechs or, for that matter, between Danes and Norwegians or Canadians and Americans; yet, however imprecise it may be, these smaller groups have a powerful sense of historic identity, a different historical experience, which still shapes the way they look at things and the way they define themselves. Group identity may even be invented - the "Nation of Islam" or Black Muslim movement in the United States is a classic example of a group seeking to give its identity, hitherto culturally unfocussed, some more precise expression. (If this is thought to have its slightly comical aspect, it is as well to remember that one highly successful and much-admired political settlement of antiquity, the Constitution of Kleisthenes in Athens, was also completely artificial, and yet was readily accepted - made-up tribes, eponymous ancestors and all.)[23]

Not that it is always necessary to separate these criteria, as there is often a combination of them involved anyway. The Tamils of Sri Lanka assert their language against the pressures of Sinhala, but also their Hinduism against the Buddhism of the majority. Symbols of this kind may be seized upon to illustrate a difference already felt but difficult to put the finger on, like the fairly recent willingness of Lowland Scots to adopt certain features of Highland culture as their own - things like national dress, once thought alien and barbarous but now seen as conveniently distinctive; many are even going to the considerable labour of learning Gaelic for much the same reason. Finally, one finds increasing use made of the social and political arguments for decentralisation. This is not, of course, confined to national and cultural minorities, but can provide a useful rationale for a more deep-seated unease.

Whatever criteria emerge as major issues, it does seem that there is a growing reluctance on the part of minorities (however defined) to be totally assimilated into a larger and stronger culture. It should not need saying, but this mood is not necessarily one of "seperatism" (whatever that means), still less one of hostility towards the majority; but, since majorities have consistently failed to understand this, and have often seen even the mildest assertions of identity by minorities as a threat or an affront, it should perhaps be spelled out: it is not a question of hostility at all, and in the normal run of things even the most vociferous of minorities are bound to maintain close links with neighbouring majorities. It is a question of identity, a preference for being oneself rather than a copy of someone else. (Being denied this may, of course, produce hostility, but that is a different matter.) As this general growth in group self-awareness, whether expressed in cultural or political terms, has been happening just at the point when the unifying pressures have seemed stronger than ever, it is necessary to speculate on possible reasons for this (on the face of it) surprising development.

One likely element in this is a growing sense of alienation from ever more remote central authority. Issues have become more complex, and central authorities (even if we assume good will on their part, which often requires some stretching of credulity) find them ever more difficult to handle sensitively. Thus, the idea that "small is beautiful" in culture and politics as well becomes more attractive. In addition, there are some practical difficulties such as pressure on parliamentary time or the cost of travel. (Someone remarked during the Referendum debate in Scotland in 1979 that one strong argument for Devolution was the cost of the air fare from Edinburgh to London, thus making it more difficult to catch the ear of the central powers in Westminster; it was swiftly pointed out that a ticket from Edinburgh to Shetland costs even more, which gives the Isles a case for particular consideration too.) Of course, considerations of this kind apply to outlying parts of majority cultures too; the difference here is that such groups may have the same sense of alienation, but lack a distinctive identity to focus their disquiet. With minorities, it is otherwise.

It is also relevant that many majority groups have lost prestige in the last few decades, the "metropolitan powers" in particular. The collapse of empires has not only meant a reduced role for countries like Britain and France, but has made it more tempting for minorities to re-examine their relationships with the larger units. The British Empire was, among other things, a means of channelling the energies of the more ambitious and well-trained Scots and Irish away from a society that was unable to make full use of their talents; but with that avenue closed, frustrations once avoided have come to the surface, including some doubts among the minorities about the acceptability of an overriding "British" identity. But apart from traumatic events like the collapse of empires, there has also been some loss of confidence among the metropolitan societies themselves that their norms are necessarily valid for themselves, let along anyone else. World recession, the shifting balance of power, the pace of change - all of these have made their mark, and have cast some doubt on the former certainties in educational thinking as well as in other fields. Contrast, for example, the worried self-doubt of the "Great Debate" with the confident, almost euphoric optimism of the post-war period in Great Britain; there are many parallels elsewhere. Ironically, one of the more positive reactions to changing circumstances, the "lifelong learning" movement, implies recognition of the permanence of uncertainty. In this atmosphere, it is perhaps not surprising that minority cultures are more prepared to look to their own norms, in education as in other things.

Finally, as already suggested, there is the inter-nationalisation of institutions, including educational ones. This may happen within formal structures like the EEC, the Nordic Council or the Pacto Andino, with their various attempts to harmonise professional qualifications, under the pressures already mentioned: the British Isles, the anglophone and francophone worlds and the Eastern European bloc are obvious examples of this type of association, in which institutions can influence each other strongly. But though these larger supra-national complexes are now a fact of life, they are too large to identify with readily, and in any case the very strength of the majority cultures within them makes homogenisation less likely. In other circumstances, one might expect the Scottish system to assimilate to the English pattern, the Bulgarian to the Soviet and even the Canadian to the American (though all of these raise some doubts); but it is harder to envisage a homogeneous culture and educational system that can embrace England, France, West Germany and Denmark[24]. Thus, major national systems themselves are going to have to collaborate in a pluralist relationship, are going to have to get used to the idea that there can be several valid ways of going about things, while still maintaining and developing points of contact.

Viewed in this way (and making the necessary though often overlooked distinction between integration and assimilation), it becomes possible to argue that European integration is quite compatible with Scottish and Welsh devolution, Basque and Catalan autonomy and similar cases of minority resurgence. The argument can be taken further; they are part of the same process - different parts, to be sure, but as closely connected as the two sides of a coin. Having recognised this, one of the main tasks of educational systems, large and small, is to find ways of meeting the double imperative: to retain and, more important, to develop their own identities, while establishing points of contact, coordination and interchange.

But having said that - and declaring in favour of internationalism, pluralism and multiculturalism is as easy, and as limited, as declaring in favour of virtue (there are difficulties of definition in either case) - one must recognise that there is a great deal more to be done. It is necessary to escape from the "either-or" cultural impasse that has caused so much trouble in the past, and recognise that such a choice is not necessary, and indeed that it is not really possible. We are all several people: one can be simultaneously human, western, European, British, Scots and Highland, for example, with some of these more prominent in the consciousness than others, but all in existence. We can all compose our own lists, and identify our own main points of emphasis, which will vary according to time and circumstance. The important thing is to recognise that they exist, and can coexist.

How, then, can identity be recognised in educational systems, in accordance with the criteria mentioned?

In the case of language, some systems have little difficulty with this. The USSR, Yugoslavia, Switzerland, Belgium and many others have, so to speak, multi-lingualism built into their population patterns, and as a rule recognise this in the organisation of their educational provision, with instruction being given in the children's mother tongue; in the last three cases, indeed, the balance of the population is such that there is not even one overriding national language taught in addition to the vernaculars. In Canada, the position is more complex[25]. At the level of the Federal

19

Government, the country is officially bilingual; but the entire range of educational provision is a provincial concern, and there policies differ considerably. Only one province is officially bilingual, namely New Brunswick; Ontario and Quebec, in spite of the present of large French-speaking and English-speaking minorities respectively, are officially unilingual, though they do make some concessions to their minorities (albeit grudgingly) in the matter of schooling. Other systems, like the Scottish and the Welsh, have moved from a position of suppressing minority languages to one of official encouragment in the first case and alleged "neutrality" on the other, though there are indications that active hostility lingers on. Other systems again, like those of the USA and Spain, are being pushed by events in the direction of linguistic pluralism, while others are still strenuously resisting this; in France, for example, the settled policy right up to the change of government was still rigidly centralist for long-standing historical reasons, and the Mitterand government has, so far, done little more than declare a change of intent; and in Malaysia there is actually a move away from linguistic pluralism, as the government seeks to advance the position of Bahasa Malaysia at the expense not only of English but of Chinese and Tamil as well[26]. In this last case, as in many others, we see linguistic-educational decisions being affected by broader political considerations, especially in countries where there is a fear of strong centrifugal tendencies that might threaten the very existence of the state. Even in systems where multilingualism is official policy, similar considerations have sometimes encouraged covert centrism, as in certain well-documented cases of Russifying pressures in parts of the Soviet Union where separatism is a matter of frequent anxiety to the authorities, notably in the Ukraine and the Baltic Republics[27].

In principle, however, this is not a great problem; it is quite possible to concede and even encourage mother-tongue instruction without having to make any changes in content, structure or policy. The Welsh system, for example, differs from the English not at all in structure; and in the USSR, for all the use of the vernaculars in non-Russian schools, the content of schooling differs hardly at all, the structure is practically identical and, most important of all, policy and ideological objectives are uniform throughout.

There are cases, however, where the structure of the system itself may reflect a distinctive philosophy, historical experience or cultural ethos. Within the United Kingdom, Scotland (but not Wales) is distinguished by certain important differences in examinations and curriculum, particularly at secondary and higher level. These (contrary to the exasperated incomprehension of many English residents and observers) are not arbitrary, but arise from a tradition of curricular breadth, as opposed to the English preference for specialisation; and this approach, seriously eroded though it has been by some of the pressures already mentioned, has been shaped by differences of social and cultural attitudes that are as deeply involved in Scottish national consciousness as language is in the Welsh. This mode of expressing identity is relatively uncommon, but should not be ignored for that reason[28]. It may well become commoner, as smaller groups become more inclined to tackle their problems in their own ways rather than copy someone else; for that reason, if for no other, the international community will have to get used to it.

In some systems, religion is officially recognised as a major determinant of identity, and allowed for accordingly in the organisation of schools. This is particularly striking in Northern Ireland, where the whole community is split along religious lines (themselves symbolising more deep-seated historical, cultural, political and, frequently, economic divisions.) The school system is therefore divided on religious criteria more than on any other; it is possible to place someone in a wide spectrum of social niches simply by identifying the person's former school. The same is true to a lesser extent in parts of Scotland, where a system of Catholic schools exists within the public system, differing only in denominational affiliation. In the Netherlands, there are in effect three parallel systems - Protestant, Catholic and the State secular system - a division which is repeated in many other institutions in Dutch society. In Quebec, there are Catholic and Protestant school boards; these used to cater almost exclusively for the French and English speaking populations respectively, but the recent influx of immigrants who are of neither tongue (and, increasingly, of neither faith) has cast doubt on the reliability of this classification for the future. In a great many other systems, this classification does not figure at all, given the official hostility to any form of religion; the same is true of the USA, for rather different reasons, within the public system at least. Finally, there are the theocratically-ruled states, Muslim, Buddhist or varieties of Christian, where the national system is religious by definition.

These criteria are readily identifiable; the real difficulties arise when group identity rests on a much less easily definable set of social values or group mores, which may or may not claim divine sanction; and this becomes even more difficult when a minority holds important, as a basic matter of identity, values that run counter to those of society as a whole. To declare in favour of pluralism and tolerance is one thing; but it needs to be asked how far any society (or, for that matter, an international community) is prepared to go.

Some societies have little difficulty with this if all

that is involved is dropping out of the educational system by
a minority, like the Amish in the USA or the Exclusive
Brethren in the United Kingdom. There remains, nonetheless, a
dilemma no less real for having been ducked: if a minority
sect or group is opposed to higher education, tolerance of
minority modes may dictate that society should not interfere
if a young person is prevented from taking it. But is this
not regarding that person as the possession of others? Is
this not a denial of his rights, as defined by the wider
community? And how can a society committed to compulsory
schooling for all react if some such group is opposed, for
whatever reason, to schooling of any kind? If this last
question seems hypothetical, it still has to be faced, for
versions of it have already turned up within the UK. Some
Muslim immigrant groups, for example, have already let it be
known that they find some of the practices of the host society
unacceptable for their daughters - coeducation, sometimes, or
physical education that involves "immodesty". This may seem
relatively trivial, but it can take more serious forms -
arranged marriages, semi-purdah, even the killing of sexually
delinquent daughters and their lovers. Whether these
practices and attitudes are essential parts of Muslim culture
is for Muslims to argue[29]; but how far can they, or even the
discouragement of girls' scholastic advancement, be accepted
in a country where sex equality is a matter of law?

In some countries, the authorities at least are quite
clear where they stand. The Soviet Union's view is summed up
(although usually without the attribution, nowadays) in
Stalin's phrase "a culture national in form but socialist in
content" - in other words, cultural pluralism is accepted and
even encouraged in language or cuisine, dress or artistic
idiom, but emphatically not in social values. Children,
therefore, may be taught in Armenian or Tadzhik or Moldavian
or whatever, but with practically the same curriculum and the
same set of socio-political values.[30] Some attention is given
to local literary and historical traditions also, as long as
they do not encourage separatist sentiments. Children in
Transcaucasia and Central Asia are taught in their own
languages, but never come across the names of Shamyl or Yakub
Beg, the charismatic leaders of resistance to (Tsarist)
Russian expansionism in the 19th Century[31].

Most of us are probably less sure of the validity of our
own norms, but the problem remains. The earnest and often
courageous men who went as missionaries to Polynesia and
Melanesia had no such doubts. We may laugh now at their
naively total conviction and their appalling prudery, and
doubt the wisdom, the necessity and the motivation of draping
brown bosoms in hideous pinafores in the name of Christ; but
would we take quite such a tolerant view of headhunting,
mutilation and ritual murder[32]? The question is not likely
to arise now in quite such an extreme form but, one way or

another, the decision will have to be made where to draw the line. Multiculturalism, after all, means not only the acceptance of different cultures, but their coexistence and cooperation. It is not possible to dissect the problems here, let alone offer solutions, but it is just as well to be ready for them.

There is another one that has already made itself obvious enough: the measures taken by a minority culture for its own defence may take a form that suppresses the identity of other groups in their turn. Thus, Hungary battled long and hard to assert its own identity - cultural, linguistic and political - against being absorbed by that of Austria under the Dual Monarchy. But, on winning autonomy within the Empire, the Hungarians promptly denied the Slovaks, Croats, Romanians and others within their own part of the Empire the very rights they had so strenuously sought for themselves. As for Quebec, it is easy to see how the French-speakers could feel threatened, first by the social and economic dominance of English, then by the tendency of immigrants coming to Montreal to learn English, the more influential of the two official languages of Canada as a whole, rather than French. In this situation, the desire to tip the balance in favour of French, even if it did mean some kind of legal action, is entirely understandable; but there are dangers in the pressures now being put on the anglophone minority under Loi 101, and there are also the usual risks of falling into bureaucratic absurdities like compelling shopkeepers to put up signs in French only, or forcing English-speaking Canadians from other provinces to send their children to French schools[33]. Like the "tokenism" of compulsory (but often ineffective) Irish, measures of this kind can be both counter-productive, and also detrimental to the rights of other minorities. The issue is not simple, but it does pinpoint the need for greater sensitivity on the part of majorities and minorities alike.

Finally, there is the danger of falling into a merely conservationist position, seeking to preserve all the aspects of a threatened culture even if this means a commitment to social and educational stagnation. This is unlikely to work in any case, in the long run; the logic of internationalisation is against it, and this too can be counterproductive. It must seem obvious enough that if the use of a minority language comes to be associated with the more backward-looking aspects of a culture, this is unlikely to enhance its standing with the younger generation on which its future depends[34]. Cultures are growing things, to be developed rather than just preserved; and they are complex things, not monolithic entities to be embraced or rejected in toto.

Now, getting educational systems to face this task - fostering and developing the children's own cultures, and at the same time preparing them for the wider world in which they will have to cope with other cultures as well, is a formidably difficult one; there are bound to be tensions, within as well as between systems. But to fail to attempt either is to rob them of an essential part of their human identity. Naturally, schools can not do this alone, but they can help by using the fact of human variety as the basis for cooperation rather than conflict. It will not be easy; but there is no really acceptable alternative if internationalisation is to mean anything more than the old dominance game re-labelled, and if identity is to mean anything more than obscurantism or self-obsession. To foster this necessary dual awareness, to build it into educational policy, and to translate it into actual decisions on the structure and content of education, will keep us, as educationists, busy enough for the rest of the present century at least. In this task, the particularly valuable contribution that comparative education can make should hardly need to be stressed.

NOTES AND REFERENCES

1. C.T. Marks, "Policy and attitudes towards the teaching of standard dialect: Great Britain,France, W.Germany". **Comparative Education.** Vol. 12, No. 3, 1976, pp.199-218.

2. Meic Stephens, **Linguistic Minorities in Western Europe** (Gomer Press, Llandysul, 1977), pp.603-632. John McNair, "The contribution of the schools to the restoration of regional autonomy in Spain." **Comparative Education,** Vol.16, No.1, 1980, pp.33-34.

3. Neil Munro, "Neutral" attitude to bilingual teaching offends. **Times Educational Supplement Scotland,** 25 December 1981. F. MacLeod and J. Murray, "The bilingual project in the Western Isles of Scotland." In Jonathan P. Sher (Ed.), **Rural Education in Urbanised Nations: Issues and Innovations** (Westview, Boulder, with OECD/CERI, Paris, 1981).

4. See the paper by Dr. Davies in the present volume.

5. For a fuller treatment of this point, see R.E. Bell and N. Grant, **Patterns of Education in the British Isles** (Allen & Unwin, 1977), Chs. 4 & 5, pp.107-158.

6. Brian O Cuív, **A View of the Irish Language** (Dublin, Stationery Office, 1977).
    Desmond Fennell, "Can a shrinking linguistic minority be saved? Lessons from the Irish experience." In E. Haugen, J.D. McClure and D. Thomson (Eds.) **Minority Languages Today** (Edinburgh University Press, 1981), pp.32-39.
    The experience of voluntary All-Irish Schools in Dublin is, however, more encouraging. (T.E. Corner, Irish case-study, in N.Grant et al., **Gaelic School Study,** G.U. Education Department, 1980.)

7. R. Edwards, "Language, politics and ethnicity as educational variables: The Quebec case." **Compare,** Vol.8, No.1, 1978, pp. 15-30.
    M.R. Lupul, "Multiculturalism and educational policies in Canada". Ibid., pp.45-50.
    Richard J. Joy, **Languages in Conflict** (McLelland & Stewart, Toronto, 1972.)
    D. Dorotich (Ed.) **Education and Canadian Multi-Culturalism: Some Problems and Some Solutions** (University of Saskatchewan, Saskatoon, 1981.)

8. Kenneth MacKinnon, **The Lion's Tongue** (Inverness, Club Leabhar, 1974.)

9. An apparent exception, the admission of Gaelic instruction in the lower classes of SPCK schools, has been interpreted as a transitional device to facilitate eventual Anglicisation. A. D. Dunlop, **Language, Schooling and Reality: The Shaping of an Educational Paradigm** (Unpubd. M.Ed. thesis, University of Glasgow,

1981.)

10. There are about 9,000 Gaelic-speakers in Glasgow, of whom some are second or even third generation in that city. There is, however, considerable linguistic erosion: the 1981 Census figure is a drop from 12,000 in 1971.

11. This is even more marked in the Bailiwicks of Guernsey and Jersey, where the political position is similar; there, teachers are recruited from "elsewhere", mainly England, as a matter of policy. See Dora M. Pickering, "Education in the Channel Islands." in R.E. Bell, G. Fowler and K. Little (Eds.), **Education in Great Britain and Ireland: A Source-Book** (London, Open University/Routledge & Kegan Paul, 1973), pp.31-38.

12. Adam J. Aitken, "The good old Scots tongue: does Scots have an identity?" In Haugen, McClure & Thomson, op.cit., pp.72-90.
J.D. McClure, "The synthesisers of Scots." Ibid., pp.91-99.

13. For examples, see Bell & Grant, op.cit.

14. For a fuller treatment, see N.Grant, **Society, Schools and Progress in Eastern Europe** (Oxford, Pergamon, 1969.)

15. Thomas Rørdam, **The Danish Folk High Schools** (Copenhagen: Det Danske Selskab, 1980.)
Poul Engberg, **De nordiske Folkehøjskoler** (Det nordiske Folkehøjskolerad, Surghøj, 1963.)

16. Treaty Establishing the European Economic Community (Rome), 27 March 1957, Articles 48, 57.

17. Uniquely (and perhaps awkwardly), Denmark belongs to both organisations.

18. Linguistic Arabisation was not total, except in the areas of the earlier conquests (the area from Iraq to Morocco and, for a time, Spain); Arabic did not replace Persian or Turkish, even less the languages of peoples converted later, such as Malay or Kiswahili. It did, however, have a profound influence on their vocabulary, grammar and (though in some cases temporarily) script.

19. For an excellent account of this topic – indeed, of the whole nationality question – see Hugh Seton-Watson, **Nations and States** (Methuen, 1977, 1982.)

20. Just in case the point has been forgotten, the proposition in favour of a Scottish Assembly did secure a clear majority of votes cast, sufficient for any other vote in the UK before or since. The rule requiring 40% of all **registered** votes (including the double-registered, the absent, the sick and the dead) was introduced for this occasion only; if it had been applied in the 1975 Referendum, the UK would not now be in the EEC. Unsurprisingly, the whole episode and its aftermath occasioned much cynicism and disillusionment in Scotland.

21. More recently, Galicia and Andalusia have also acquired a measure of regional autonomy.

22. D. Dorotich,"Ethnic diversity and national unity in Yugoslav education: the socialist autonomous province of Vojvodina". **Compare**, Vol.8, No1.1, 1978, pp.81-92.

23. See H.D.F. Kitto, **The Greeks** (Harmondsworth, Penguin, 1952.)

24. This point is more fully argued in N.Grant, "European unity and national systems". in Brian Simon and William Taylor (Eds.), **Education in the Eighties: The Central Issues** (Batsford, 1981), pp.92-110.

25. See note 7. Also Alison d'Anglejean, "The education of minorities in Canada: an examination of policies." in J. Megarry, S. Nisbet & E. Hoyle (Eds.), **World Yearbook of Education 1981: Education of Minorities** (London, Kogan Page, 1981), pp. 85-97.

26. J.T. Platt, "The Chinese community in Malaysia: language policies and relationships." in Megarry, Nisbet & Hoyle, op.cit., pp. 164-176.
Keith Watson, "Eduation and cultural pluralism in south East Asia, with special reference to peninsular Malaysia." **Comparative Education**, Vol.16, No.2, 1980, pp.139-158.

27. The position in the USSR is extremely complex, with many differences in trends from one area to another. See N.Grant, "The education of linguistic minorities in the USSR". In Megarry, Nisbet & Hoyle, op.cit., pp.67-84.

28. See, for example, A. McPherson and G. Neave, **The Scottish Sixth** (Slough, NFER, 1976) and N. Grant, **The Crisis of Scottish Education** (Edinburgh, Saltire, 1982.)

29. The Qur'ān makes no mention of the veil - or the **chador**, now virtually required wear for women in Iran (unless I have missed something.)

30. It is necessary to distinguish between Russification and Sovietisation; the first is strenuously denied, the second (which of course can proceed through the indigenous tongue) is openly pursued. See W. Medlin, W.M. Cave and F. Carpenter, **Education and Development in Central Asia: A Case Study on Social Change in Uzbekistan** (Leiden, E.J. Brill, 1971.)

31. Shamyl in Transcaucasia and Yakub Beg in Central Asia occupy a place in their peoples' histories comparable with those of William Wallace or Wilhelm Tell.

32. Some are not as rare as was once thought. Infibulation, for example, is still widely practiced in Africa and much of the Muslim world.

33. Montreal has an enormous diversity of ethnic minorities, and signs in shops, banks, restaurants, etc., usually reflected this by having versions in French, English and as many as a dozen other languages. When the provisions of Loi 101 outlawing bilingual notices were brought into effect in 1978, shopkeepers and restaurateurs simply put masking-tape - not always very securely - over the

English version, leaving the others untouched.

34. There are still signs that some young people in Ireland and Scotland are turning from Gaelic for this very reason - just as others, with different perceptions, are trying to learn or re-learn the language.

2 DEVELOPING PERCEPTIONS OF MULTICULTURALISM IN THE BRITISH ISLES

TREVOR CORNER

Introduction

The cultural diversity of British society has changed considerably over the past 30 years. In trying to change from a monocultural to a multicultural system, educational systems throughout the British Isles have had to adapt the educational philosophies and change the schools' curricula and policies. This chapter reviews both the extent and limitations of these changes so far as they can be gauged with any certainty. The evidence seems to suggest that the early 1970s, when economic and political conditions were for a time in a state of flux, provided an opportunity for the implications of a British pluralist society to be appraised. Since that time there has been a substantial growth of interest, research and information into the possibilitites of multicultural schooling.

The frequent interchange of use of the terms (Great) Britain, the British Isles, United Kingdom indicates a certain degree of uncertainty of identity and the fact that the constituent parts - Scotland, Wales, Northern Ireland, England, Republic of Ireland, Isle of Man, Channel Islands etc have identifiably different education systems makes the point of established social and political diversity.[1] The Celtic minorities, along with European and Black communities, are considered here as making up a continuum of time and pluralism with common interests, but substantive differences. After reviewing the extent of cultural pluralism in the British Isles, this chapter goes on to outline some important legislation in Europe and Britain and finally suggests some possible future developments.

The Celtic Communities

A full coverage of the Celtic communities should include the Republic of Ireland and, for a comprehensive picture, the Brittany peninsular of Brythonic speakers, or Bretons. For the purpose of this very brief survey, however, whilst the

Irish community is considered, the Bretons have to be excluded, at the same time noting that of the six identifiable Celtic cultures, Welsh, Breton, Kernow (Cornish) - linguistically the P-Celtic group, and Irish, Scots Gaelic and Manx - the Q-Celtic group, two of them, Manx and Kernow have effectively disappeared as community languages since the nineteenth century. All the Celtic cultures in Britain enjoyed their greatest epoch between the 9th - 16th centuries (opinions differ as to the extent and relative powers of the civilisations), whilst all have, from 1600 onwards, been pressed more and more on to the western seaboard regions of the islands and the Brittany peninsular of France. They are thus the most ancient of all surviving ethnic groups in Britain and Ireland, though perhaps more recent newcomers could claim equally ancient roots by association with their mother civilisations.[2]

Because of their effective existence as minorities for over 400 years, the Celtic groups are important in establishing both a historical and contemporary picture of multicultural society. Educational systems have tended to weaken rather than sustain their cultures; by excluding them from any meaningful part in developing state education from the 1850s onwards 'educational dependency' was created which has parallels with the condition of some more contemporary minorities in Britain.[3] Interest in Celtic culture and language has enjoyed a renaissance over the past twenty years as a result of new attitudes to biculturalism.

Around 1600 Irish was still the language of the whole of the country of Ireland outside Dublin and a few other English settlements; it was the everyday means of communication and contained a rich literary heritage. The Scots Gaels were originally immigrants from the Celtic north of Ireland, around the 5th century onwards, and by assimilation of the Brythonic Celts who were settled in present-day Strathclyde became the major civilisation in Scotland; their power and influence was gradually weakened through increasing Norman and English influences until, by the eighteenth century, Scotland was perhaps half Gaelic and half Lowland Scots. In Wales, the Act of Union of 1536 saw the advent of English political power which had the overt intention to extirpate the Welsh language and culture; this happened within the ruling aristocracy but Welsh people retained the language to the extent that over two hundred years later perhaps two-thirds of the population spoke Welsh with about half monolingual.

Several common trends were thus acting where the Celtic cultures predominated. Their political power was eroded and finally broken during the 17th and 18th centuries; the language of the people became divorced from government, law and business; the status of the languaes became diminished, the more so after the education acts of the 1840s to 1890s which promoted a monolingual English culture. The western areas of

the British Isles were severely depopulated through voluntary
and forced emigration to the New World; the Highland
clearances were a significant factor in weakening the Gaelic
community in Scotland, whilst the 'opening-up' of the north
and south of Wales caused English immigration and Welsh emigration, surrounding and isolating the Welsh heartland.
Perhaps the most severely affected of all was Ireland where
the effects of the 1840s famine and the continuous emigrations
to England and America effected a decline in population that
only within the past two decades has been reversed. (Table 1)
The Celtic communities thus experienced a haemorrhage of
people which inevitably weakened the base of their cultures;
English boroughs and towns established at strategic trading
points further weakened the social and administrative
cohesion.

TABLE 1

Emigration: Ireland 1881-1971

	Northern Ireland	Irish Republic
1881-1891	140,670	597,325
1926-1936	57,651	166,751
1951-1961	92,228	408,766
1961-1966	37,781	80,605
1966-1971	33,141	53,096

Source" Edwards, R.D. **An Atlas of Irish History,** (Methuen,
London, 1973.)

With greater isolation came fragmentation of the
languages, this being the most prenounced in Ireland where no
agreed standardised Irish became established and to a lesser
degree in Scotland where communications between the Highlands
and Islands was difficult.[4] Welsh fared better through being
absorbed into the non-conformist evangelical movement and into
the industrialised areas; this helped to diversify the
language base and aided the revival of Welsh during the 1920s
and the present time.[5] Nevertheless, until very recently,
perhaps the past ten years, the trend in numbers of Welsh-
speakers has been consistently downwards.

There were important periods of renaissance of the Celtic
cultures within this general picture of decline. The Irish
Gaelic League mounted a strong revival of interest in Irish
culture and language at the turn of this century.[6] The
foundation of the Irish Free State in 1921 and the Republic in
1939 gave the Irish language official status with English;
education was seen as a major instrument in a revival of the

TABLE 2

The numbers and Populations of Welsh Speakers in Wales
1901 - 1971

Welsh	Speakers	%age of total population
1901	929,800	49.9
1911	977,400	43.5
1921	922,100	37.1
1931	909,100	36.8
1951	714,686	28.9
1961	656,002	26.0
1971	542,402	20.8

Source: Jones, B.C. "Welsh Linguistic Conservation and Shifting Bilingualism" in Haugen, E. **et.al** (Eds) **Minority Language Today,** Edinburgh U.P. 1981, p.43.

TABLE 3

The percentage decline/increase of the bilingual population as a percentage of the entire population

	1891–1901	1901–1911	1911–1921	1921–1931	1931–1951	1951–1961
Wales	-5.3	-5.5	-1.9	-0.0	-18.0	-4.8
Scotland	-18.1	-11.5	-12.5	-14.2	-66.6	-25.0
Ireland	0.0	-0.0	+14.2	+31.2	-10.5	+36.8

(Quoted in: Durkacz, V.E., **The Decline of the Celtic Languages,** John Donald, Edinburgh, p.226.

language through Irish medium and bilingual schools.[7] There were limited post-war revivals in Scotland and Wales, though Welsh became the more stronger through factors mentioned above and an association with Nationalism which fuelled the aspirations of Welsh literarists. There was, and is, an important Gaelic literary movement in Scotland but the culture as a unity was unable to fully assimilate the Protestant reformation, nor until perhaps very recently, remove official apathy towards the culture.[8]

The current renaissance, since about the middle 1960s has several similarities with earlier ones. An 'ethnic' revival of interest in music and festival traditions (the Gaelic **Mòd** and Welsh **Eisteddfod** for example) expanded to become a broader movement to revive the language. The academic centres of Celtic Studies were drawn into supporting a more populist approach to the languages with some, such as in Aberystwyth and Galway which already offered higher education through Welsh and Irish acting as catalysts to create new learning methods. But there are also important differences. Large sections of the Celtic communities are now city-dwellers in the connurbations of Dublin, Cardiff, London, Glasgow, etc and the "rural image" they obtained is now only part of the picture. For social and educational networks to be maintained attention now needs to be focussed on urban Celts as well as on their remote communities. Grant has shown that, in Scotland, over half the total of Gaelic speakers now live outside the 'official Gàidhealtachd' (see Table 4), and in Dublin the growth of Irish medium schooling has been strongly assisted by Irish Gaels originating of the western Gaeltacht. Even smaller Celtic communities have established a number of mother-tongue medium schools such as the Shaws Road Irish-medium school in Belfast and the Welsh school in central London.[9]

The media are now more than ever vital to the maintenance of minority languages. The Celtic languages have a long way to go in this regard and Welsh T.V.s **Sianel Pedwar** has a symbolic as well as practical significance; Ireland's Radio Telefis Eireann carries a proportion of Irish-medium broadcasting and regional radio such as Scotland's Radio Highland broadcast a percentage of programmes in Gaelic. Local and national surveys now show a fairly consistent support for further development of the languages and culture such as play groups and nursery schools.[10]

MacKinnon's survey on Gaelic opinion in Scotland showed a strong positive opinion by Gaelic speakers for increasing financial and media support, not surprisingfor whilst 2 million pounds is spent on promoting Welsh, one-twentieth of this amount is spent in direct support of Scots Gaelic.[11] Even in Ireland the amount of financial and official support is often found wanting.[12] As with other minorities in Britain, continuing financial and official support over the next ten years will be crucial if this renaissance is to be sustained.

TABLE 4

Gaelic Speakers in Scotland. 1981

A. Gaelic Speakers in Highlands and Lowlands, 'official
    Gàidhealtachd (W. Isles + Highlands)   40,687

    Galldachd (all other regions)   41,719

B. Gaelic Speakers and access to any form of Gaelic-medium
    teaching.

    Areas with bilingual schooling   28,755
     of which W. Isles   23,589
     Skye and Lochalsh   5,166

    Areas with no bilingual schooling   53,651
     of which: in Highland Region   11,932
               in Argyll   6,408
               in Galldachd   35,311

(Source: Grant, N. "Multicultural Education in Scotland" in
Comparative Education, Vol 19, No 2, 1983, p.136. Adapted)

TABLE 5

ATTITUDES TOWARDS SCOTS GAELIC IN SCOTLAND

Degree of Ability in Gaelic	% Proportion of sample in agreement with:-		
	Official Recognition	Increased Public Financial Support	Increased Media Time
Fluent	88.0	80.0	90.4
Intermediate	82.4	70.6	78.4
Minimal	68.8	62.3	70.1
None	53.0	44.6	36.3
Average (weighted)	54.2	45.9	39.3

(Source: MacKinnon, K., Scottish Opinion on Gaelic. Hatfield
Polytechnic, SSOC Paper 6, 1981, p.27. Adapted).

The Europeans within Britain

Approximately six and a quarter per cent of the population of the United Kingdom has been born overseas. Table 6, which has been extracted from figures given in the 1981 U.K. Census, [13] shows those countries that contribute more than a half per cent of the total overseas born, but by no means shows the full range of diversity of overseas communities within Britain. 'Country of origin' itself is but one indication of cultural background; labels such as 'Indian' or 'Canadian' give only the merest clues to language, religion, and general cultural background. The information therefore needs some elaboration and discussion, not only because of its limited and fragmentory nature, but also because British census data on nationality and language are highly unreliable. [14]

The most numerous of the overseas born groups, about one sixth of the total, originate from the Republic of Ireland; possibly a further 200,000 persons from Northern Ireland have settled throught the island of Britain. A great proportion of the Irish in Britain originate from the rural west of Ireland, such as Donegal or the province of Connaught, often having travelled via Dublin or Belfast. Work opportunities in the urban centres encouraged settlement of the majority of the Irish-born around the major connurbations - Liverpool, Birmingham, London, Glasgow etc. As O'Connor has noted, waves of Irish emigration from the famine of the 1840s and the post-war economic booms of this century have led him to estimate that about four million Britons are of Irish one-generation extraction. [15] Over time the 'Irish in Britain' have become part of the major community, though particular identifications or associations are often retained; a typical example is the support of football teams in Liverpool, London, or Glasgow (where the Celtic and Rangers affiliations are famous, if not on occasions notorious). Many, retain a strong Catholic allegiance which sometimes becomes a main badge of identity in parts of the west of England and Scotland; it can appear in an extreme symbolic form, as in the 'green' and the 'orange' in sections of the Northern Irish Community. But there are many Irish families in Britain who over two or three generations, (as with sections of Polish, Italian and Central European migrant workers) followed the paths of the railway construction companies, or took on seasonal agricultural work. Their modern equivalents in the post-second-war era are the road construction programmes, or the present off-shore oil explorations around the British coast. [16]

Five of the most numerous of the Europeans living in Brtiain and born overseas are shown in Table 7. Of these the Italians have been probably the most researched, particularly the community in Peterborough. Around 25 millions of Italians have emigrated to other countries; the figure of 108,980 given in the table is possibly only one-third of the actual figure

TABLE 6 : OVERSEAS BORN POPULATION OF BRITAIN BY SELECTED
COUNTRIES OF BIRTH 1981.

Total Overseas Born Population 3,359,825 (6.27% of total
resident population)

Country of Birth	Number	% of Overseas Born Population
Republic of Ireland	606,651	18.06
India	391,874	11.66
Pakistan	188,198	5.60
Germany (F.D.R. + D.D.R.)	176,436	5.25
Jamaica	164,119	4.88
U.S.A.	118,079	3.50
Kenya	102,144	3.04
Italy	97,848	2.91
Poland	93,369	2.98
Cyprus	84,327	2.51
Canada	62,051	1.85
Australia	61,916	1.84
Hong Kong	58,917	1.75
Rep.of South Africa	54,207	1.61
Bangladesh	48,517	1.44
Uganda	45,937	1.37
Malaysia	45,430	1.35
Spain	40,041	1.19
France	39,052	1.16
U.S.S.R.	35,900	1.06

Countries with 0.5 - 1.0% : Barbados, Egypt, Ghana, Guyana,
Iran, Maltat Gozo, Mauritius, Netherlands, New Zealand, Nigeria,
Rep.of China, Singapore, Sri Lanka, Tanzania.

(Adapted from 1981 Census, H.M.S.O. London, 1983)

settled often in quite small communities around Britain.
Farrell suggests that the transfer to English occurs within
one generation of Italian families; many were from small rural
villages in southern Italy and in any case did not speak the
Tuscan dialect which only recently became accepted as the
national language. Italians also often saw emigration as
permanent and made attempts to integrate into the schools and
social structures of the home community. "It is a matter of
observation", says Farrell, "that every community in Scotland,
from the mining villages of Fife to the prosperous commuter
suburbs around Glasgow and Edinburgh, had an Italian cafe."[17]
    If the 'invisibility' of the European communities in
Britain reduced overt persecution, it should not be assumed
that this necessarily assured acceptance or equality of
status. Many migrants were initially from poor, rural communities and the adjustment to living in central, highly
industrialised centres needed a considerable effort of the
first generation to secure employment and housing meant that
cultural life may quickly be weakened. Religious and social
activities may help, but the Polish community, for example,
often had to create two lifestyles, Polish for the social club
and family home and English or Scottish for life at school and
when in the city or town. Where a community has a particularly strong base, and in contact with the 'home' country as
in London, German, French, Italian, Greek, etc., schools have
been established. In the main, however, the specific
development of bilingual and bicultural communities has not
been a major development until the past decade. Similar to
other ethnic groups there is a growing interest in creating
mother-tongue pre-schools and primary schools. Organisations
have developed which administer a range of schools which like
the Asian and West Indian 'supplementary' schools can vary
enormously in size and support. McLean quotes examples of the
Greek Orthodox Church schools with over 5,000 pupils in
1980, the Greek Parents Association (OESEKA) running classes
with about 3,000 pupils; the Central Council for Jewish
Religious Education supervised supplementary classes for over
30,000 pupils in 1976-77. There are an estimated 50 voluntary language classes in Chinese over the country.[18] It may
take well beyond one generation for networks to be
sufficiently strongly established for such developments to
take place.
    Small isolated communities with no power to establish
their language and culture, may find the creation of biculturalism almost impossible. The massive emigration from
Lithuania at the turn of the century of perhaps three-quarters
of a million people, became scattered in small communities
around the world. Perhaps up to 6,000 Lithuanians settled in
Scotland with migrant labourers settling where work was
available. The relatively sudden appearance of 'immigrant'
colonies often caused resentment and the Lithuanians, just
as the Irish and Spanish, sometimes became scapegoats for all

TABLE 7 : DISTRIBUTION OF THE POPULATION BORN IN SELECTED EUROPEAN COUNTRIES, BY SELECTED CONURBATIONS, BRITAIN 1971

Area of Residence		Germany	Italy	Poland	Spain	Malta & Gozo
				Country of Birth		
Great Britain		157,680	108,980	110,925	49,470	33,840
GLC		34,300	32,545	32,505	25,640	8,305
Derby	(CB)	-	-	1,220	-	-
Bristol	(CB)	1,070	1,000	1,010	-	-
Portsmouth	(CB)	-	-	-	-	1,180
Peterborough, New Town		-	2,065	-	-	-
Manchester	(CB)	1,185	(910)	2,015	-	-
Leicester	(CB)	-	-	1,505	-	-
Nottingham	(CB)	-	1,090	1,725	-	-
Birmingham	(CB)	1,605	1,000	2,250	-	-
Coventry	(CB)	-	-	1,255	-	-
Bradford	(CB)	-	-	1,940	-	-
Leeds	(CB)	1,185	-	1,885	-	-
Edinburgh (City of)		1,455	1,240	-	-	-
Glasgow (City of)		1,015	3,785	-	-	-
Bedford District		-	-	-	-	-

(Source: Campbell-Platt K., Linguistic Minorities in Britain. Runnymede Trust, London 1978)

the ills in society. Under such conditions independence became at a premium:-

> "The men were normally good joiners or carpenters. In fact my father (Antonas Augustaitis) ... used to make tables and he made a violin. He built a violin for my brother and a golf club. The were self-sufficient among themselves, they worked hard"[19]

Such a community is perhaps able to establish a strong ethnic identity with the language and culture preserved intact, but with no contact with the homeland, an almost complete change of identity becomes necessary to be accommodated in the 'host' community; after three generations the Lithuanian community has now disappeared almost without trace. The European communities for the most part opted to integrate into the British way of life, there being no real alternative. Political barriers often made contact with the home country tenuous, and the two world wars sometimes led to the total estrangement of these communities.

The Rom, or Gypsies, are a group whose whole social history has taught them to resist assimilation. Local authorities have been known to try enforced settlement, or perhaps, now with a more enlightened attitude, set up travelling schools. The estimated 50,000 Romanies in Britain and a further 10,000 in Ireland, (out of perhaps 4 million in Europe), have found any form of nomadic life more and more difficult to practise; the 1954 Highways Act states "If without lawful authority or excuse...a gypsy...encamps on a highway he shall be guilty of an offence". Sometimes referred to as the 'first blacks of Europe' the 'Zigeuner' were, along with the Jews, part of the 'final-solution' of Nazi-Germany, with possibly up to half a million exterminated.[20]

Such extremes of persecution have led to organisations such as the World Romani Congress to fight at intertnational level for human rights. Some countries, The Netherlands and parts of Britain for example, are now providing networks of caravan sites. Although there has been a certain amount of research into the lives of contemporary Romani and Travelling Peoples at local and national levels, there is still much to be learnt about their language, occupations and daily life.[21] Travelling people in Scotland, particularly in the Highlands have a mixture of origins - Celtic, Norse and Anglo-Saxon, and are often keen to be dissociated from the Rom. Travelling classrooms, talks in schools by members of the travelling community and curriculum materials are being developed which will at least serve the section of the travelling community that wish to live a more permanently settled way of life.

The Black Community in Britain

Within the plural society that has existed in Britain over the past several thousand years it has always been possible to include members of what is today referred to as

TABLE 8 : CHARACTERISTICS OF HOUSEHOLDS WITH HEADS BORN IN NON-EUROPEAN COMMONWEALTH, COMPARED WITH UK BORN

Birthplace of household head	Caribbean	India	Pakistan	Bangladesh	East Africa	Far East	Mediterranean	UK
No. of persons with wife	545,744	673,704	295,461	64,561	181,321	120,123	170,078	48,290,586
% of total population	1.03	1.27	0.56	0.12	0.34	0.23	0.32	91.5
% UK born	50	39	40	26	27	33	47	98
mean size of household	3.5	4.1	4.9	4.9	3.8	3.1	3.3	2.7
% single parent	10.4	1.4	1.8	1.3	1.8	2.0	2.5	2.0
% with 3 + children	11.5	19.5	40.1	35.2	11.4	10.1	9.1	4.7
% with 3 + adults	35.0	40.3	40.3	45.5	37.9	30.0	32.7	21.9

This omits people born elsewhere in the Commonwealth, or in Europe, Ireland, N.America, etc; Cyprus and Malta are here 'non-European'.
(Source: Ballard, R. "Race and the census: what an 'ethnic question' would show" in New Society, 12.5.83, p.212)

TABLE 9 :   LANGUAGES OTHER THAN ENGLISH, WHERE SPOKEN BY ONE OR MORE PUPILS, IN LONDON

European	African	South Asian	Mid-Eastern	Far Eastern	Other
Greek	Yoruba	Gujorati	'Iranian'	Cantonese	French Creoles
Turkish	Hausa	Bengali	'Morrocan'	Chinese new	Dominican
Italian	Ibo	Punjabi	'Arabic'	standard	St. Lucian
Spanish	'Gambian'	Hindi		Mandarin	Guyanese
German	Gur	Urdu		Japanese	Mauritian
Portuguese	Swahili	Katchi		Malay	Maori
French	Twi	Nepalese			Maltese
Dutch	Zulu	Pustitu			Romany
Finnish	Afrikaans	Sinhalese			
Hungarian		Tamil			
Polish					
Swedish					
Serbo-Croat					
Slovene					
Armenian					
Latvian					
Yiddish					
Hebrew					

(Source: Teacher Reported Survey in Inner London Schools, Rosen and Burgess, 1980. Adapted).

the Black community. It was however in the post war period
that the black population in Britain, and particularly
England, began to increase in sizeable numbers; over a million
black workers were attracted to Britain during the 1950s and
1960s either to seek work independently, or very often as the
result of recruitment campaigns by British companies seeking
labour from the Caribbean, Pakistan and India. The first
census to give anything like a clear picture of the incidence
of the black population and its social characteristics was in
1971, though only very broad variables like country of birth
were employed. An estimate taken from this census and
including blacks born in Britain is possibly around 1.4
million.[23] There were attempts to increase the sophistication
of the questions on ethnic origin in the 1981 Census but these
proved unsuccessful. Using the 1981 data and making
assumptions on numbers of heads of household and size of
family Ballard has estimated that the most numerous groups are
Indians, followed by Caribbeans, Pakistanis, East African
(Asians), Mediterraneans (Cyprus and Malta), Far East Hong
Kong and Singapore (Chinese), and Bangladeshis.[24] (See Table
8). Estimates are also given in this table of the proportion
of British-born blacks, 26% in the case of Bangladeshis, 50%
for the Caribbeans. Each group has its own characteristic age
profile because of the differing times and circumstances of
original immigration; it is likely that the third-generation
Afro-Caribbean will be born over the next few years with other
groups following soon after, as the second generations reach
child bearing age. It seems to be a general characteristic of
the groups given in the table that family size is higher than
the United Kingdom average and there are also indications of
strong kinship ties (i.e. the %age with +3 adults).

The interpretation of such statistics needs to be done
with great caution even when the figures are accurate, which
any national figures on ethnicity are certainly not. The
great diversity of attitudes across and within the ethnic
black communities also means, as in any other display of
social statistics, there can be many suggested avenues for
action.[25]

More accurate and detailed information, which was also
valid for education was necessary to broaden the picture that
individual teachers were meeting each day in inner-city
schools. Rosen and Burgess surveyed the first-year pupils of
28 London secondary schools through their teachers, who
reported that a small percentage (about 6%) spoke over 50
languages between them (see Table 9) which further studies
have increased to well over 100. In Glasgow 53 different
languages other than Gaelic and English are in use by
children; the most numerous is Punjabi, following by
Cantonese, Hakka, Urdu and Bengali. The figures, when
presented as country of origin with level of school come out
as shown in Table 10. The Scottish Education Department has
not collated information for the whole of Scotland, but

TABLE 10 : CHILDREN WHOSE LANGUAGE IS NOT ENGLISH (GLASGOW 1982) BY COUNTRY OF ORIGIN AND LEVEL OF SCHOOL (SUMMARY)

	Nursery	Primary	Secondary	Total
Pakistan	321	1503	807	2631
India	108	540	305	908
Hong Kong	74	249	127	450
Nigeria	20	22	2	44
Bangladesh	16	11	7	34
Vietnam	10	20	1	31
Papua/New Guinea	30	-	-	30
Italy	3	16	10	29
Egypt	5	14	1	29
Others (45 listed)	54	124	44	222
Total 1982	655	2522	1304	4481

Source: Strathclyde Regional Council, Department of Education; Glasgow District Statistical Summary, September 1982

TABLE 11 : CHILDREN WHOSE FIRST LANGUAGE IS NOT ENGLISH (SCOTLAND 1979) MAIN NATIONALITIES AND SELECTED REGIONS (SUMMARY)

	Central	Fife	Grampian	Highland	Lothian	Strathclyde	Tayside
Pakistan	32	28	14	18	198	2230	166
India	7	4	8	2	162	1045	49
(Hong Kong	25	61	43				
(Cantonese					23	467	
(China			27	37	75	89	63
Italy	1	2	2		92	52	1
Bangladesh	1		4		3	36	9
Nigeria	2	2	2		10	30	

Regions with none or insignificant numbers omitted: Borders, Dumfries & Galloway, Orkney, Shetland, Western Isles.

Source: Jarvie & Petrie, Moray House

something of an indication of the national picture was given by Petrie and Jarvis at Moray House College of Education (Table 11). However, as for the earlier surveys in London, the reliability of these figures is open to question.

The Linguistic Minorities Project, set up at the Institute of Education in London in 1979 to investigate patterns of bilingualism in Bradford, Coventry, Peterborough, Haringey and Waltham Forest, covered a range of linguistic minorities, including those from Eastern and Southern Europe, South and East Asia. The detailed findings have yet to be published (1984) but, for example, Table 12 shows the extent of second language acquisition and bilingualism in some of these communities; the high levels of claimed bilingualism of Gujerati and Urdu speakers in Coventry, Bradford and London are quite noticeable. [26]

The complex ethnic background of the Caribbean region is replicated in the British West Indian community. Colin Brock discusses in chapter 8 the extent of diversity and imposed dependency in Caribbean region; equally there has been a remarkably slow appreciation of the languages of West Indian migrants which differed in some important respects from standard English. The French and English creoles, which have some common grammatical features, though different vocabularies, are spoken to different degrees of sophistication by British West Indians dependent on the island of ancestry or the extent to which a group, family or individual has retained the language.[27] The disadvantage through the lack of recognition of language differentiation in schools was reinforced by poor housing, discrimination in jobs and straightforward racial prejudice in everyday living. The Rampton Report [28] brought attention to the importance in promoting positive social and educational attitudes in both white and West Indian communities, though the survey by Little and Willey of 70 local Education Authorities showed that only a small number have so far made serious attempts to fully evaluate the needs of West Indian pupils. [29] It is particularly in the case of the British West Indian community that the immediacy and extent of the failure of traditional education is most acute where straight-forward prejudice becomes most directly expressed. In the urban areas where certain of the West Indian communities have become established since the early 1960s such as West London and environs, Bristol, West Brampton, Leicester, Sheffield, Manchester, Liverpool, etc., developing unemployment, serious poverty and inner-city tensions have exascerbated the racial undertones in British society. Many of the "anti-racist" statements now being issued by certain education authorities, and discussed later in this chapter, evidence this. Most modern commentators agree that racial prejudice, which has many sources and rationalisations, takes on a special significance with people whose ancestral roots are African. The racial slavery of 18th century England and ensueing attitudes traceable up to the

TABLE 12		LANGUAGE SKILLS OF PEOPLE LIVING IN MINORITY LANGUAGE HOUSEHOLDS *		
		Minority Language	English	Bilingual
Bengali				
Coventry	n = 308	80	71	57
London	n = 802	75	57	47
Chinese				
Coventry	n = 213	49	55	26
Bradford	n = 233	66	18	16
London	n = 504	82	61	51
Greek				
London	n = 673	82	79	63
Gujerati				
Coventry	n = 973	87	79	69
London	n = 383	85	80	68
Italian				
Coventry	n = 387	58	89	50
London	n = 339	76	86	65
Punjabi (G)				
Coventry	n = 993	89	75	68
Bradford	n = 471	87	75	67
Punjabi (U)				
Coventry	n = 472	79	66	54
Bradford	n = 941	86	67	62
Polish				
Coventry	n = 465	71	93	65
Bradford	n = 401	79	83	61
Portuguese				
London	n = 592	78	69	50
Turkish				
London	n = 761	87	80	70
Ukranian				
Coventry	n = 132	80	80	62

* % of persons reported as knowing minority language or English, or both, 'very well' or 'fairly well'.

(Source: London Institute of Education Linguistic Minorities in England. Tinga Tinga 1983. p. 142.)

present day are perhaps indicative of their reproduction of education when the mythological origins are no longer questioned. As mentioned at the beginning of this section there is evidence of a sizeable Black community in Britain since the 17th century which developed a culture and a substantial literature of its own well before this, according to Edwards, [30] Africans travelled to Britain with the Viking invasions, Roman conquests (as merceneries) and via Southern Europe though the merchant and developing slave trade; Edwards also records that the Edinburgh court of King James had several 'more lassis' or 'blak ladyes' quoting Dunbar's poem 'Ane Blak Moir' (The Black Moor) as evidence.

Legislation on minority rights

On a European scale, and perhaps on a world scale, 1973 has proved to be the turning point in the interpretation of human rights as applied to ethnic and regional minorities. The United Nations Declaration of Human Rights, by this time 35 years old had established, in theory at least, human rights on the recognition of language, race, sex, political opinion and religion (Article 2) whilst Article 26 referred specifically to language rights in education, with the later additional reinforcement that their religions and culture should be defined by the minority itself (1966). Sections of the U.N.E.S.C.O. Convention of 1960 specifically referred to rights against discrimination in education, and the rights of members of minorities, in the organisation of schools and 'general educational matters'; this was later reinforced to include the right to education through the mother-tongue.

The above legislation in itself could not be of direct assistance to many migrant and regional minorities because of their economic and social dependence on the host countries. The Council of Europe Convention on the Problems of Regionalisation, or the Bourdeaux Declaration' of 1978 advocated: the development of autonomy in regional cultural affairs with the necessary financial resources allocated to ensure this; development of regional press and media and a review of the legal rights of cultural and linguistic minorities, amongst other matters.[31]

Between the United Nations and the Council of Europe initiates there was a growing concern within EEC countries that the 13 million 'foreign workers' and their dependents (perhaps about two million children) could no longer be easily accommodated within the traditional educational systems and structures of the EEC countries. A conference in Paris (The Children of Migrant Workers in Europe) began to investigate the implications of the cultural and linguistic diversity of the migrant workers, and brought attention to their social class composition, proportionately at a lower level than the host communities. A greater knowledge and understanding of the cultural norms of both the host and immigrant societies was required and special provision in functional language teaching to achieve successful performance in school.[32] At this time in the 1970s a large proportion of ethnic minority children in all European countries were reported as making only spasmodic school attendance, whilst some children were being kept away from schools quite deliberately on grounds of racial prejudice or religious observance. The continuing growth of these social pressures, as a general European phenomenon forced, legislation to widen its remit to give special consideration to education, social and vocational problems. Because the Treaty of Rome, the basis of all EEC legislations, does not include educational affairs, these have to be integrated into the development of social and vocational opportunities. Since 1974 the European Social Fund has been applicable to 'operations which facilitate the basic and advanced training of welfare workers and teachers responsible for integration courses for migrant workers or their children.[33]

In the case of migrants in Britain much of the EEC legislation was mostly ineffective and inapplicable. The former because the British government has been one of the slowest in adopting or applying European legislation, and the latter because, until the change in immigration legislation many Commonwealth citizens were U.K. citizens as of right, and thus not 'foreign nationals' or migrant workers. It has to be noted here how the interpretation of the European Community Legislation on migration, initially intended to encourage intra-European immigration, has been changed by the presence of the migrant workers, a situation not foreseen when the Treaty of Rome was originally drafted. There was however, a growing awareness of European legislation that could be used to foster minority aspirations in the face of national legislation and inertia; pressure groups, either associations of parents, or religious groups, were more prepared to appeal to the European Court of Human Rights. They point out, for example, that the EC Directive mentioned earlier and which became law in July 1981 states:-

"Member States shall, in accordance with their national circumstances and legal systems, and in cooperation with states of origin, take appropriate measures to promote, in coordination with normal education, teaching of the mother tongue and culture of the country of origin." (Article 3)

Interpretations of this Directive may well fall short of of expectations; the Scottish Education Department's interpretation is for example:-

"For education authorities in this country, this implies they should explore ways in which mother tongue teaching might be provided, whether outside or during school hours, but not that they are required to give such tuition to all individuals as of right"[34]

Research by Allardt has indicated the plight for many of the regional minorities in Europe. In identifying 58 languages and cultures in Western Europe he suggested 27 languages were clearly in irreversible decline, 15 were stable and 16 were expanding slowly.[35] A consequence of this research led to the Arfe Report which called on EEC states to ensure teaching of lesser-spoken languages and cultures with an emphasis on pre-schools, and an emphasis towards the establishment of history and literature courses.[36] On the activation of such a policy O'Brien has suggested the need for collaboration of the EEC and Council of Europe to provide finance, and, in addition pointed to the need for demographic data, the importance of media in minority languages, the necessity for strong academically supported formal schooling, and a philosophy of emphasis and value of cultural pluralism.[37] as a measure of the extent of autonomy minorities have, or may hope to aspire to, Lewis has suggested, from survey work in Wales and the U.S.A. that the following criteria are a useful guide as to whether the language and culture are given adequate recognition:-

1.   Officially recognised in courts of law.
2.   Officially recognised in public administration.
3.   Required for official appointments.
4.   Taught in primary and secondary schools.
5.   Taught in colleges and universities.
6.   Used to teach other subjects in schools.
7.   Used to teach other subjects in colleges and universities.
8.   Used frequently on radio and T.V.
9.   Used frequently in nationally recognised press.
10. Used in scientific publications.
11. Used frequently in business and commerce.
12. Used in public worship.[38]

British ethnic minorities may well hope to aspire to such autonomy but the reality is that to reverse the trend from casual assimilation of into a traditional mainstream British society, even the first stages of recognition of cultural pluralism have to be fought for. As the Commission for Racial Equality has put it:

"Although education for a multi-racial society has made some headway, the linguistic diversity of British society has so far been either ignored or viewed rather as a liability than a national resource. Furthermore, the potentiality and positive aspects of bilingual education programmes (English **and** mother-tongue or language of the ethnic minority communities) have not merited significant attention either"[39]

Over the last two or three years local authorities, aware that ethnic minority associations are actively reviewing their educational rights, have sought to issue statements which provide guidelines for schools and colleges. The Inner London Education Authority has issued a directly worded statement covering anti-racist policies in schools. Whilst recognising that each establishment will determine its own policy it recommends:

1. A clear, unambiguous statement of opposition to any form of racism or racist behaviour.

2. A firm expression of all pupils' or students' rights to the best possible education.

3. A clear indication of what is not acceptable and the procedures, including sanctions, to deal with any transgressions.

4. An explanation of the way in which the school or college intends to develop practices which both tackle racism and create educational opportunities which make for a cohesive society and a local school or college community in which diversity can flourish.

5. An outline of the measures by which development will be monitored and evaluated. [40]

The National Association for Multi-racial Education focus in their statement on "the need for radical change in teacher education" and propose that "teacher training departments and institutions shall supply evidence that their courses are designed to prepare students to teach in a multicultural society". The statement concludes:-

"A policy of drift and neglect will only confirm the predictions of those who deny the possibility of a serious commitment to the elimination of injustice and racism among those bodies and sections of society in whose interests the existing and unjust and racist structures and processes may be seen to operate. The extent of the changes required in the management and content of pre-service and in-service teacher education must not be under-estimated. In some institutions and for some people these changes may be painful but to ignore these issues will permanently endanger the prospects of achieving a just and vigorous multiracial and multicultural society in Britain." [41]

The call for radical organisational and curriculum revision in education brings cautious furrows across the brows of educational administrators. Contrast the statement below, taken from a Scottish Inspectorate Report of 1983, with the previous quote:-

"The Authority has already responded to growing pressure for mother-tongue teaching by mounting pilot studies in some Glasgow secondary schools, and assistant home-visitors recruited from ethnic minority groups have been used to promote mother-tongue at nursery and early primary stages. In addition to the maintenance of culture and strengthening of self-image, recent research suggests that recognition and use of the first language at the early stages eases transition from home to school, and from first to second language." [42]

A certain amount of reserve is to be expected from authorities, if only because policy implementation rests on their shoulders. But it is also an area where educational "experts" can genuinely find themselves at a loss. Thus the construction of "statements of policy" **can** act as a safety valve to release pressure on the legislative, and illustrate an intention of goodwill, but lack the strategy and resources to realise implementation. Reference to the condition of regional minorities in Britain makes the point that 'neutral' legislation is insufficient to support the full rights of minorities vis-à-vis the majority, at least in a representative, as opposed to proportionate, democracy.

Some Possible Future Developments

Multicultural education has now gained a toe-hold, if a somewhat insecure one, on the educational systems of the British Isles. There is every reason to be cautious in suggesting further development, as progress in bilingualism, curriculum change, attitude-change, anti-racist teaching, bias in text books, local, regional and national legislation has been fragmentary and uneven. The good research that has been done particularly in the English cities may not apply to other areas of Britain; indeed there is a danger, in times of economic stringency when research money is hard to obtain, that generalisations may be made about multi-cultural education without regard to both local and international conditions.

The extent of racism in British schools is still only half-realised and inherited attitudes are hard to change (in host **and** minority populations). 'British' history as taught in most parts of the educational systems, and as portrayed through the media, can encourage an 'empire-building' attitude entirely at odds with modern reality. Rushdie, in disucssing what he calls 'the new empire within Britain', shows that appeals to past greatness are still part of the armoury of national politics:

"The people who thought we could no longer do the great things which we once did...that we could never again be what we were. There were those who would not admit it... but - in their heart of hearts - they too had their secret fears that, it was true: that Britain was no longer the nation that had built an Empire and ruled a quarter of the world. Well, they were wrong". (Margaret Thatcher, July 1982)[43]

The debates about devolution during the 1970s perhaps helped to create an intellectual climate where such attitudes could be openly challenged and when the question of national and political identities of the whole population thought through. Maybe what the 1980s in their turn are showing is that the balance between traditional conservatism and democratic socialism is more unstable in British society than at any time since the 1940s.[44]

DIAGRAM
I

DICHOTOMIES IN THE APPROACH TO
MULTICULTURAL RESEARCH STRATEGIES.

A.   SPONSORED 'OFFICIAL' RESEARCH

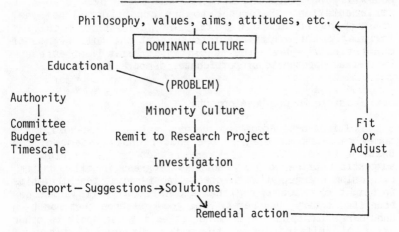

B.   INDIGENOUS ACTION

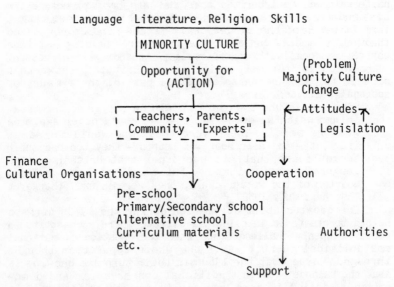

52

During this period there was a split in the approach to investigations into multiculturalism. Educational authorities have been prone to see the growing cultural diversity of children in schools as a problem which should be researched to find a remedial solution. Such an approach had several short-comings: the change in the nature of pluralism, even locally, far outpaced the rate at which research could respond if carried out in the established fashion as the background expertise of educational administrations, used to working in a monocultural environment, was simply inadequate. Educational authorities tended to respond to educational needs rather than anticipate educational change and they have been unable to take full advantage of the opportunities which growing cultural pluralism offered. Even if educational systems in the British Isles had the political freedom to respond, it seems that the bureaucratic inertia and lack of autonomy within the teaching professions have severely limited this response. Comparisons made at this level with the Scandinavian countries, the Netherlands, Canada and many other countries make it clear that progress in Britain has been slow and rather painful.

The strong indigenous action by minorities has played a great part in changing educational policies and sometimes even school practice. In cases where this has not been possible supplementary schools have been created to fill the gap. By mobilising parental opinion, engaging the services of teachers both from within and outwith the ethnic community, pressure has broadened to act at local authority level. And, as out-lined in the previous section appeal to international legislation has given minorities a broader stage to play out their case. Diagram I attempts to outline in a generalised way the essential differences in approach between educational authorities and minority pressure groups. The impact in this dichotomy goes further than one of contrasting methods of approach. Cultural pluralism is demonstrably an area where 'expert' knowledge crosses the established boundaries of power and authority for in a real sense, minorities simply know more about their own cultures. There are universals of knowledge which are evidenc across many, if not all cultures which provide unity and concensus. Thus "multicultural education does not mean, indeed cannot mean that anything and everything goes, but it does offer a more objective, open and deliberate means of deciding what goes within a multicultural society."[45]

The cooperation between ethnic minorities and education authorities should not be underestimated. Many research initiatives have stemmed from the enthusiasm of teachers who came into daily contact with ethnic minority children; the language centres in most major cities and community relations councils have acted as foci of opinion and information; multi-cultural centres have created in-service courses which set out to increase the level of conceptual analysis to inform policy and practice.[46] Nevertheless, in the evolution of

DIAGRAM 2 : PHASES IN THE EVOLUTION OF MULTICULTURAL AWARENESS

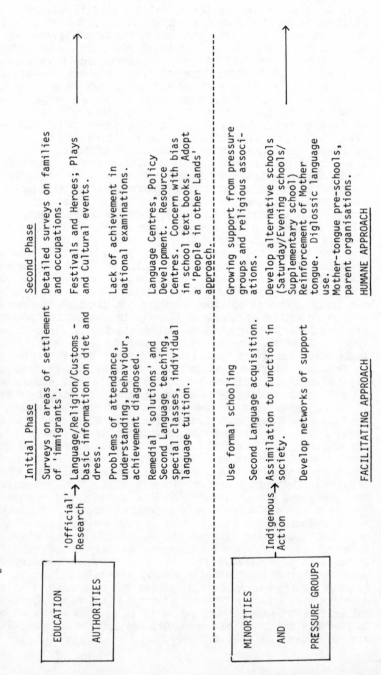

	Initial Phase	Second Phase
EDUCATION AUTHORITIES	'Official' Research → Surveys on areas of settlement of 'immigrants'.	Detailed surveys on families and occupations.
	Language/Religion/Customs - basic information on diet and dress.	Festivals and Heroes; Plays and Cultural events.
	Problems of attendance, understanding, behaviour, achievement diagnosed.	Lack of achievement in national examinations.
	Remedial 'solutions' and Second Language teaching, special classes, individual language tuition.	Language Centres, Policy Development. Resource Centres. Concern with bias in school text books. Adopt a 'People in other Lands' approach.
MINORITIES AND PRESSURE GROUPS	Indigenous → Action Use formal schooling	Growing support from pressure groups and religious associations.
	Second Language acquisition.	Develop alternative schools (Saturday/Evening schools/Supplementary school)
	Assimilation to function in society.	Reinforcement of Mother tongue. Diglossic language use.
	Develop networks of support	Mother-tongue pre-schools, parent organisations.
	FACILITATING APPROACH	HUMANE APPROACH

DIAGRAM 2 Continued

Third Phase

Detailed commissioned surveys on housing and social class.

Extra-classes for cultural subjects. 'New' Language Syllabuses adopted into optional curriculum.

Development of proficiency testing and teaching.

The beginnings of coordination of policies between local authorities.
Multicultural Research Centres.

Lobbying to change legislation.

Bilingual and Medium pre-schools and primary schools.

Bilingualism/Trilingualism established in secondary school generation.

Interests in HE and Pro-fessional careers.
Community Action/Economic Support

Fourth Phase

National and local data on pluralist population.

Whole-school policies and multicultural curriculum. New syllabuses available throughout age range.

Teachers culturally representative of population

Multilingual resources of teachers and materials.

Legislation at national and international levels.
Bilingual education through-out and linked into formal sectors.

Achievement through the school system.

International links within cultural groups.

FULL RECOGNITION OF A PLURALIST SOCIETY

COOPERATION AT COMMUNITY AND LOCAL AUTHORITY LEVELS BY ETHNIC AND LINGUISTIC MINORITIES.

—— TOWARDS —CULTURAL— PLURALISM ⟶

multicultural education in Britain it is possible to delineate the developments made by the educational authorities and those by the minorities themselves. The early phases of a 'facilitating approach' and 'humane approach' (Diagram 2) have proved inadequate and represent possibly the present level of evolution in Britain. It is suggested here that if the cooperation between these two streams of action can be improved, further steps in the trend towards cultural pluralism could be achieved.[47]

Several changes are taking place within British society which make further efforts more urgent. Economic conditions continue to worsen, making youth employment a major problem, exacerbated in the case of many minorities by apparent discrimination. Evidence produced from work done in the 1960s and 1970s was often concerned with newly-arrived minorities; as this chapter hopefully demonstrates the range and diversity of minorities requires programmes that consider the medium and long term future, as well as immediate ad-hoc arrangements. Issues such as bilinguaslim, mother-tongue teaching, status of minority languages, differential attainment and employment, curriculum and 'whole-school' policies, anti-racist teaching and many others are in the first stages of being mapped out. The question for the future of multicultural education in Britain is whether the educational effort will be sufficient to make multicultural education a reality for all.

NOTES AND REFERENCES

1. Bell, R. and Grant, N. **Patterns of Education in the British Isles,** Unwin, London 1977.
2. For a general treatment of the Celtic languages and communities see Stephens, M. **Minorities in Western Europe** Gomer Press, 1979. A comparative linguistic analysis of the languages is given in Gregor, D.B. **Celtic: A Comparative Study,** Oleander Press, Cambridge, 1980.
3. Durkacz, V.E. **The Decline of the Celtic Languages,** John Donald, Edinburgh 1983, Chapter 4.
   Lewis, E.G. **Bilingualism and Bilingual Education,** Pergamon London, 1981. Chapter 3.
4. For further discussion see:
   Greene, D. **The Irish Language: An Ghaeilge,** Mercier, Dublin 1966.
   O'Cuiv, B. **A View of the Irish Language,** Stationary Office Dublin, 1969.
   Corkery, D. **The Fortunes of the Irish Language,** Mercier, Dublin 1968.
   MacThomais, R. **Gàidhlig ann an Albainn, Gaelic in Scotland** Gairm Glaschu 1976.
   Aitken, A. and McArthur, T. **Languages of Scotland,** Chambers, Edinburgh, 1976.

MacKinnon, K. **The Lions Tongue,** Club Leabhar, Inbhirnis, 1974.

5   Lewis, E.G. **op.cit.** pp.114-116.

6. O'Tuama, S. **The Gaelic League Idea,** Mercier, Dublin 1972.

7. O'Buachalla, S. "The Language in the Classroom" in **The Crane Bag** (Special Edition on Irish Language and Culture) Co. Dublin 1981.

8. Durkacz, V.E. **op.cit.** pp.224-6.

9. Grant, J.H. "An Investigation into the Feasibility of establishing Gaelic/English Bilingual Primary Schools on the Mainland of Scotland". **M.Phil. Thesis,** Department of Education, University of Glasgow, 1983.

10. See, for example, **All Irish Primary Schools in the Dublin Area: Report,** Institiuid Teangeolaiochta Eireann, Dublin, 1979.

11. Information supplied by An Comann Gàidhealach, Inverness.

12. Lyons, E.S.L, **Ireland Since the Famine,** Fontana/Collins, Glasgow, 1973, p.637.

13. The United Kingdom Census information is collected for bureaucratic rather than educational purposes, which imposes a strict limitation on its usefulness.

14. The Select Committee on Race Relations and Immigration said in March 1978: "There are no reliable figures about immigrants now resident in the United Kingdom: no reliable statistics which can be described as indicators of immigration". Such remains the case for immigration, but also for reliable information on matters of language, race and ethnicity within the total U.K. population.

15. O'Connor, K. **The Irish in Britain,** Gill and Macmillan, Dublin, 1974, pp.151-155.

16. See, for example, Kay, B. "From the Gorbals to the Gweedore: The Story of the Glasgow Irish" in Kay, B. (Ed) **Odyssey,** EUSPB, Edinburgh 1980.

17. Farrell, J, 'Italian' in McClure, J.D, **Minority Languages in Central Scotland,** Association of Literary Studies, Aberdeen, 1983, pp.15-21.

18. McLean, M. "Ethnicity Initiatives in Education: Private Supplementary Schools with Special Reference to England and Wales". Paper given at the C.E.S.E. 11th Conference Wurzburg, July 1983 and Commission for Racial Equality, **Ethnic Minority Community Languages: A Statement,** London 1982.

19. Rodgers, M. "The Lanarkshire Lithuanians" in Kay, B. (Ed) **Odyssey, op.cit,** p.21.

20. Puxan, G. **Rom: Europe's Gypsies,** Minority Rights Group, London 1973.

21. Some examples are: Reiss, C. **Education of Travelling People,** Macmillan (Schools Council) 1977; Scottish Development Department, **Scotland's Travelling People,** H.M.S.O. Edinburgh 1971. Bewley, V. **Travelling People,** Veritas, Dublin 1974; **Report of Government Commission on Itineracy,** (Republic of Ireland), Dublin 1963.

22. Neat, T., "The Summer Walkers" in **Seer**, Dundee College of Art, 1978.

23. Runnymede Trust, **Britain's Black Population,** Heinemann London 1980, p.3.

24. Ballard, R. Race and the Census: What an 'ethnic question' would show, **New Society** 12.5.83. p.212.

25. The Runnymede Trust, Commission for Racial Equality and other interested bodies publish materials which assist in this task. Some examples are:- Runnymede Trust, **Inner Cities and Black Minorities** 1979, Lomas, G. **The Coloured Population of Great Britain,** 1973, CRE: **Ethnic Minorities in Britain: Statistical Background and Ethnic Minority Youth Unemployment.**

26. University of London Institute of Education, **Linguistic Minorities in England,** Tinga Tinga, London 1983.

27. Edwards, V. **Language in Multicultural Classrooms,** Batsford, London 1983. Chapter 4. See also, Bailey, B.L. **The Transformational Grammar of Jamaican Creole,** Cambridge U.P. 1966. Edwards, V. **The West Indian Language Issue in British Schools: Challenges and Responses,** R.K.P. 1979 and Sutcliffe, D. **Black British English,** Blackwell, Oxford, 1982.

28. Rampton, A. **West Indian Children in Our Schools,** (Interim Report) H.M.S.O. London 1981.

29. Little, A. and Willey, R. **Multi-Ethnic Education: The Way Forward** Schools Council Pamphlet, No.18, 1981.

30. Edwards, P. "Africans in Britain Before 1560". Paper presented to the International Conference on the History of Blacks in Britain, Edinburgh 1981, and Edwards, P. and Walvin, J. **Black Personalities in the Era of the Slave Trade,** Macmillan, London 1983. William Dunbar's poem 'Ane Blak Moir' can be found in Kinsey, J. (Ed) **The Poems of William Dunbar,** Oxford, 1979.

31. Zachariev, Z. "Droits Linguistiques et Droits à l'éducation dans les Sociétés Pluralistique" in **International Review of Education,** Vol 24, 1978, pp.260-265.

32. Commission of the European Communities: Studies Document No 1. **The Children of Migrant Workers,** Brussels, 1977.

33. Commission of the European Communities, **Directive on the Education of the Children of Migrant Workers,** Brussels, 1977.

34. Scottish Education Department, **Circular 1071,** August 1981 quoted in Barty, L. and Hashmi, H. **Multicultural Education - What needs to be done?** Lothian Community Relations Council, Edinburgh, undated.

35. Allardt, E. "Implications of the Ethnic Revival of Modern Industrialised Society". **Commentiones Scientiarum Socialium,** 12, 1979. Societas Scientiarum Fermica, Helsinki. See also Petrella, R. **La Rennaissance des Cultures Regionales en Europe,** Editions Entent, Paris 1981. Stephens, M. **Linguistic Minorities in Western Europe,**

Gomer Press, London, 1976. Bernard, P. **Region and Culture**, Council of Europe, Strasbourg, 1978.

36. Commission of the European Communities. "A Community Charter of Regional Cultures and a Charter of rights of ethnic minorities". (Arfe Report) **Working Document**, 1-965/80/Corr, March 1981.

37. O'Brien, T. "The Activation of a European Cultural Policy". Paper presented at a Seminar, **The Lesser-Spoken Languages of the European Community**, Gael Linn, Dublin, 1981.

38. Lewis, E.G. **Bilingualism and Bilingual Education**, Pergamon, London 1981. p.270.

39. Commission for Racial Equality. **Ethnic Minority Community Languages: A Statement**. London, 1982, p.1.

40. Inner London Education Authority. **Race, Sex and Class: Anti Racist Statement and Guidelines**, London, 1983, p.5.

41. National Association for Multi-racial Education, **Teacher Education For a Multicultural Society: A Statement**, Glasgow 1983.

42. Scottish Education Department, **The Education of Ethnic Minorities in Strathclyde Region**, December 1983.

43. Rushdie, S. "The New Empire within Britain", **New Society**, 9.12.82. p.417.

44. For two points of view on the British devolution debate see: Nairn, T. **The Break-Up of Britain: Crisis and Neo-Nationalism**, NLB, London, 1977 and Dalyell, T. **Devolution: The End of Britain?**, Cape, London, 1977.

45. Lynch, J. **The Multicultural Curriculum**, Batsford, London 1983, p.15.

46. See for example, **Report on Activities 1982-83**, Centre for Multicultural Education, Institute of Education, London. There are now possibly over a dozen such centres throughout Britain.

47. The phases in the evolution of multicultural education (in the Netherlands) are outlined in Kokhuis, S. "The Theory of Education in a Transcultural Perspective: Some Consequences for Teaching". Paper read at the Comparative Education Society in Europe Conference, Würzburg, July 1983.

3 LANGUAGE AND CULTURE IN A MULTI-CULTURAL SOCIETY

ALAN DAVIES

Language and culture are difficult to separate. Let us start with some obvious statements which may help us understand something of their relationship.

1. all cultures are made up of sub-cultures.
2. all languages are made up of sub-languages.
3. 'my' culture means being at home.
4. home is where they have to take you in.
5. knowing a culture is behaving socially without thinking.
6. knowing a language is behaving verbally without thinking.
7. membership of one culture does not preclude membership of others.
8. members may be members of more than one speech community.

We must distinguish two common meanings of culture: the evaluative meaning and the life style meaning. The evaluative meaning can be illustrated by sayings like 'so and so has no culture' or 'he's a very cultured person' or 'the trouble with this city is that it has no culture'. This meaning contrasts a high culture (either the doings of the 'folk' as in folk song, or working class entertainment and leisure, or simply the absence of a high culture). The life style meaning of culture can be illustrated by sayings as 'Americans made a new culture in 300 years' or 'In some cultures the cow is sacred', or' Culture is learnt in early childhood'. In this paper I shall be concerned only with the second meaning of culture, the life style meaning, the meaning which is summed up by the third statement at the beginning of the paper: 'my culture means being at home'.

Leach makes a direct analogy between culture and language:

"the various dimensions of culture, such as styles in clothing, village lay-out, architecture, furniture, food, cooking, music, physical gestures, postural attitudes and so on are organised in patterned sets so as to

60

incorporate coded information in a manner analogous to the sounds and words and sentences of a natural language."[1]

The phrase 'patterned sets' is crucial in that it indicates that cultures must be learned (like language) and that they cannot easily be assumed; there is no instant acculturation. The 'real content of culture' is "how people organise their experiences conceptually so that it can be transmitted as knowledge from person to person and from generation to generation"[2]. We may say that a culture is an exchange (or communication) of primary messages, eg. linguistic ones, or auxialiary messages, eg. goods, services, and mates. Just as knowing a language implies the ability to communicate verbal messages with other members of the speech community, so knowing (being part of) a culture implies the ability to exchange all kinds of social (including verbal) messages.

One view of the speech community is that it is made up of people who talk the same way. But it is very difficult defining what 'the same way' is. A more helpful definition, (suggested by Gumperz), is that the speech community is made up of those who share a set of social norms about language[3]. Such an attitudinal definition places speech community firmly within sociolinguistics. Speech communities, like cultures and like languages, need to be seen as overlapping groupings, ie, we may belong to more than one speech community. And as Labov and others have shown, social attitudes towards language are uniform throughout a speech community. Macaulay provides evidence for this kind of uniformity within the Glasgow speech community.[4]

Language is very obviously part of an embracing culture. Part of being Japanese is knowing the Japanese language, part of being Spanish is speaking Spanish and so on. Many distinctively cultural representations are mediated through a particular language - songs, myths, poems, folk tales. Hence the problem of translation and the denial of its possibility. Language may be used as a means of symbolising the culture through rallying the faithful. Note the enthusiasm with which nationalist movements (as in Norway, Ireland, Wales, Brittany, the Basque area of Spain) seize on a distinct language as evidence of their separate culture. Scotland is interesting here in that it lacks a national Celtic language; it has Gaelic, of course, but Gaelic belongs historically to the Highlands and not to the Lowlands. It seems unlikely that a nationalist movement in Scotland would give credence to Scots. Nationalism in Scotland seems to accept that its vehicle must be Scottish English, distinctive mainly in pronunciation from the various Englishes spoken south of the Border. At least the Scots can console themselves that the Americans achieved their independence without a distinct language of their own.

Furthermore the Scots can observe with some relief that the Irish, 50 years after independence, have accepted tacitly that Irish cannot be the major functional language in Ireland. The Welsh poet, Saunders Lewis, warned the nationalist movement in Wales in the early 1960s not to make the Irish mistake which was to secure independence before the restoration of the language. The result, he insisted, was the loss of the language.

Culture is less obviously part of language. One analysis of language is that it consists of an array of speech acts which range from the highly ritualised items which are concerned with religion, naming etc. (eg. 'I pronounce you man and wife', 'I name this ship') to the more frequent 'I promise', 'I swear' etc. Insults and curses are heavily culture loaded and need to be expressed in precise ways in order to count as insults etc. Otherwise they may fail in their intent and be rejected. Again the central cultural area of kinship depends on language for its articulation since we tend to name lexically (uncle, aunt, etc) those relations prominent in our culture.

Culture and language can also be viewed separately. Culture can be seen as a set of important behaviours which culture members know about and practise as second nature eg. cooking, dress, colour symbolism (what for example 'red' means) and the relative importance of noise and silence. The salience of these cultural features shows that a culture does not need a separate language though the distinctive nature of a culture is probably more obvious if it can display a separate language. In other words language and culture are not the same thing. Thus while the remarks above about Japan and Japanese are probably true it is less clear that the Spain-Spanish example is equally well made. Spain contains both a number of languages (Spanish itself, Basque, Catalan) but since the Basque language (for example) and the Basque culture are not necessarily in a one to one relation 'Basques' may not in fact be speakers of Basque and yet see themselves as Basques. A Basque may speak Basque and adopt the Spanish culture or he may speak Spanish and yet cling to the Basque culture. Similarly English contains a number of groups who all speak the same language but who surely belong to different cultures, eg. Scottish, English, American Indian. Thus, the 'many cultures within one language' model is more likely than the converse. One culture is less likely to express itself in a number of different languages. However the outsider notices variety less than the insider. The Americans and the English may themselves see their languages as very different from one another just as the Chinese may see themselves as made up of quite distinct cultural groups. Both language and culture are variable and any boundary drawn between language X and language Y is always an arbitrary one.

Learning a language certainly involves learning how to be

a member of a culture. There are, of course, dangers in learning a language too well linguistically and not being acculturated - telling jokes in a foreign language is hard because jokes depend on cultural assumptions to make their point. But it is not only in jokes that the foreign learner is at risk. As soon as his command of the language code becomes like that of a native speaker then expectations will be set up that his command of the cultural code is equally proficient. It is in this way that many highly skilled foreign learners (of, of course, any language) come to grief. Writing about the Subanun, Frake points to the difficulties of getting under the skin of a culture. In the Subanun culture, he says,

> "one of the most crucial sets of instructions to provide would be that specifying how to ask for a drink... To ask appropriately for a drink among the Subanun it is not enough to know how to construct a grammatical utterance in Subanun translatable in English as a request for a drink. Rendering such an utterance might elicit praise for one's fluency in Subanun but it probably would not get one a drink. To speak appropriately it is not enough to speak grammatically or even sensibly"[5]

A foreign visitor once called to see me. I happened to be in the corridor when he arrived. I greeted him, ushered him into my room, offered him a chair and took his coat. Then I said 'I'll just shut the door', to which he replied 'Why bother?'. His remark was, of course, meant to be polite but it unsettled me. I shut the door feeling strongly that in my room I decide when to shut the door. Thinking about the incident afterwards I wondered why I had been upset. It seemed to me that my visitor had in fact spoken inappropriately. What he said was perfectly correct English but it was out of context. He may have meant 'Don't bother!' or he may indeed not have understood the implications of 'Why bother' which in my idiolect suggests an equality of status and so on. My own (unspoken) reaction was probably typical of a native speaker's spontaneous reaction in such a situation. My visitor's English was excellent. He sounded so much like a native speaker of English that his use of 'Why bother?' was understood by me as meaning what I would have meant by saying it rather than what it probably was, a mistake. My visitor did not lack linguistic competence but he was lacking in communicative competence, the appropriate use of language, or the right language in the right siutation[6].

Attitude, as we have seen in our discussion of speech community, is central to considerations of language and culture. What determines membership of a speech community is primarily one's view of oneself as a member and only secondarily one's possession of the various accoutrements of membership (eg. cultural behaviours, speaking the language). Indeed these can always be acquired.

Language Culture in a Multicultural Society

The issue that faces us is the role of language in a multi-cultural society. The term multi-cultural is awkward. If it means that a society consists of a series of overlapping and embracing cultures then that is fine, indeed it is the general case. If it means that some societies have a set of parallel cultures, all equally equal and discrete then I challenge it since such a situation would surely break up a society. If it simply means that some societies have groups of people from different racial groups who want to belong both to the majority culture and still retain something of their own then that seems to me valid but I would prefer to call it a multi-racial society, or even better a multi-ethnic society. Culture and language can be viewed as ethnic characteristics or ethnicities and parallel therefore to colour, race, religion, tribe, common history. These are all qualities which social groups use as symbols for common membership, as ways of identifying with one another. Ethnicity is a recent term as Glazer and Moynihan point out[7]. The 1933 edition of the Oxford English Dictionary contains only an obsolete meaning of the word, 'heathendom, heathen superstition'. It is not until the 1972 Supplement to the O.E.D. that we get a more modern meaning, viz. 'ethnic character or peculiarity' with a quote from David Riesman, 'the groups who by reason of rural or small-town location, ethnicity or other peculiarities, feel theatened by the better educated middle class people'. But, again as Glazer and Moynihan note, it is to the American Heritage Dictionary (A.H.D.) of 1973 that we have to look for the meanings we now use ethnicity for, viz. '1. the condition of belonging to a partiular ethnic group'. The A.H.D. does have a second meaning, that of, '2. ethnic pride'. This may be the sense of those uses of ethnic (and therefore of ethnicity) to refer to clothes and artefacts, eg. 'that's a very ethnic skirt you're wearing' which seems to mean something like belonging to a proud cultural tradition not our own where handicrafts are still valued. But ethnic and ethnicity have come out of the closet in the last decade, no doubt partly because they provide convenient generic terms for movements and forces that indicate primary and now refound identities. Ethnicity is in, not only in academic discussion; all the O.E.D. Supplement's citations are to academics. We are all into ethnicity as Alex Haley's 'Roots' on television a few years ago showed with its record audiences. That television series struck a chord, not least among majority and mainstream groups (WASPS and their equivalents), indicating a widespread need to trace one's roots, to belong.

I began with a series of statements. I want to end with a set of questions.

1. Can culture exist without language? Different cultures can exist within the same language. Ireland and England (or Scotland and England) are sufficiently distinct culturally and yet the language they all speak is English.

Culture is not isomorphic with language, then, it can exist in its own right. Of course, as we have also mentioned earlier, this raises the question of what one means by the '<u>same</u>' language. Is the English of Ireland, Scotland, England, etc the 'same' language?

2.   Can language exist without culture?   Different languages can exist within the same culture. Scots Gaelic, Scots English, perhaps, are examples of speakers of both languages seeing themselves as all united within a Scottish culture. A strong religious culture (eg. Islam) can provide a similar kind of overall unity, even though groups of members may use quite different languages, eg. Malay, Farsi Arabic, Turkish. Islam is interesting in that it does at the same time carry with it the acceptance of Arabic, the language of the sacred revelation as a unifying language among the initiated. So we can accept different languages within one culture, but still with some reservation. Again we must raise the question what is the <u>same</u> culture? Do Farsi speakers in Persia and Malay speakers in Malaysia etc. see themselves as the same in any major cultural way?

3. How important are members' attitudes? In both culture in language and language in culture the view members take of themselves is important. No doubt separateness is easier, as we have noted earlier, when members can find multiple sources of distinction, not just language but religion, history, colour, political organisation etc. Boundaries between groups are easier to maintain when more than one symbol can be appealed to. But it is possible, even so, for boundaries to persevere without more symbolic attachment: thus in India there is a kind of common culture and yet groups within India speak many different kinds of language. And the boundary between the USA and Canada persists (as does that between Germany and Austria) in spite of a common language, suggestive that there is a flimsy separateness of culture. It is just possible for a community to be divided with no overt symbol (no language difference, no religious difference, no cultural difference) other than the political reality eg. the two Germanies. Over time no doubt cultural (and perhaps language) differences will grow and add to the political separateness.

4. How common are plural societies? Plural societies, plural culturally (with the proviso above), plural racially and plural linguistically are the norm not the exception. But political stability seems to require a normative approach to difference i.e. a homogenising process. In the flux of time there is a double tendancy apparent, for separation between societes and sameness within societies. Our task and our problem is to reserve these tendencies so that societies do not become so different from one another that they become unintelligible culturally and linguistically and, more important, and perhaps more possible, so that societies exercise extreme tolerance towards different groups within

their boundaries and slow up or halt the unifying process. In the USA and in the UK we must find some way of being both unified, the same, and different, being American **and** Chicano or British **and** Pakistani, speaking both English and Spanish or English and Urdu etc. That is politically desirable and it is also politically novel.

5. Finally how can one balance between minority language and culture maintenance and majority language and culture acquisition be established in present day multi-ethnic societies. The assumption we make is that in the increasingly obvious ethnicities of European cities we are seeing renewal, viz. that minority ethnicities are not going to fade away. What this view does is to provide a dilemma for the liberal who chooses not to explain stratification in terms of ethnicity and prefers economic explanations. Thereafter it becomes impossible to seek amelioration in terms of positive ethnic discrimintion. And yet if we do not wish to take action in that way where does that leave issues such as mother tongue maintenance? In such situations there is often a congruence of marked ethnicity and low economic status. But such congruence is not always present and then the liberal has to face squarely his attitude to positive discrimination on grounds of ethnicity alone. It is a real dilemma. As Glazer and Moynihan point out it is only recently that we were removing indications of ethnic membership because the very labelling was thought discriminatory[8]. And with a fine paradox discrimination can become inverted as in the case of Wales or Malaysia or Canada. It is not necessary to have to choose between maintenance and acquisition. Statements 7 and 8 at the head of this paper indicated that membership in both culture and language may be (and normally is) overlapping; to repeat:

7. membership of one culture does not preclude membership of others.

8. members may be members of more than one speech community.

Some comments on multi-ethnic society involve an essentially homogenised view. Little and Willey see the need for a new multi-ethnic society which incorporates all the ethnicities in some coherent mass (hence the arguments for a multi-cultural or multi-ethnic education)[9]. My own view is that that is wrong; that the only multi-ethnic society we can have - and the only one we will have - is one which, like an onion, or a family, combines smaller units within larger ones. The small are not lost: all are equally part of the whole.

NOTES AND REFERENCES

1. Leach, E. **Culture and Communication**, Cambridge University Press, 1976, p.10.
2. Frake, C.O. "The Ethnographic Study of Cognitive

Systems" in **Anthropology and Human Behaviour**, Gladwin, T. and Sturtevant, W.C. (Eds) Anthropological Society of Washington D.C., 1962.

3. Gumper, J.J. "The Speech Community" in **International Encyclopedia of Social Science**, Vol.9, 1968. pp. 381-386.

4. Macaulay,R. and Trevelyan,P. **Language, Education and Employment in Glasgow**, University of Edinburgh Press, 1977.

5. Frake, C.O. "How to ask for a drink in Subanun" in **American Anthropoligist**, 66/6, part 2. 1964.

6. Hymes, D. **"On Communicative Competence"**, University of Pennsylvania Press, Philadelphia 1971: also Pride, J.B. and Holes, J. (Eds) **Sociolinguistics**, Penguin, 1972.

7. Glazer, N. and Moynihan, D.P. (Eds) **Ethnicity, Theory and Experience**, Harvard University Press 1975.

8. **Ibid.**

9. Little, A. and Willey, R. **Multi-ethnic education: The Way Forward**, Schools Council Pamphlet 18, 1981.

4 MULTIETHNIC EDUCATION IN THE U.S.A.: PRACTICES AND PROMISES

JAMES BANKS

The Goals of Multiethnic Education

Multiethnic education assumes that ethnicity is a salient part of American life and culture. It also assumes that ethnic diversity is a positive element in a society because it enriches a nation and increases the ways in which its citizens can perceive and solve personal and public problems. Ethnic diversity also enriches a society because it provides individuals with more opportunities to experience other cultures and thus to become more fulfilled as human beings. When individuals are able to participate in a variety of ethnic cultures they are more able to benefit from the total human experience. Multiethnic education is a reform movement designed to make some major changes in the education of children and youths; its advocates believe that many school practices related to race and ethnicity are harmful to students and reinforce many of the ethnic stereotypes and discriminatory practices in American society.

Individuals who only know, participate in, and see the world from their unique cultural and ethnic perspectives are denied important parts of the human experience and are culturally and ethnically encapsulated. Alice Miel, in **The Shortchanged Children of Suburbia**,[1] tells an anecdote about an economically and culturally encapsulated child:

"The story is told about a little girl in a school near Hollywood who was asked to write a composition about a poor family. The essay began: 'This family was very poor. The Mommy was poor. The Daddy was poor. The brothers and sisters were poor. The maid was poor. The nurse was poor. The butler was poor. The cook was poor. And the chauffeur was poor...'"[2]

---

*This paper appeared in a slightly different form as **Multiethnic Education: Practices and Promises** (Bloomington, Indiana: Phi Delta Kappa Educational Foundation, 1977. Reprinted with permission of the Foundation.

Culturally and ethnically encapsulated individuals are also unable to fully know and to see their own cultures because of their cultural and ethnic blinders. We can get a full view of our own cultures and behaviours only by viewing them from the perspectives of other racial and ethnic cultures. Just as a fish is unable to appreciate the uniqueness of his aquatic environment, so are many Anglo-American children unable to fully see and appreciate the uniqueness of their cultural characteristics. A key goal of multiethnic education is to help individuals to gain greater self-understanding by viewing themselves from the perspectives of other cultures.

Multiethnic education attempts to acquaint each ethnic group with the others' unique culture and to help ethnic group members to see that other ethnic cultures are just as meaningful and valid as their own. With increasing acquaintance and understanding, respect may follow. A major goal of multiethnic education is to provide students with cultural and ethnic alternatives. Both the Anglo-American child and the Filipino American child should be provided with cultural and ethnic options in the school. Historically, the school curriculum has focused primarily on the culture of the Anglo-American child, whilst the school itself was, and often is, primarily an extension of the Anglo-American child's home and community culture and did not present him/her with cultural and ethnic alternatives.

The Anglo-Centric curriculum, which still exists to varying degrees in most American schools, has harmful consequences for both Anglo-American children and ethnic minorities such as Afro-Americans and Mexican Americans. By teaching the Anglo-American child only about his or her own culture, the school is denying him or her the richness of the music, literature, values, life styles, and perspectives which exist among ethnic groups such as Blacks, Puerto Rican Americans, and Asian Americans. Anglo-American children should know that Black literature is uniquely enriching, and that groups such as Native Americans and Mexican Americans have values which they may freely embrace. Many of the behaviors and values within these ethnic groups may help Anglo-American students to enrich their personal and public lives.

The Anglo-Centric curriculum negatively affects the ethnic child of color because he or she may find the school culture alien, hostile, and self-defeating. Most ethnic minority communities are characterized by some values, institutions, behavior patterns, and linguistic traits which differ in significant ways from those within the dominant society and in the schools. Because of the negative ways in which ethnic students and their cultures are often viewed by educators, many of them do not attian the skills which they need to function successfully within the wider society. All students should be provided with the skills, attitudes, and knowledge they need to function within their ethnic culture, the mainstream culture, as well as within and across other ethnic cultures. The Anglo-American child should be familiar with Black English; the Afro-American child should be able to speak and write standard English and to function successfully within Anglo-American institutions.

Another major goal of multiethnic education is to reduce the pain and discrimination which members of some ethnic and racial groups experience in the schools and in the wider society because of their unique racial, physical, and cultural characteristics. Groups such as Filipino Americans, Mexican Americans, Puerto Ricans and Chinese Americans often deny their ethnic identity, ethnic heritage, and family in order to assimilate and to participate more fully in America's social, economic, and political institutions. Individuals who are Jewish Americans, Polish Americans, and Italian Americans also frequently reject parts of their ethnic cultures when trying to succeed in school and in society. As Mildred Dickeman has insightfully pointed out, schools force members of these groups to experience "self-alienation" in order to succeed.[3] This is a high price to pay for educational, social, and economic mobility.

When individuals are forced to reject parts of their racial and ethnic cultures in order to experience success, problems are created for both individuals and society. Ethnic peoples of color, such as Afro-Americans and Mexican Americans, experience special problems because no matter how hard they try to become like Anglo-Americans (the idealized ethnic group in the United States) most of them cannot totally succeed because of their skin color.

Some Blacks become very Anglo-Saxon in speech, ways of viewing the world, and in their values and behavior. These individuals become so Anglicized that we might call them "Afro-Saxons." However, because of their skin color, such individuals may still be denied jobs or the opportunities to buy homes in all-white neighborhoods. They may also become alienated from their own ethnic communities and families in their attempts to act and be like white Anglo-Americans, becoming alienated from both their ethnic cultures and the mainstream Anglo culture; such individuals are often referred to as "marginal" persons.

Those who belong to such groups as Jewish Americans and Italian Americans may also experience "marginality" when they attempt to deny their ethnic heritages and to become Anglo-Americans. Although they can usually succeed in looking and in acting like Anglo-Americans, they are likely to experience a great deal of psychological stress and identity conflict when they deny and reject family and their ethnic languages, symbols, behavior, and beliefs. Ethnicity plays a cogent role in the socialization of ethnic group members; ethnic characteristics are part of the basic identity of many individuals, and when such individuals deny their ethnic cultures they are rejecting an important part of their own self.

The Melting Pot

The Melting Pot, a play written by the English Jewish author Israel Zangwill opened in New York City in 1908.[4] The great ambition of the play's composer-protagonist, David Quixano, was to create an American symphony that would personify his deep conviction that his adopted land was a nation in which all ethnic differences would mix and from this a new person, superior to all, would emerge. The Melting Pot became a tremendous success because it embodied an idea that was pervasive in the United States at the turn of the century.

What in fact happened, however, was that most of the imimmigrant and ethnic cultures stuck to the bottom of the mythical melting pot. Anglo-Saxon culture became dominant; other ethnics groups had to give up their ethnic traits. Rather than a melting pot, Anglo-conformity existed.

The American school, like other American institutions, embraced Anglo-conformity goals. One of its major goals was to rid ethnic groups of their ethnic traits and to force them to acquire Anglo-Saxon values and behavior. Ellwood Patterson Cubberley,[5] the famed educational leader, clearly stated the school's goal near the turn of the century:

"Everywhere these people (immigrants) tend to settle in groups or settlements and to set up their own national manners, customs, and observances. Our task is to break up their groups and settlements, to assimilate or amalgamate these people as part of the American race, and to implant in their children, as far as can be done, the Anglo-Saxon conception of righteousness, law, order and popular government, and to awaken in them reverence for our democratic institutions and for those things which we as a people hold to be of abiding worth".[6]

The Salad Bowl: Cultural Pluralism

Philosophers and writers at the turn of the century, such as Horace Kallen, Randolph Bourne, and Julius Drachsler, strongly defended the rights of the immigrants that were entering the United States, and rejected the assimilationist argument made by leaders such as Cubberley.[7] They argued that a political democracy must also be a cultural democracy and that the thousands of Southern, Eastern, and Central European immigrant groups had a right to maintain their ethnic cultures and institutions in American society. They used a "salad bowl" argument, maintaining that each ethnic culture would play a unique role in American society but would contribute to the total society. Arguing that these ethnic cultures would enrich American "civilization", they called their position "cultural pluralism", and said that it should be used to guide public and educational policies.

The arguments of the cultural pluralists were a cry in the wilderness. American's political, business, and educational leaders continued to push for the assimilation of the immigrant and indigenous racial and ethnic groups, feeling that only in this way could they make a unified nation out of so many different ethnic groups with histories of wars and hostilities in Europe. The triumph of the assimilationist forces in American life were symbolized by the Immigration Acts of 1917 and 1924.[8]

The Immigration Act of 1917, designed to halt the immigration of Southern, Central and Eastern European groups, such as Poles, Greeks, and Italians, required immigrants to pass a reading test to enter the United States.[9] When this act was passed but failed to substantially reduce the number of immigrants from these nations, the nativist groups pushed for and succeeded in getting another act passed, the Immigration Act of 1924.[10] This act drastically limited the number of immigrants that could enter the United States from all nations except Western Europe and ended the era of massive immigration to the United States and thus closed a significant chapter in American history.

The New Pluralism

Assimilationist forces and policies dominated American life from about the turn of the century to the beginning of the 1960s. This idea was almost totally unchallenged during this long period. Most minority group leaders, as well as most dominant group leaders, saw the assimilation of America's ethnic groups as the proper societal goal. True, there were a few voices in the wilderness who talked about separatism and ethnic cultures, such as Marcus Garvey in the 1920s.[11] However, these lone voices were successfully ignored or silenced. Garvey, for example, ended up behind bars.

By the late 1950s and early 1960s, the combined forces of discrimination in such areas as employment, housing, and education, and rising expectations, caused Afro-Americans to lead an unprecedented fight for their rights which became known as the Black Revolt. The American assimilationist policy shaped a nation from millions of immigrants and from diverse Native American groups. The United States did not become an ethnically balkanized nation, though this could well have happened. For ethnic peoples who are white the assimilationist idea also worked reasonably well; however, it did force many of them to become "marginal" and to deny family and heritage. This should not be taken lightly, for denying one's basic group identity is a very painful and psychologically unsettling process. For the most part white ethnic groups have been able, in time, to climb up the economic and social ladders.

The assimilationist idea has not worked nearly as well for ethnic peoples of color. This is what Blacks realized by the early 1960s. The unfulfilled promises and dreams of the assimilationist idea was a major cause of the Black civil rights movement of the 1960s when many Blacks who had become highly assimilated Afro-Saxons were still unable to fully participate in many American institutions and when they were still being denied many opportunities because of their skin color. They searched for a new ideal; many endorsed some form of "cultural pluralism." An idea born during the turn of the century was refashioned to fit the hopes, aspirations, and dreams of disillusioned ethnic peoples in the 1960s. It was during this period that Blacks demanded more control over the institutions in their communities and that all institutions, including the schools, more accurately reflect their ethnic cultures. They demanded more Black teachers and administrators for their youths, textbooks which reflected Black culture, and cafeteria foods more like those which their children ate at home.

Educational institutions, at all levels, began to respond to the Black Revolt, and its apparent success caused other alienated ethnic groups of color, such as Mexican and Asian Americans, and Puerto Ricans, to make similar demands for political, economic, and educational change. As a result, Mexican American Studies and Asian American Studies courses which paralleled Black Studies courses emerged. The reform movements initiated by the ethnic peoples of color caused many white ethnic groups that had denied their ethnic cultures in the past to proclaim ethnic pride and to push for the inclusion of more information about white ethnic groups in the curriculum. This movement became known as the "new pluralism." Judith Herman writes,[12]

"[It] has been described as reactive, as "me too", and essentially opportunistic and false. For some, it may have been. But for many, especially the new generation of ethnic leaders, it was a real response. It was in part a sense that the requirement for success in America seemed to be an estrangement from family and history; that for all its rhetoric about pluralism, America didn't mean for ethnicity to go beyond the boundaries of food, a few statues or parades honoring heroes, of colorful costumes and dances."[13]

In a sense, the Black civil rights movement legitimized ethnicity and other alienated ethnic groups began to search for their ethnic roots and to demand more group and human rights.

Multiethnic Education: Practices and Problems

The ethnic movements of the 1960s and 1970s stimulated needed reform in educational institutions at all levels, from kindergarten to the university. However, some unfortunate practices, ideas, and assumptions also resulted from these movements, and many of these ideas and practices still negatively affect school programs related to ethnicity. I will review and critize these ideas and practices, and later describe some of the salient characteristics of the idealized multiethnic school.

Programs to Silence Protest

Many school districts, more anxious to silence "militant" ethnic students and teachers than to reform the curriculum, structured hurriedly and poorly conceptualized ethnic studies programs and hired anyone with a visible claim to ethnic group membership to teach them. Consequently, these programs were often poorly taught, highly politicized, and often emphasized how ethnic peoples of color had been victimized by institutional racism. These programs focused on only one ethnic group; thus Black Studies units and courses were usually taught in predominantly Black schools; Puerto Rican Studies courses and units in predominantly Puerto Rican schools. The assumption was that only Blacks needed to study about Blacks and that only Puerto Ricans needed to study about Puerto Ricans in the United States. While both the politicized nature and monoethnic character of ethnic studies programmes have waned tremendously in recent years, monoethnic programs and practices still haunt the multiethnic education movement. School districts often point to their Asian American Studies or Black Studies courses to explain whey they have not attempted to reform the general course of study. Courses such as Chicano Studies and Black Studies are usually electives, taken by only a small percentage of the school population. While specialized ethnic studies courses can and often do serve essential needs of students, the total curriculum should be changed to reflect ethnic diversity.

Children Learn What They Live

Teachers often assume that children are unaware of racial differences, and that they will merely "create" problems by making the study of ethnicity an integral part of the curriculum. This idea is widespread among many teachers probably because they are not acquainted with the research on the racial attitudes of children and/or have not carefully observed children in interracial settings and situations.

Over the years, research has consistently shown that very young children, even before they enter kindergarten, are aware of racial differences and very soon internalize the evaluations of different races that are widespread within their culture. Studies by researchers such as Kenneth B. and Mamie Clark, Mary Ellen Goodman, and J. Kenneth Morland have shown that very young children are aware of racial differences.[14]

Children learn about race long before they enter school form their parents, television, cartoons, and movies. All of these experiences, which Carlos E. Cortes calls the "societal curriculum", teach children many ideas and attitudes toward ethnic and racial groups.[15] Unfortunately, many of the ideas and attitudes which children learn from the wider society are negative, stereotypic, and damaging, to children themselves and to the victimized groups. Research by Morland, for example, indicates that both black and white nursery-school children tend to prefer white to black playmates.[16] Other research has demonstrated the negative images about different racial groups which children learn from television and the mass media. Research by Charles Y. Glock and Associates indicates that by adolescence ethnic and racial bias is widespread. They write, "Prejudice is rampant in school populations... not only racial prejudice but anti-Semitism and a virulent but especially neglected class prejudice as well."[17] Other research has highlighted the negative images about different ethnic and racial groups which children learn from television and the mass media.

Thus, contrary to what many teachers believe, children are keenly aware of racial differences and have developed many attitudes toward different racial and ethnic groups by the time they enter school. It is true,however, that the racial attitudes of a five year old are not as crystallized as those of a teenager. This suggests that if the curriculum is going to have any significant impact on the racial and ethnic attitudes of children, it should be multiethnic beginning in the pre-school years.

The teacher, as we have seen, cannot determine whether children will learn ideas about ethnic and racial groups, though the teacher can decide whether or not to take an active part in the child's ethnic education and help to counter some of the prejudices and stereotypes which children learn from the media, adults, and the wider society.

We Treat Them All The Same

Many teachers say that they do not get involved in problems related to race and ethnicity because they don't see the colors and racial characteristics of their students. Such teachers claim that they "treat them all the same, whether they are black, brown, blue or red." Those who make this claim usually have the best intentions, see themselves as good teachers, and want to treat all of their students fairly. However, in their attempts (which I feel cannot be successfully attained) to deny the ethnic and racial problems which result from their ethnicity, though the special needs of some, means that the teacher must carefully and sensitively respond to the unique needs of each child.

The Mexican American student who comes to school speaking primarily Spanish does not need a teacher who will treat him or her exactly like all of the Anglo students who are fluent in English. Rather, he or she needs a teacher who recognizes, respects, and appreciates his/her unique cultural differences and who has the attitudes, skills, and abilities to respond to them in a positive and helpful way. The Black or Jewish American child who is experiencing an ethnic identity problem will best be helped by the recognition of his/her problem rather than the approach of "treating everyone the same". When a teacher treats students the same who have very different and unique needs he/she is denying them an equal chance to succeed.

A Black child who was attending a predominantly white school that had a white principal was experiencing acute racial identity problems. He was also having a great deal of difficulty adjusting to the racial climate of the school, which was often hostile and self-defeating. One day while in class, the child's pain overcame him and he ran out of his classroom and down the hall. The principal stopped him and asked, "Robert L. what's the matter?" The child cried out anguishly, "I'm Black, I'm Black!" The principal responded, "You know, I had never noticed." The principal had very benign intentions and was trying to make the child feel more comfortable in the school. However, his response, in effect, denied the root of the child's problem and his very identity.

Us and Them

Many teachers say that they would like to teach about ethnicity and race but they don't have any Blacks or other ethnic minority students in their classes. These kinds of teachers, like those described above, have good intentions but have some misconeptions about the nature of ethnicity and about the goals of multiethnic education. They assume that ethnic studies is the study of "them", meaning ethnic peoples of color, and that American Studies is the study of "us", meaning Anglo-Americans.

Ethnicity is a broad concept which is often misunderstood by educators. Social scientists define an ethnic group as a group with a unique culture, heritage, tradition, and some unique value orientations, beliefs and behavior. An ethnic group is also a political and economic interest group. This broad definition of an ethnic group suggests that all Americans are members of ethnic groups, including Anglo-Americans, Irish Americans, and German Americans. However, many white ethnic group individuals who have experienced total assimilation are ethnically Anglo-Americans. Also, a person's level of identity with his or her ethnic group may vary from zero to total identification. Some Afro-Americans and Mexican Americans are highly assimilated and have almost no identity with their ethnic group; other members of these groups, in all social class groups, identify strongly with them. The same is true for white ethnic group members.

When a broad definition of an ethnic group is used to conceptualize and design school programs related to ethnicity, ethnic studies becomes the study of both "us" and "them", and not just the study of ethnic peoples of color or ethnic minority groups. A major goal of ethnic studies, conceptualized in this way, is to help the individual to better understand their own self by looking at his/her culture and behavior through the perspectives of another culture. Kluckhohn, the eminent American anthropologist, wrote that "[cultural studies] holds up a great mirror to man and lets him look at himself in his infinite variety".[18] Better self-understanding is one of the key goals of multiethnic education. In a sound multiethnic curriculum, the teacher helps each child to see that he or she is a member of many different groups and that the ethnic group is one of the many groups to which he or she belongs. Figure 1 illustrates the many different groups to which each individual belongs.

One's attachment and identity with these various groups varies with the individual, the times in his or her life, and the situations and/or settings in which an individual finds himself/herself. Some individuals, such as many Afro-Americans, have a strong identity with their ethnic group in large part because they usually do not have the option to identity or not to identify with it. However, a Black person's identity with his or her ethnic group may vary with region, social class, or educational level. Other individuals, such as many Norwegian Americans, have little or no identity with their ethnic group, in large part because they usually have an option whether to identify or not identify with it. Other groups, such as religious, social class, or occupational group, are much more important to some individuals than their ethnic group.

The teacher must look at each individual in his/her class, and determine which groups for that individual are the most important and determine their teaching implications. Ethnicity will be very important for some students, of little or no importance to others. The teacher cannot assume that just because a child is Black or Chicano, he or she is necessarily interested in or strongly identified with the ethnic groups to which he/she belongs. Ethnic identification should not be forced on children; to do so would probably do more harm than good. Nor should ethnicity be artificial or romanticized. Many students, especially many white students, are culturally Anglo-Saxons, even though their ancestors may have come from Southern or Central Europe. The teacher should

FIGURE 1 : THE INDIVIDUAL AS A MEMBER OF MANY GROUPS

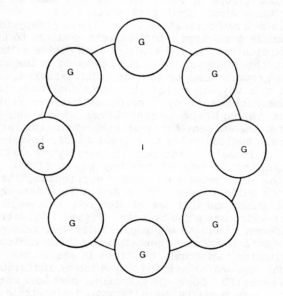

(I = Individual; G = Group)

Figure 1 illustrates the relationship of groupness to
individuality. The large middle circle (I) represents
the individual. The small surrounding circles (G)
represent the groups to which that individual belongs.[19]

characteristics of their students, they may be failing to
respond to the uniqueness of many of the Black, Mexican
American, Filipino American, and Jewish American students.
Many students who belong to these ethnic groups have no

be careful not to force these students to "find" their ethnic roots. Forcing students to identify ethnically can be psychologically unsettling and embarrassing. In one classroom, a teacher told the children to group themselves by their ethnic groups to complete an assignment. After the groups had been formed, Susie was sitting alone at her desk. The teacher said "Susie, why aren't you in a group? Where is your group?" Susie answered in tears, "I don't have a group Miss Bandini!" Miss Bandini certainly did not mean to shame or to hurt Susie, but that's exactly what she had done, despite her benign intentions and concern for teaching about ethnicity.

Heroes and Holidays

Many teachers see ethnic studies as essentially additive to the major curriculum thrust. They believe that multiethnic education consists primarily of adding facts about ethnic minority heroes to the list of Anglo-American heroes that are already taught. Thus, Martin Luther King and Cesar Chavez are studied along with George Washington and Thomas Jefferson.

There are several problems with the "hero approach" to teaching about race and ethnicity. It tends to emphasize the experiences of selected heroes, many of whom are of questionable historical significance, rather than the total experiences and problems of ethnic groups, viewed from a comparative, conceptual, and interdisciplinary perspective. Often children learn little about the experiences of an ethnic group when they only study its heroes.

The "hero" approach to teaching about ethnicity is also problematical because it too often emphasizes the memory of isolated facts about famous people and does not help children to develop higher level thinking skills or to learn how to resolve value-related personal and social problems. The curriculum should help students master higher-level concepts and generalizations and to rationally resolve social issues. Isolated facts about Crispus Attucks don't help students to develop these kinds of skills and abilities any more than isolated facts about Abraham Lincoln or George Washington. The "hero" approach to ethnic studies is clearly insufficient.

Changing the curriculum so that it reflects the ethnic diversity within American society provides a tremendous opportunity to implement the kinds of radical curriculum reforms which are essential, such as conceptual teaching, interdisciplinary approaches to the study of social issues, value inquiry, and providing students with opportunities to become involved in social action and social participation activities. Thus multiethnic education can serve as a vehicle for general and radical curriculum reform. This is probably its greatest promise. We can best view multiethnic education as a process as well as a reform movement that will result in a new type of schooling that will present novel views of the

American experience and help students to acquire the knowledge, skills, and commitments needed to make our nation more responsive to the total human condition.

Tepees and Chitlins

Some teachers view multiethnic education primarily as the study of the "strange" and "exotic" customs and behavior of ethnic groups and as the celebration of ethnic holidays and birthdays. Teachers who view multiethnic education in this way often have students build tepees and igloos, and make and eat ethnic foods such as chitlins, enchiladas, and chow mein. We might think of this as the "chitlin and tepee" approach to multiethnic education.

In many schools, most of what is taught about ethnic groups is in the forms of specialized days and celebrations. Some schools have Black week, Indian day and Chicano "afternoon". On these special occasions, students prepare ethnic foods, build tepees, venerate ethnic "heroes", sing ethnic songs, and perform ethnic dances. Ethnic community people might also be invited to the school to give talks that "tell it like it is".

This approach to multiethnic education is problematical for several reasons. By focusing on the experiences of ethnic groups only on special days and holidays, teachers are likely to reinforce the notion that ethnic groups are not integral parts of American society and culture. Students are likely to conclude that "Black history" and "American history" are separate things. Rather than being isolated on special days, Black history, as well as Chicano and Jewish history, ought to be integral parts of the daily instructional program. Thus, everyday in the classroom ought to be Black day, Chicano day, and Jewish American day. I am not suggesting that ethnic holidays should not be celebrated in the school. Rather, I am recommending that content about ethnic groups becomes an integral part of the daily curriculum. When this happens, the celebration of ethnic holidays becomes an important and integral part of a total school program in multiethnic education.

Focusing on the "strange and exotic" traits and characteristics of ethnic groups is likely to reinforce stereotypes and misconceptions. The making of tepees does not reveal anything significant about contemporary American Indian values, cultures or experiences. It merely adds to the classical Indian stereotype, which is so pervasive on television and in the wider society. Willard Bill calls the prototype stereotypic Plains Indian the "museum Indian".[21] Rather than focusing on the "exotic" characteristics of ethnic groups, the teacher should emphasize the common needs which all human groups share and the diverse ways in which American ethnic groups have solved the problems of survival.

By approaching the study of ethnicity in this way, students are more likely to develop a sophisticated appreciation for the common human bonds which they have with all humans and the ways in which they differ. This type of learning is likely to make students less rather than more ethnically encapsulated and intolerant.

Multiethnic Education: Nature and Promises

Many educators, when they think of "multiethnic education", think of the school's formalized course of study. Thus, Black Studies and Chicano Studies courses immediately come to mind when many educators hear the term "multiethnic education". Educators also tend to think of social studies and of racially mixed schools when they think of multiethnic education. Ethnic studies, which is part of the formalized course of study, is only a small but important part of multiethnic education.

Multiethnic education is designed for all students, of all races, ethnic groups and social classes, and not just for schools which have racially and ethnically mixed populations. A major assumption made by advocates of multiethnic education is that it is needed as much if not more by the Anglo-American middle class suburban child as it is by the Mexican American child who lives in the barrio.

Multiethnic education reaches far beyond social studies. It is concerned with modifying the total educational environment so that it is more reflective of the ethnic diversity within American society. This includes not only the study of ethnic cultures and experiences but making institutional changes within the school so that students from diverse ethnic groups have equal educational opportunities and the school promotes and encourages the concept of ethnic diversity.

Thus the broader concept which multiethnic education implies is towards total school reform; educators who want their schools to become multiethnic must examine their total school environment to determine the extent to which it is monoethnic and Anglo-Centric, and take appropriate steps to create and sustain a multiethnic educational environment. The ethnic and racial composition of the school staff, its attitudes, the formalized and hidden curricula, the teaching strategies and materials, the testing and counseling program, and the school's norms are some of the factors which must reflect ethnic diversity within the multiethnic school. These and other variables of the school environment which must be reformed in order to make the school multiethnic are illustrated in Figure 2.

The reform must be system-wide to be effective. While any one of the factors in Figure 2 may be the initial focus for school reform, changes must take place in all of the major

FIGURE 2 :   TOTAL SCHOOL ENVIRONMENT

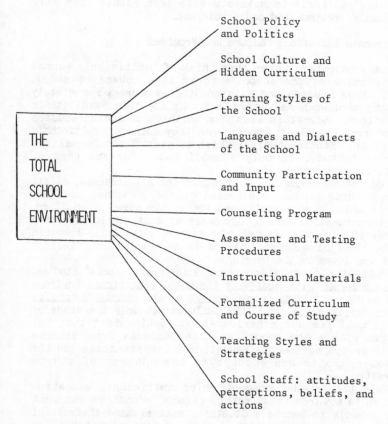

THE
TOTAL
SCHOOL
ENVIRONMENT

School Policy
and Politics

School Culture and
Hidden Curriculum

Learning Styles of
the School

Languages and Dialects
of the School

Community Participation
and Input

Counseling Program

Assessment and Testing
Procedures

Instructional Materials

Formalized Curriculum
and Course of Study

Teaching Styles and
Strategies

School Staff: attitudes,
perceptions, beliefs, and
actions

This figure conceptualizes the total school environment
as a system consisting of a number of major identifiable
variables and factors, such as school culture, school
policy and politics, and formalized curriculum and course
of study. In the idealized multiethnic school, each of
these variables reflects ethnic pluralism. While any
one of these factors may be the focus of initial school
reform, changes must take place in each of them to create
and sustain an effective multiethnic educational
environment. [20]

school variables in order for multiethnic education to be successfully implemented. The American experience from the ethnic studies movements of the 1960s teaches us that little substantial changes take place when you simply give teachers multiethnic materials but do not train them how to use them or help them to acquire new conceptual frameworks for viewing American culture and society.

The total school environment must be the unit of change, and not any one element, such as materials, teaching strategies, the testing program, or teacher training. While teacher training is very important, other changes must take place in the school environment in order to reform the school. Many teachers attain new insights, materials, and multiethnic teaching strategies during summer workshops, and subsequently are eager to try them in their schools. However, they become very discouraged when they return to their schools in the fall where traditional norms toward ethnic diversity often exist and where they frequently get no support from their administrators or peers. Without such support, teachers with new skills and insights give up and revert back to their old behaviors and attitudes.

In the next section of this chapter, I will discuss the characteristics of the idealized multiethnic school. Goals which all schools can strive to achieve will be presented. The major variables which must be reformed in order to make a school multiethnic will be highlighted.

Characteristics of the Multiethnic School: A Philosophy of Ethnic Pluralism

Historically, the American school has accepted the "melting pot" idea. It has rejected the ethnic culture of the ethnic child, ridiculed it, and forced him or her to accept Anglo-Saxon values, beliefs, and behavior.

The multiethnic school rejects the melting pot idea and recognizes and accepts the child's ethnic culture. It is guided by a philosophy which may be called ethnic pluralism. This philosophy recognizes that ethnicity is a cogent factor in many students lives. It also recognizes that the ethnic child must learn to function effectively in both his or her ethnic culture and in the mainstream culture. The school, according to this position, should help students to develop the skills, attitudes, and abilities which they need to function in their ethnic culture, as well as within the mainstream culture. The school should also help the ethnic child learn how to function successfully within and across different ethnic cultures.

The philosophy of ethnic pluralism also assumes that the Anglo child should also be helped to acquire the skills, attitudes, and knowledge needed to function in his or her ethnic culture as well as in and across various ethnic cultures. Thus, the effective multiethnic school helps all students, regardless of their ethnic, racial, or social class characteristics, to function successfully within their own ethnic cultures and within and across other ethnic cultures. Figure 3 summarizes this philosophy.

A Multiethnic School Staff

The multiethnic school has a racially and ethnically mixed school staff which respects and values ethnic diversity. Students learn important lessons about ethnicity by observing the adults in the school environment. Their racial and ethnic composition and their interactions and behavior teach students attitudes and values about ethnicity and race. When students walk into a school in which all of the "significant adults", such as teachers, principals, and counselors are white, they learn something about the school's attitude toward racial and ethnic diversity. Lengthy didactic lessons about the need for an ethnically diverse society are not likely to have much impact on students in a school which has a monoethnic professional and supportive staff and institutional norms which reflect the "melting pot".

The school staff is not only racially and ethnically mixed in the multiethnic school. Its members have positive attitudes toward ethnic youths and high academic expectations for them. Teacher attitudes and expectations have a profound impact on students' perceptions, academic behavior, self-concepts, and beliefs.

Studies by researchers such as Ray Rist, Thomas P. Carter, and Geneva Gay indicate that teachers typically have negative attitudes and low academic expectations for their Black, Mexican American, and Indian students. [22] Other research suggests that teachers, next to parents, are the most "significant others" in children's lives, and that teachers play an important role in the formation of children's racial attitudes and beliefs.

Parsons, in an important study, found that the teachers within a school he studied in a Mexican-American community held many stereotypes about Mexican-American children. [23] He felt that the schools reinforced the negative images of the Mexican-American that were widespread in the community and helped to maintain their lower class status. He quotes one teacher who explains why she put an Anglo boy in charge of a small group of Mexican-American pupils:

"I think Johnny needs to learn how to set a good example and how to lead others. His father owns one of the big farms in the area and Johnny has to learn how to lead the Mexicans. One day he will be helping his father and he will have to know how to handle Mexicans. I try to help whenever I can." [24]

An extensive review of the research suggests that changing

FIGURE 3 :   THE SOCIOCULTURAL ENVIRONMENT OF ETHNIC YOUTHS

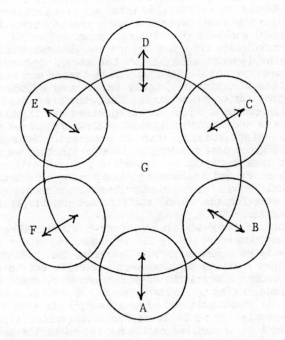

The ethnic minority youth functions within two socio-ethnic
environments, that of his or her ethnic subsociety and
that of the mainstream society. The circles labeled A
through F represent ethnic minority subsocieties. The
circle labeled G represents the mainstream society. The
school should help all children to learn to function
successfully within their own ethnic subsociety, other
ethnic subsocieties, and the mainstream society.

the racial attitudes of adults is a cumbersome task.[25] To maximize the chances for successful intervention, experiences must be designed specifically to change attitudes. Courses with general or global objectives are not likely to be successful, and courses which consist primarily or exclusively of lecture presentations have little effect. Diverse experiences, such as seminars, visitations, community involvement, committee work, guest speakers, films, multiethnic materials, and workshops, combined with factual lectures, are more effective than any single approach. Community involvement (with the appropriate norms in the social setting) can be a powerful technique.

Some behaviorally oriented theory and research suggest that changing teacher **behavior** is far more important than changing their personal attitudes. This theory and research indicate that behavior is highly influenced by the norms within an institution or setting. Thus, the prejudiced individual will tend to act in a non-prejudiced way if there are powerful norms and sanctions against acting prejudiced within a particular institution, such as a school. Behaviorist theory has a great deal of merit. It suggests that we should concentrate less on trying to change the personal attitudes of the school staff and spend more time trying to change the institutional norms of the school. These norms should make it non-reinforcing for the school staff to act negatively toward ethnic students.

A strong policy which reinforces ethnic diversity, supported and implemented by the key administrators in the district, will go a long way toward changing the institutional district might start by issuing a policy statement on ethnic pluralism. Several model statements, issued by professional organizations, exist. They are "No One Model American: A Statement on Multicultural Education",[26] issued by the American Association of Colleges for Teacher Education, and the much more comprehensive statement issued by the National Council for the Social Studies, _Curriculum Guidelines for Multiethnic Education_.[27] A school district, interested in issuing a policy statement, could adapt one of these statements or, using them as models, develop its own statement. Both the Minneapolis Public Schools, and the Michigan State Department of Education have issued policy statements on multicultural education.

Multiethnic Perspectives

The curriculum in the multiethnic school helps students to view American society and history from diverse ethnic perspectives rather than primarily or exclusively from the points of view of Anglo-American historians and writers. Most school courses are currently taught primarily from Anglo-American perspectives and points of view. These types of courses and experiences are based on what I call the **Anglo-American** Centric Model or Model A (See Figure 4). Many school districts which have attempted to reform their curriculum to reflect ethnic diversity, have moved from a Model A type curriculum to Model B, the **Ethnic** **Additive** **Model**. In courses and experiences based on Model B, ethnic content is an additive to the major curriculum thrust, which remains Anglo-American dominated. Asian American Studies courses, Puerto Rican Studies courses, and special units on ethnic groups in the elementary grades are examples of Model B types of curricular experiences.

In the multiethnic school, the curriculum reflects Model C, the **Multiethnic** **Model**. In courses and experiences based on Model C, the students study events and situations from several ethnic points of view. Anglo-American perspectives are only one group of several and are in no way superior or inferior to other perspectives. However, I view Model D (The **Multinational** **Model**), types of courses and programs as the ultimate goal of curriculum reform. In this curriculum model, students study events and situations from multiethnic and multinational perspectives and points of view. Since we live in a global society, students need to learn how to become effective citizens of the world community. This is unlikely to happen if they study historical and contemporary events and situations only or primarily from the perspectives of ethnic cultures within their own nation.

When studying a historical period, such as the Colonial period in American history, in a course organized on the Multiethnic Model (Model C), the inquiry would not end when the students viewed the thirteen English colonies in North America from the perspectives of Anglo-American historians, as is usually the case. Conceptualizing the Colonial period as only the study of the English colonies is limiting and Anglo-Centric.

Long before the English colonists were successful in settling Jamestown, the Spaniards had established colonies in Florida and New Mexico. Also, the French established a colony in Louisiana during the Colonial period. When the Spanish and the French colonies are studied in addition to the English colonies, the students are able to see that the region which became the United States was highly multiethnic during this period. Not only were many different European nationality groups in North America during the Colonial period, but there were many different groups of Indians as well as Blacks. To gain a full understanding of the Colonial period, students must view it from the perspectives of the English, Spanish and French colonists, as well as from the points of view of the many different groups of Indians and Blacks. The era of colonization had very different meanings for the Pueblo Indians and the Spanish colonists. It also had different meanings for the Black slaves, the free Blacks, and for the

FIGURE 4: ETHNIC STUDIES AS A PROCESS OF CURRICULUM CHANGE

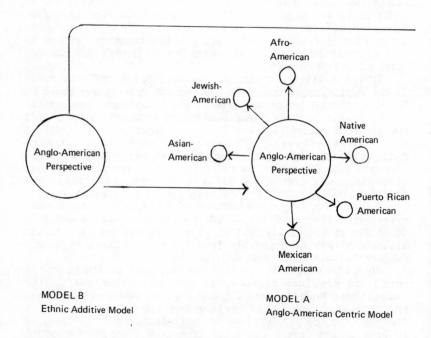

MODEL B
Ethnic Additive Model

MODEL A
Anglo-American Centric Model

Ethnic studies is conceptualized as a process of curriculum reform which can lead from a total Anglo-American perspective on our history and culture (MODEL A), to multiethnic perspectives as additives to the major curriculum thrust (MODEL B), to a completely multiethnic curriculum in which every historical and social event is viewed from the perspectives of different ethnic groups (MODEL C). In MODEL C the Anglo-American perspective is only one of several and is in no way superior or inferior to other ethnic perspectives. MODEL D, which is multinational, is the ultimate curriculum goal. In this curriculum model, students study historical and social events from multinational perspectives and points of view. Many schools that have attempted ethnic modification of the curriculum have implemented MODEL B types of programs. It is suggested here that curriculum reform move directly from MODEL A to MODEL C and ultimately to MODEL D. However, in those districts which have MODEL B types of programs, it is suggested that they move from

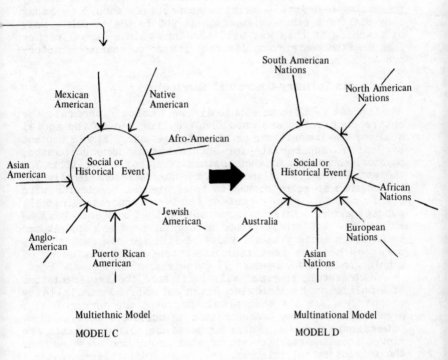

Multiethnic Model
MODEL C

Multinational Model
MODEL D

MODEL B to MODEL C and eventually to MODEL D types of curricular organizations.

English settlers. These diverse perspectives and points of view should be studied within a sound multiethnic curriculum.

I am not suggesting that we eliminate or denigrate Anglo-American perspectives on American society. I am merely suggesting that Anglo-American perspectives should be among many different ethnic viewpoints taught in the schools. Only by teaching in this way will students gain a global rather than an ethnocentric and limited view of our nation's history and culture.

An Interdisciplinary–Conceptual Curriculum

Content related to ethnic diversity should permeate the entire curriculum and should not be limited to the social studies, the humanities, or the language arts. Ethnic content is just as appropriate for such areas as home economics, physical education, science, mathematics, and art as it is for the social studies. Although it is often very challenging for the science or math teacher to integrate the curriculum with ethnic content, ethnic content can be incorporated into all subject areas. This is important so that students will be able to see how ethnic groups have influenced and contributed to American society in all walks of life and how each subject area can help us to better understand the experiences of ethnic groups and consequently ourselves.

A conceptual approach will facilitate the implementation of a multiethnic curriculum which cuts across disciplinary boundaries. In the conceptual approach, the curriculum is organized around key concepts such as culture, socialization, power, and scarcity. Whenever possible, these concepts are viewed from the perspectives of disciplines and areas such as the various social sciences, art, music, literature, physical education, communication, the sciences, and mathematics.

Let's look at an example using the concept of culture. In reading and literature, the students can read such novels as Farewell to Manzanar, House Made of Dawn, and Bless Me Ultima. They can determine what these novels reveal or do not reveal about the cultures of Japanese Americans, American Indians, and Mexican Americans. In drama, the students can create a dramatization of the epic poem I am Joaquin and discuss how it expresses Chicano history, contemporary life and culture. The students can examine the works of ethnic artists such as Jacob Lawrence, Charles White, and Roberto Lebron in art. The language arts can focus on the various ways in which symbols and communication styles differ between and within ethnic groups and how standard American English is influenced by the ethnic cultures within the United States.

In science, the students can examine the physical characteristics of the various ethnic groups and try to determine ways in which the physical traits of ethnic groups influence how other groups respond to them, their interactions with each other, and their total culture. In mathematics, the students can study the cultural roots of our base ten number system and discuss ways in which the number system within a society reflects its culture. They can also research the contributions which various ethnic groups have made to our number system.

Many excellent opportunities exist within the curriculum for teaching concepts from an interdisciplinary perspective. These opportunities should be fully explored and used. However, interdisciplinary teaching requires the strong cooperation of teachers in the various content areas. Team teaching will often be necessary, especially at the high school level, to organize and implement interdisciplinary units and lessons.

The Linguistic Characteristics of Ethnic Students

Because of the communities in which they grow up, many ethnic group children come to school with some values, beliefs, and behavioral characteristics which differ from those of other children and from those expected in the school. Language is one of these characteristics. A large number of Mexican American students speak Spanish when they enter school. Other ethnics, such as many Filipino Americans, Chinese Americans, Italian Americans, and some groups of American Indians, also come to school speaking a language other than English. Many lower class Black children speak a dialect of English which some linguistics, such as Geneva Smitherman and William Labov, call "Black English."[20] According to these linguistics, Black English is a valid communication system, with rules and a logical system of its own. Thus, there is a correct way to speak Black English.

In the past, and too frequently today, the school responded to the unique languages of ethnic children by rejecting them and trying to **replace** them with standard English. In many South-western schools in past years, the "No Spanish Rule" existed. Mexican American students were not allowed to speak Spanish in the school; if they did, they were punished, sometimes severely.

In the multiethnic school, the professional staff has positive attitudes toward the linguistic characteristics of ethnic students. Their languages are viewed as valid communication systems which they need to survive in their families and communities. No attempt is made to replace their languages with standard English. Rather, teachers introduce the students to the concept of **alternative** languages and dialects. They are taught that some languages are appropriate in some social situations and settings and inappropriate in others. The minority student who speaks barrio Spanish or Black English is helped to master standard English. However, it is presented to him/her as an alternative rather than as a replacement way of speaking and writing.

Many advocates of multiethnic education believe thatall children in the multiethnic school should learn to speak a second language, such as Spanish. Students in the multiethnic school become acquainted with the languages and dialects of minority groups and view them as valid communication systems. They also learn how these languages and dialects have influenced standard English and how they have been influenced by standard English. The assumption is made that students from diverse ethnic and cultural groups should understand and appreciate other languages and dialects.

The students in the multiethnic school also learn that languages are in the process of change and that a language system relfects the values and culture of a people. Thus, when you reject an individual's language or force him/her to reject it, you are rejecting an important part of that person or forcing him/her to reject part of the self. Students should also learn that the ways in which languages and dialects are viewed within a society reflects its power structure. The language and dialects spoken by groups with power within a society tend to be positively viewed; those spoken by groups that exercise little power tend to be rejected and ridiculed.

Multiethnic Testing

In the multiethnic school, the testing and assessment procedures reflect the ethnic and cultural characteristics of the students. Many students who are socialized within ethnic minority cultures find the tests and other aspects of the school setting alien and intimidating. Consequently, they tend to perform poorly on such tests and are placed in low academic tracks, special education classes, and low reading groups. Research indicates that teachers who teach in these kinds of situations tend to have low expectations for their students and often fail to create the kinds of learning environments which will enable them to master the skills and abilities needed to function successfully in society.

Standardized intelligence testing often serves to deny minority youths equal educational opportunities. The results of such tests are frequently used to justify the noneducation of minority youths and to relieve those who are responsible for their learning from accountability. We desperately need to devise novel approaches to assess the abilities of minority youths, and tests which will reflect the cultures in which they are socialized. However, it will do little good for us to create novel assessment procedures which reflect their cultures unless, at the same time, we implement curricular and teaching practices which are also multiethnic and multiracial. Students who score well on an ethnically oriented intelligence test are not likely to achieve well within an alien school culture which has a curriculum that is unrelated to their feelings, perceptions, and cultural experiences. Jane R. Mercer has identified some changes which multiethnic testing necessitates,

"... a multicultural perspective would recognize the integrity and value of different cultural traditions. It would not assume that the Anglo-American culture is necessarily superior to other traditions, or that Anglo-conformity is imperative for social cohesion. It would accept the fact that there are multiple cultural mainstreams in modern America and that individual citizens have the right to participate in as many of these mainstreams as they wish. Differences in life styles, language, and values would be treated with respect, and persons from minority cultures would not be regarded as culturally disadvantaged, culturally deprived, or empty vessels."[29]

A Final Note

Events within the last decade have dramatically indicated that we live in a world society that is beset with momentous social and human problems, many of which are related to ethnic hostility and conflict. Effective solutions to these tremendous problems can be found only by an active, compassionate, and ethnically sensitive citizenry capable of making sound public decisions that will benefit our ethnically diverse world community.

The current school curriculum is not helping most of our youths to prepare to function within a world community of the future. Many of our students grow up within middle class Anglo communities and attend all-white middle class schools. Their world is very different from the world society in which they will be required to function in the future. The white race is a world minority. Five out of six persons in the world are non-white and most are non-Christian. Because the birth-rate of non-whites greatly exceeds that of whites, white Christians will be an even smaller world minority by the year 2000. The school should present all students, from all racial, ethnic, and social class groups, with cultural and ethnic alternatives, and help them learn how to live in a world society that is ethnically and racially diverse. It should be an imperative to help all people to develop the vision and the commitment needed to make our world more humane.

NOTES AND REFERENCES

1. Alice Miel with Edwin Kiester, Jr. **The Shortchanged Children of Suburbia** (New York: American Jewish

Committee, 1967.)

2. Miel with Kiester, **ibid**, p.5.
3. Mildred Dickeman, "Teaching Cultural Pluralism", in James A. Banks, (Ed.), **Teaching Ethnic Studies: Concepts and Strategies**. Washington, D.C.: National council for the Social Studies, 1973, pp.5-25.
4. Israel Zangwill, **The Melting Pot**, New York: The Macmillan Company, 1909.
5. Ellwood Patterson Cubberley, **Changing Conceptions of Education**, Boston: Houghton Mifflin, 1909.
6. Cubberley, **ibid**, pp.15-16.
7. Horace M. Kallen, **Culture and Democracy in the United States: Studies in The Group Psychology of the American Peoples** (New York: Boni and Liveright Publishers, 1924); Randolph S. Bourne, "Trans-National America", **The Atlantic Monthly**, Vol. 118, July, 1916; Julius Drachsler, **Democracy and Assimilation: The Blending of Immigrant Heritages in America** (New York: Macmillan, 1920).
8. "Immigration Restriction: Laws of 1917 and 1921," in Henry Steele Commanger, (Ed.) **Documents of American History**, Volume II, Since 1898. Englewood Cliffs, N.J.: Prentice-Hall, 1973, p.135; "Immigration Act of 1924", in Commanger, p.192.
9. Commanger, **ibid**, p.135.
10. Commanger, **ibid**, p.192.
11. E. David Cronon, **Black Moses: The Story of Marcus Garvey and the Universal Negro Improvement Association**, (Madison: University of Wisconsin Press, 1955).
12. Judith Herman, **The Schools and Group Identity: Educating for a New Pluralism** (New York: American Jewish Committee, 1974).
13. Herman, **ibid**, p.15.
14. Kenneth B. Clark and Mamie P. Clark, "Racial Identification and Preference in Negro Children," in Theodore M. Newcomb and Eugene L. Hartley, (Eds.) **Readings in Social Psychology** (New York: Henry Holt, 1947); Mary Ellen Goodman, **Race Awareness in Young Children** (New York: Collier Books, 1952); J. Kenneth Morland, "Racial Self-Identification: A Study of Nursery School Children", **The American Catholic Sociological Review**, Vol.24. (Fall, 1963), pp.231-242.
15. Carlos E. Cortes, "The Societal Curriculum: Implications for Multiethnic Education", in James A. Banks, (Ed.) **Education in the 80's: Multiethnic Education**, (Washington, D.C.: National Education Association, 1981), pp.24-31.
16. Morland, **op.cit.**
17. Charles Y. Glock, Robert Wutnow, Jane A. Piliavin, and Metta Spencer, **Adolescent Prejudice** (New York: Harper and Row, 1975), p.172.

18. Clyde Kluckhohn, **Mirror for Man** (Greenwich, Conn.: Fawcett, 1965,) p.19.

19. Reprinted from Carlos E. Cortes with Fay Metcalfe and Shartyl Hawke, **Understanding You and Them: Tips for Teaching About Ethnicity** (Boulder, Colorado: Social Science Education Consortium, 1976). Reprinted with permission of the Consortium.

20. James Banks (Ed.) Education in the '80's: Multiethnic Education (National Education Association,Washington, D.C., 1981), p.22. Reprinted with permission of the N.E.A.

21. William Bill, "Teaching About the American Indian", Lecture presented at the University of Washington, Seattle, May, 1977.

22. Ray C. Rist, "Student Social Class and Teacher Expectations: The Self-Fullfilling Prophecy in Ghetto Education", **Harvard Educational Review**, Vol.40 (August, 1970), pp.411-451; Thomas P.Carter, **Mexican Americans in School: A History of Educational Neglect** (New York: College Entrance Examination Board, 1970); Geneva Gay, "Differential Dyadic Interactions with Black and White Pupils in Recently Desegregated Social Studies Classrooms: A Function of Teacher and Pupil Ethnicity", Washington, D.C.: National Institute of Education, 1974).

23. Theodore, W. Parsons, Jr. "Ethnic Cleavage in a California School, unpublished Ph.D. Thesis, Stanford University, August, 1965. Quoted in Carter, pp.82-84.

24. Quoted in Carter, pp.82-84.

25. James A. Banks, "Racial Prejudice and the Black Self-Concept", in James A. Banks and Jean D. Grambs (Eds.) **Black Self-Concept: Implications for Education and Social Science** (New York: McGraw-Hill, 1972), pp.5-35.

26. "No One Model American: A Statement on Multicultural Education", (Washington, D.C.: American Association of Colleges for Teacher Education, November, 1973).

27. James A. Banks, Carlos E. Cortes, Geneva Gay, Ricardo L. Garcia and Anna S. Ochoa, **Curriculum Guidelines for Multiethnic Education.** (Washington: D.C.: National Council for the Social Studies, 1976).

28. Geneva Smitherman, **Talkin and Testifyin: The Language of Black America** (Boston: Houghton Mifflin, 1977); William Labov, "The Logic of Nonstandard English", in Frederick Williams (Ed.) **Language and Poverty: Perspectives on A Theme** (Chicago: Markham Publishing Company, 1970), pp.153-187.

29. Jane R. Mercer, "Latent Functions of Intelligence Testing in the Public Schools", in Lamar P. Miller, (Ed.) **The Testing of Black Students** (Englewood Cliffs, N.J. : Prentice-Hall, 1974), p.91.

5 MULTICULTURAL EDUCATION AND SOCIETY IN CANADA AND YUGOSLAVIA

DAN DOROTICH AND WERNER STEPHAN

Any attempt at fully understanding the phenomenon of multiculturalism is fraught with a host of interrelated complex problems which, at times, appear to be insurmountable. First and foremost, of course, there is the question of meaning. Not only do anthropologists and sociologists of different schools of thought find it difficult to agree on a definition of culture as a concept, but even if some kind of consensus could be reached, the problem of what is meant by a multicultural society would likely engender new controversies. The same applies to multicultural education. There is a wide range of meanings of the concept[1], and different segments of the public, such as administrators, teachers, students, and parents, hold different views as to what multicultural education is supposed to accomplish.

Despite such difficulties, multicultural policies have been in effect for many years in a great number of countries, and schools have increasingly been charged with the responsibility of promoting social change through emphasis on certain aspects of multicultural education. The underlying principles have been stated implicitly rather than explicitly, and the resulting ambiguity has led to a great variety of curricular and extra-curricular programmes.

Following a descriptive account of multiculturalism and multicultural education in Canada and Yugoslavia, this study will try to derive some of those underlying sociolcultural and sociopolitical principles. It is our hope that this approach will also vividly portray the role of education in two different multicultural societies and point out the complexities of their respective policies.

In order to facilitate a comparative assessment, a number of assumptions have to be made and examined. First, in both

The authors wish to express their appreciation to Dr. A.B. Anderson, University of Saskatchewan for his valuable comments.

countries, multiculturalism is a "political" fact. The governments have recognized the multi-ethnic composition of their peoples and promised active support for what might be called "unity in diversity". Second, the two countries accept multiculturalism as a "social" fact. Cultural differences are not seen, at least by the governments, as a divisive force, but as a means of achieving social cohesion. Third, multiculturalism is also seen as an 'economic' fact. Attempts are being made to share evenly both production and consumption of material and non-material goods among the various segments of the multi-ethnic society through policies of equalization and the principle of equal opportunities. In the case of Canada, "equalization" applies to the provinces, and forms of "affirmative action" have been provided for ethnic and other minority groups. Fourth, both countries recognize multiculturalism as a "cultural" fact. The multicultural policies aim beyond cultural pluralism, in the sense of mere co-existence of diverse ethnic groups, acceptance of differences in life-styles, and tolerance. Rather, multiculturalism entails an interpenetration of existing value orientations and an extensive interaction among majority and minority groups. Finally, multiculturalism is a "pyschological" fact. Endorsement and publicity of multicultural policies by governments and other public institutions is expected to lead to change in attitudes and behaviours of individuals and, ultimately, to overcoming discrimination, stereotyping, and ethnocentrism.

THE POLITICAL DIMENSION OF MULTICULTURALISM

In 1971, the Canadian Prime Minister announced his government's multicultural policy within a bilingual framework as the most suitable vehicle for assuring the cultural freedom of Canadians. He promised that the government would lend support to cultural groups to develop a capacity to grow and to contribute to Canada, to overcome cultural barriers to full participation in Canadian society, to promote creative encounters and interchange, and to acquire at least one of the country's two official languages.[2] Ostensibly, the political objective of multiculturalism was the promotion of national unity through the strengthening of national allegiance.[3]

The new policy did not come unexpectedly. During the preceding years, the Royal Commission on Bilingualism and Biculturalism had toured the country to establish means by which English-French relations could be improved. But pressure from the "other" ethnic groups to have their contributions to Canada's development recognized prompted the Commission to publish an additional, fourth volume of its report, in 1969, in which these contributions were acknowledged. A perusal of the Tables 1, 2 and 3 will reveal the significance of the regional distribution of the various ethnic groups in Canada.

TABLE 1: POPULATION BY ETHNIC GROUP, 1951 and 1971

Ethnic group	1951		1971	
	No.	%	No.	%
British Isles	6,709,685	47.9		
English	3,630,344	25.9		
Irish	1,439,635	10.3		
Scottish	1,547,470	11.0	9,624,115	44.6
Welsh and other	92,236	0.7		
French	4,319,167	30.8	6,180,120	28.7
Other European	2,553,722	18.2	4,959,680	23.0
Austrian	32,231	0.2	42,120	0.2
Belgian	35,148	0.2	51,135	0.2
Czech & Slovak	63,959	0.5	81,870	0.4
Danish	42,671	0.3	75,725	0.4
Finnish	43,745	0.3	59,215	0.3
German	619,995	4.4	1,317,200	6.1
Greek	13,966	0.1	124,475	0.6
Hungarian	60,460	0.4	131,890	0.6
Icelandic	23,307	0.2	27,905	0.1
Italian	152,245	1.1	730,820	3.4
Jewish	181,670	1.3	296,945	1.4
Lithuanian	16,224	0.1	24,535	0.1
Netherlands	264,267	1.9	425,945	2.0
Norwegian	119,266	0.8	179,290	0.8
Polish	219,845	1.6	316,425	1.5
Portuguese			96,875	0.4
Romanian	23,601	0.2	27,375	0.1
Russian	91,279	0.7	64,475	0.3
Spanish			27,515	0.1
Swedish	97,780	0.7	101,870	0.5
Ukrainian	395,043	2.8	580,660	2.7
Yugoslavic	21,404	0.2	104,950	0.5
Other	35,616	0.2	70,460	0.3
Asiatic	72,827	0.5	285,540	1.3
Chinese	32,528	0.2	118,815	0.6
Japanese	21,663	0.2	37,260	0.2
Other	18,636	0.1	129,460	0.6
Other	354,028	2.5	518,850	2.4
Eskimo	9,733	0.1	17,550	0.1
Nat. Indian	155,874	1.1	295,215	1.4
Negro	18,020	0.1	34,445	0.2

Canada and Yugoslavia

TABLE 1 (cont'd)

Ethnic group	1951		1971	
	No.	%.	No.	%.
W. Indian			28,025	0.1
Other and not stated	170,401	1.2	143,620	0.7
Total	14,009,429	100.0	21,568,310	100.0

Source: Canada Year Book 1980-81. Statistics Canada, Ottawa.

TABLE 2: NUMERICAL AND PERCENTAGE DISTRIBUTION OF THE POPULATION SPEAKING ONE OR BOTH OF THE OFFICIAL LANGUAGES, BY PROVINCE, 1971.

Year and province or territory	English only		French only		English and French		Neither English nor French	
	No.	%	No.	%	No.	%	No.	%
1971								
Newfoundland	511,620	98.0	510	0.1	9,350	1.8	625	0.1
Prince Edward Island	101,820	91.2	680	0.6	9,110	8.2	30	-
Nova Scotia	730,700	92.6	4,185	0.5	53,035	6.7	1,035	0.1
New Brunswick	396,855	62.5	100,985	15.9	136,115	21.5	600	0.1
Quebec	632,515	10.5	3,668,020	60.9	1,663,790	27.6	63,445	1.1
Ontario	6,724,100	87.3	92,840	1.2	716,065	9.3	170,090	2.2
Manitoba	881,715	89.2	5,020	0.5	80,935	8.2	20,585	2.1
Saskatchewan	867,315	93.6	1,825	0.2	45,985	5.0	11,110	1.2
Alberta	1,525,575	93.7	3,310	0.2	81,000	5.0	17,990	1.1
British Columbia	2,054,690	94.1	1,775	0.1	101,435	4.6	26,725	1.2
Yukon	17,130	93.2	5	-	1,210	6.6	35	0.2
N.W.Terr.	25,000	73.3	100	0.3	2,120	6.1	7,085	20.4
Canada	14,469,540	67.1	3,879,255	18.0	2,900,155	13.4	319,160	1.5

TABLE 3: POPULATION BY SELECTED ETHNIC GROUPS, CANADA AND THE PROVINCES, 1971, IN PERCENT

	New-found-land	Prince Edward Island	Nova Scotia	New Bruns-wick	Quebec	Ontario	Mani-toba	Sask-atch-ewan	Alberta	British Co-lumbia	Canada
British*	93.9	82.7	77.5	57.7	10.8	59.3	41.9	42.1	46.7	57.8	44.6
French	3.0	13.8	10.1	37.1	79.1	9.6	8.9	6.1	5.8	4.4	28.7
German	0.5	0.9	5.2	1.3	0.9	6.2	12.5	19.4	14.2	9.0	6.1
Italian	0.1	0.1	0.5	0.2	2.8	6.0	1.1	0.3	1.5	2.5	3.4
Ukrainian	—	0.1	0.3	0.1	0.3	2.1	11.6	9.3	8.3	2.8	2.7
Dutch	0.1	1.1	1.9	0.8	0.2	2.7	3.6	2.1	3.6	3.2	2.0
Polish	0.1	0.1	0.4	0.1	0.4	1.9	4.3	2.9	2.7	1.4	1.5
Indian (Native)	0.2	0.3	0.6	0.6	0.5	0.8	4.4	4.4	2.7	2.4	1.4
Jewish	0.1	0.1	0.3	0.2	1.9	1.8	2.0	0.2	0.4	0.6	1.4
Norwegian	0.1	0.1	0.3	0.2	0.1	0.3	0.8	3.9	3.2	2.4	0.8
Other	1.9	0.7	2.9	1.7	3.0	9.3	8.9	9.3	10.9	13.5	7.4

Source: Adapted from Statistics Canada, Cat. 92-762. The figures of the 1981 census have not yet been released.

*The British group comprises the English, Scots, Irish and Welsh who, in fact, might display very strong national identities. Therefore, to group them together as British is misleading to some extent.

Canada is mainly a land of immigrants. Her native peoples, namely the Indians, Metis, and Inuit (Eskimos) comprise only 1.4 percent of the total population of about 24.5 million. The last three centuries have witnessed various immigration patterns. Initially, the French and British settled in the eastern parts of the country and then in British Columbia. Toward the end of the 19th and the early 20th centuries, the western Canadian prairies were largely settled by East Europeans. Following World War II, many European refugees came in, succeeded by a massive influx of Italians and Portuguese, and, lately, by waves of immigrants and refugees from Asia, Africa, Latin America and the West Indies.

Despite claims to the contrary, the so-called 'ethnics' have never become a Third Force that could or would affect the political power structure of the country. Earlier attempts by immigrant workers to form trade unions or political organizations along ethnic lines were severely dealt with by the authorities.[4] Key positions of political decision making and control of the economy are predominantly in the hands of British, and, to a lesser degree, of French Canadians.

The effects of the overall political culture on the educational system are obvious. Although education is primarily a provincial responsibility, and although the provincial governments jealously guard their autonomy, the principles of political socialization as a process of legitimizing the mechanisms and the processes of political control are similar if not identical throughout Canada. With respect to multicultural education, there is undeniably an increasing recognition of the members of various ethnic groups as significant contributors to social life. School textbooks try to avoid stereotyping, and special programmes in support of the cultural heritage of given ethnic groups proliferate, especially in urban centres where ethnic groups are concentrated.

The Yugoslavian Constitution, like the recent Canadian Constitution, recognizes the cultural diversity of the component segments of the population, though in much more explicit and detailed ways. As shown in Table 4, a distinction is made between "nations" or "peoples", such as Croats, Serbs, Moslems, Slovenes, Macedonians, and Montenegrins and "nationalities", such as Albanians, Hungarians, Turks, etc. (comparable to Canadian ethnic groups).[5] Accordingly, the 'nations' form the majority of the population in each of the six republics, while "nationalities" are found in varying degrees of density in the republics and the two autonomous provinces within Serbia. Some Albanians, who form the majority in the province of Kosovo, have lately been demanding a status of republic for their province.

In contrast to the Canadian political system, the Yugoslav Constitution has opted for the delegate system as the basis of

Canada and Yugoslavja

TABLE 4: POPULATION BY NATIONS AND NATIONALITIES, YUGOSLAVIA, 1971.*

	%	Number
NATIONS:		
Serbs	39.7	8,143,246
Croats	22.1	4,526,782
Moslems	8.4	1,729,932
Slovenes	8.2	1,678,032
Macedonians	5.8	1,194,784
Montenegrins	2.5	508,843
NATIONALITIES:		
Albanians	6.4	1,309,523
Hungarians	2.3	477,374
Turks	0.6	127,920
Slovaks	0.4	83,656
Bulgarians	0.3	58,627
Rumanians	0.3	58,570
Czechs	0.1	24,620
Italians	0.1	21,791
Ruthenians	0.1	24,640
Other	2.7	554,120

Source: Adapted from Federal Statistical Office Beograd (1972), Statistical Bulletin 727.

* Although some figures for 1981 are available, the 1971 - census figures are given here to match the 1971 - figures in Table 3.

103

all socio-political structures.[6] Each republic, regardless of the size of its population, delegates an equal number of representatives to the two chambers of the federal parliament, thereby ensuring the full equality of the nations and nationalities of the country.

In Yugoslavia, languages is considered to be a key element of ethnic identity. Although the Croats, Serbs, and Montenegrins together form an overwhelming majority of the country, their common language, the Serbo-Croatian, or Croato-Serbian, is not considered as the lingua-franca of Yugoslavia; only within the army is it used as the official language of communication.

The multicultural education practised in the various Yugoslav republics and provinces is centred around the linguistic rights of the ethnic groups involved: each political entity, even at the municipality level, determines which language or languages will be recognized for administrative and educational purposes.[7] The cost of implementing these policies, including the provision of textbooks in a multitude of languages, is enormous; and yet, such a sacrifice is considered as acceptable in the pursuit of achieving the higher value of national unity through equality.

THE SOCIAL DIMENSION OF MULTICULTURALISM

Even the casual visitor to Canada will be surprised at the ease with which members of different ethnic groups interact. The foundation for the acceptance of the culturally different person was laid well before the announcement of the government's multicultural policy. The years since 1971 have witnessed a strengthening of the public image of ethnic groups as "legitimate" Canadians. And yet, the fact remains that ethnic stratification greatly affects social stratification. Natives and recent immigrants (particularly of non-anglophone or Oriental backgrounds) usually rank at the bottom of the scale, whereas the new and the old 'establishment', mostly of British stock, occupy the upper portions of the ranking system.[8]

It is within this social class, or stratification system, that the new multicultural policies can best be understood. Social mobility in Canadian society is still influenced by ascriptive factors, of which ethnic membership is one. Greater recognition of ethnic groups, achieved partly through financial support of scholarly research of ethnic histories and inter-ethnic relations, and partly through sponsorship of ethnic festivals, has been the result of governmental efforts at both the federal and provincial levels.[9] Some critics of multiculturalism view these expenditures as counterproductive and they believe that stressing diversity endangers the goal of national cohesion; other critics perceive multicultural policies as a paliative for social inequality, designed to legitimize the preservation of the <u>status quo</u> [10] Many more years will be needed to assess the full impact of multiculturalism on Canada's social fabric.

Two aspects of multicultural education have to be discussed in this context. First, the government's insistence that multiculturalism can only be pursued in a bilingual framework necessitates that either English in Quebec or French in the other provinces be offered in schools as so-called second languages. While this policy recognizes the historical roots of the Canadian Confederation, it also acknowledges implicitly that language can be instrumental in furthering social integration and in facilitating social mobility. Yet, there is strong opposition to English in francophone Quebec, just as there are many anglophone Canadians who resent the official status of French as a second national language in Canada. In this squabble, other languages have been grossly neglected and have no official status.

The second point follows from there: Ethnic minority groups have begun to establish their own private schools, often operating only on weekends, mainly to preserve their language and cultural heritage. In this, they seem to follow a model set by the two "charter groups", or the so-called "founding nations" who have used private schools for more than a century to serve their particular social, political, and cultural needs and objectives.

The socio-political changes that have taken place in Yugoslavia since 1945 have also had a most decisive impact on the country's system of social stratification. Similar to Canadian society, there is a hierarchical ranking system. Political and economic leaders form the upper echelon, while the peasants occupy the lowest rung of the social ladder. [11] In contrast to Canada, social mobility in Yugoslavia is determined by contest or achievement more than by inherited status or other kinds of sponsorship. Based on the equality of nations and nationalities, ethnic origin has little, if any, effect on one's social position. Conflicts between Serbs and Croats appear to be related to political and economic issues and not to socio-cultural inequalities. [12]

Nevertheless, disparities continue to exist in the levels of prosperity along regional lines and, to that extent, also ethnic lines. As Bicanic has argued, the variation in gross national product per capita between the most advanced republic (Slovenia) and the least advanced (Bosnia-Herzegovina) is in a ratio of 3:1; while at district level it rises even to 10:1. [13] The national policy to assist underdeveloped areas also has a socialist motive; attempts are made to distribute the national income in such a way as to have all parts of the country progress towards socialism at an equal pace, with socialist solidarity being the ultimate goal. [14]

Educational provisions for members of given ethnic groups are based on the principle of self-management. On the one hand, this enables the individual to form and express his interest in the sphere of education, culture, and science, while, on the other hand, it entitles the individual to participate actively in shaping and carrying out educational and cultural policies, thus ensuring the cultural development of nationalities on a broad and democratic basis.[15] The right to unhindered development of national cultures is guaranteed by the Constitution, which states, in Article 170, that "citizens shall be guaranteed freedom of expressing membership of a nation or nationality, free expression of national culture and free use of their language and alphabet".[16] This provision is also contained in the constitutions of all the republics and provinces.

THE ECONOMIC DIMENSION OF MULTICULTURALISM

An exploration of the implications of economics for multiculturalism in the Canadian context has to take into account the fact that large sectors of the economy are owned by multinational corporations whose headquarters are located outside Canada. Their respective policies - for example in the publishing industry or the film industry - undeniably have an effect on the cultural self-concept of Canadians. Furthermore, the proximity of the United States and the close trade relations with that country, especially in the areas of the print and electronic media of mass communications, as well as the influence of American universities on shaping the views of political, economic, and cultural leaders in Canada, tend to foster an ideology of unilingual North American continentalism, rather than a Canadian mutliculturalism, in a bilingual, let alone multilingual framework.

Another salient feature, pertinent to this discussion, is the insistence among Canadian economic leaders on the principle of free enterprise which appeals to the entrepreneurial spirit of individuals rather than of groups. As a result, members of ethnic groups compete in the market place individually, and it is only on the local level that they can expect to draw on the support of other group members in establishing themselves and in serving the specific needs of their clients or customers.[17]

The historical advantage, especially prior to Confederation in 1867, enjoyed by British merchants and, in particular, their access to capital in Britain has laid the foundation for an over-representation of Anglo-Canadians in the economic elite. The so-called "WASPS", the White Anglo-Saxon protestants, constitute 86.2 percent of the elite, but only 44.7 percent of the entire population. By contrast, the comparative figures for French-Canadians are 8.4 percent and 28.6 percent, and for the other ethnic groups 5.4 percent and 26.7 percent respectively. Among the latter, the 5.4 percent figure can further be subdivided into 4.1 percent for the

Jewish community, and only 1.3 percent for all the other ethnic groups.[18]

The implications for multicultural eduction are far-reaching, indeed. First, as a result of the fact that the production of material and, especially, non-material goods is almost exclusively controlled by foreign corporations whose primary objective is financial gain rather than cultural enrichment, even the inclusion of multicultural materials in textbooks and other instructional materials is marginal. More often than not, it is geared towards the North-American, and not specifically the Canadian market. Second, as a result of the predominance of English as the main, if not the sole, language of Canadian economic life, the study of other languages, with some exceptions of French, is relegated merely to the fringes of academic pursuits. In other words, the learning, or the retention of ancestral languages has, at best, only a symbolic value within multicultural eduation. Third, the recruitment of the economic elite from prestigious private schools, attended almost exclusively by the "WASP", diminishes otherwise genuine efforts on the part of the public eduational system to provide equal opportunities for all.

As Horvat has argued, the Yugoslav economic system is unique in that, while it has abolished private ownership and decentralized decision making, it has also rejected state ownership of the means of production. As a result, the Yugoslav model could most accurately be described as "associationist socialism", based on the principle of social ownership.[19] Contrary to the Canadian situation, entrepreneurial functions are exercised not by individuals but, for better or worse, by the collective of workers. Self-management within a decentralized economic system implies that members of the respective nations and nationalities become fully involved in the decision-making process. Foreign ownership, especially control, and even ownership and control by Yugoslavs living outside a given republic or province, is thus made impossible. Wherever financial aid is needed in underdeveloped areas or districts, aid from the Federal Government's solidarity fund is allocated to strengthen the local economy[20], somewhat like equalization payments in Canada.

The level of relative regional development or underdevelopment is, however, one of the factors affecting the equality of workers, aswell as of students in terms of educational opportunities. Such disparities are, at times, a cause for tensions in Yugoslavia's internal relations, as evidenced by complaints voiced in parliament by delegates from Croatia and Slovenia who claimed that they had to take a major share in providing support for the less developed republics, such as Macedonia, Bosnia-Herzegovina, and Montenegro[21]; or by such events as had taken place in the Autonomous Province of Kosovo in the Spring of 1981.

It is interesting to note, however, that, in terms of educational opportunities, the less developed republics provide, at the post-secondary level, proportionately more students than the richer republics, suggesting that the university acts as an agent for social mobility if alternative avenues are blocked, especially since higher education is free.[22] The foregoing argument does not, on the other hand, mean that equality of educational opportunity has been achieved. Although the proportion of children from rural or working-class backgrounds at university has increased, children from larger urban centres with a greater number of university-trained parents are more strongly represented.[23]

THE CULTURAL DIMENSION OF MULTICULTURALISM

Canadians are generally in agreement that the American metaphor of the "melting-pot" has not reflected the cultural policy of Canadian governments during the last few decades, but that the image of a "mosaic", "quilt", or "salad bowl", more acurately portrays the persistence of cultural manifestations of the component ethnic groups. In more academic terms, the issue centres around such concepts a assimilation, accommodation, and integration. As Anderson and Frideres have cogently argued, the meaning of "assimilation" has undergone considerable change.[24] In the Canadian context, it is virtually synonymous with Anglo-conformity which, in the more recent past, has been rejected in favour of cultural pluralism. Here, integration, in the sense of cultural differentition and reciprocity, allows for the maintenance of ethnic identity. Accommodation, on the other hand, intervenes between segregation and assimilation, while implying the mutual acceptance of some integration. At least in theory, they point out,

" a multi-national state should rest upon the principle of sanctioning cultural variability and group differences within the context of national federalism furnishing the means of integrating minorities and encouraging some sort of national unity."[25]

Canadian society, perceiving itself as pluralistic rather than multi-national, has not fully adopted this notion of accommodation, as indicated by the special linguistic status granted to the British and French "charter groups". Spokesmen of ethnic minority groups claim, however, that accommodation would enable each group to contribute the most valuable aspects of their cultural heritage, thus making it part of the national culture.[26]

Multicultural education in Canada reflects the ambiguity that still surrounds the notion of multiculturalism. As mentioned above, recent instructional materials tend to present a more balanced picture of cultural values espoused by various ethnic groups, for example, of natives and other minorities, such as the Hutterites. The financial support of full-time or part-time schools catering to the needs of minority groups also points at multiculturalism as an accommodative response. An example for viewing multiculturalism as favouring assimilation is the growing number of agencies involved in teaching English as a second language (or second dialect). The most recent language legislation in Quebec (Bill 101) points in the same direction. So-called heritage days, on the other hand, seem to reflect the integrationist perspective, where the aspect of cultural differentiation, as the persistence of specific cultural identities, is most pronounced.

In attempting to discuss and analyse the cultural dimensions of the Yugoslav multinational society, brief reference has to be made to historical circumstances. The impact of Austrian, Hungarian, and Turkish cultural influences, to name just a few, created a vast diversity of customs and traditions. An even greater variety could be found in comparing levels of development among those cultures, with some possessing highly sophisticated forms of cultural expressions, while others, before 1944, have even lacked a fully developed and recognized literary language, e.g. in Macedonia.

At present, the officially endorsed equality of national cultures and, thus, the right to cultivate specifically national characteristics, also extends to the nationalities, as expressed in the statement of the Central Committee of the League of Communists of Yugoslavia in 1959. The nationalities retain their features as part of the nation

"to which they belong ethnically and whose specifics, primarily those of cultural nature, they carry themselves mingling them with those of the environment in which they live...but the national minorities are not only a part of the nations from which they are derived, but are bound to the country in which they live, all the more so inasmuch as they are guaranteed an equal status and unhindered development."[27]

It is significant that this statement was made by a Hungarian, the deputy minister of education in the Province of Vojvodina. The accommodative thrust of the policy is quite obvious. It provides for a free and comprehensive flourishing of the national cultures, while, at the same time, linking them to the overall environment for mutual stimulation and enrichment. This right to cultural self-expression, according to a Yugoslav scholar, no longer has as its unifying element a "unitary socialist Yugoslav culture", as once proclaimed by Tito, but merely has to be exercised within the framework of a 'Yugoslav socialist commonwealth'[28].

Education in Yugoslavia is the responsiblity of the republics and provinces, each with its own laws and regulations based on their own constitutions within the general framework of the federal constitution. Each republic and province, and even municipality, determines which language or languages will be recognized for administrative and educational purposes. They are called languages of the social environment. The province of Vojvodina, for example, has five such languages.

While provision for elementary education in the languages of the nationalities is "guaranteed" by the constitution, secondary and higher education, on the other hand, is only "made possible". Nevertheless, whenever numbers warrant, both secondary and more advanced levels of education are provided for the nationalities, as well as for the nations. The Albanians of Kosovo, for example, today can acquire their entire education in their mother tongue; before 1945 their language was not used even in the elementary grades. The language of the Macedonians, today one of the nations of Yugoslavia, before liberation in 1944 was not recognized as a language but merely a dialect of Serbian. Today the Macedonians have their own Academy of Sciences.

Although the unified public school is the rule, there are some private schools, such as the Seventh Day Adventist School in Croatia. However, these, too, must satisfy the curriculum requirements of regular schools. Included in the curricula for nationalities are subjects such as history, music, and artistic education relating to their cultural heritage. Complete sets of textbooks and readers are published in the languages of nationalities. While, for subjects like mathematics and the natural sciences, the content is identical in all languages, in subjects such as nature and social studies, history, and even geography, textbooks are modified or even designed separately for each nationality. In addition to the history of all of Yugoslavia, they contain material from the cultural and historical heritage of the specific nation and nationality.[29] Other cultural activities aim at developing the national culture, contributing to the overall culture of the Yugoslav community, enriching the nationalities' own culture with the cultural values of other peoples and nationalities and with the values of world culture, and, finally, becoming a bridge between the cultures of the Yugoslav peoples and the culture of the mother culture.[30]

THE PSYCHOLOGICAL DIMENSION OF MULTICULTURALISM

The question of how an individual feels about his own ethnicity and of others can be related to issues such as self-concept formation, personal values versus group values, religious views, and perception of reality, to name just a few. Other concepts such as racism, ethnocentrism, discrimination, and ethnic stereotyping also belong in the same overall category.

In the Canadian context, the most effective multicultural programs and activities have been developed recently in major metropolitan centres, such as Toronto, Vancouver, Edmonton, and Winnipeg. The concentration of members of various ethnic groups, particularly pronounced in these cities, facilitates the preservation of language and customs, but, at times, also creates tensions and outbursts of racism. Hard economic times tend to increase the polarization among ethnic groups, especially if recent immigrants and refugees are involved. Immigrants are often seen as competing for the same jobs and are made scapegoatsfor the rising rate of unemployment. Measures have been initiated by the authorities to combat discrimination and stereotyping, most notably through publication of ethnic newspapers, establishment of ethnic radio and television programmes, and public endorsement of ethnic folklore. Leaders of active ethnic communities have become more involved in municipal affairs, others have been elected to serve in provincial or federal parliaments, and some have even been appointed to the Senate.

An example of how an individual can be positively affected by a multicultural policy is the following comment by a young student of Ukrainian descent who visited her relatives in the Ukraine as part of an exchange programme:

"Although we live in two very different worlds, we all experienced a closeness that was heightened by the maintenance of a common cultural heritage. My relatives were pleased to find that, although our family has been in Canada for three generations, I could speak the language and therefore participate in the culture meaningfully. It was at this time that I fully experienced the deep personal satisfaction that results from maintaining close ties with one's cultural roots, and I felt grateful both to my parents and to my country, Canada, for nuturing within me a pride in one's heritage within a multicultural society."[31]

Ethnic group values, however, do not necessarily determine a person's self-concept. Many Canadians consider the emphasis on 'outlandish' traditions as being detrimental to developing a truly Canadian identity, arguing that immigrants by opting for Canada as their new homeland have implicitly also opted for identifying with Canadian values. But, the example cited above suggests that one set of values does not necessarily exclude other values. A more valid argument against multiculturalism is that maintenance of ethnic differentiation tends to lead to social and economic discrimination.

Multicultural education reflects this controversy in many ways. There can be no question that the students' identification with Canadian political and social values is paramount in the socialization process. Especially, students who have recently come to Canada tend to experience the syndrome of marginality, being neither fully committed to their ancestral traditions (as possibly their parents still are), nor being fully accepted by their new class-mates. The perceived need to satisfy the expectations of their parents as well as those of the peer-group is likely to produce enormous psychological stress, with as yet undetermined consequences. The still unresolved problem seems to be that students feel they have to make a choice between two sets of values. This is, possibly, an important area where multicultural education has to intervene.

Some of the issues outlined above can also be applied to Yugoslav society. For example, many Yugoslavs refuse to identify themselves at census time as members of given nations or nationalities and claim "Yugoslav" as their nationality. Although they are still a minority of slightly more than five percent of the total population, the census lists them simply as what they prefer to be, namely Yugoslavs. On the other hand, remnants of the traditional rivalries among some of the major national groups, coupled with differences of temperament, tend to colour in some cases their views of the political and social reality in different ways, leading to charges of discrimination and patronage along ethnic lines. According to Doder, these tensions appear to affect the older generation more than the younger Yugoslavs who have grown up within the multi-national state and who share many positive experiences (in common) in contrast to their elders' past experiences.[32]

Over the last four decades, the expansion of a network of radio and television stations to serve specific ethnic groups supplemented the policy of providing magazines, newspapers, and books in all the major languages for all age-groups. The intent appears to be to strengthen the identity of members of given nations and nationalities, but also to demonstrate the equality of all these groups within the broad family of Yugoslav society.

Within the school system, the provision of curricula for any number of ethnic groups even within one school creates administrative problems. If there are more than fifteen students of a given nationality per class, they can legally expect to be educated, at least in part, in their own language, including the use of textbooks. Students and parents have come to expect that their views, customs, and traditions will be respected in schools, as well as at the working place and in all social institutions, not excluding the parliament itself.[33]

CONCLUSIONS

As has been stated at the beginning, the issue of inter-ethnic or multicultural relations is extremely complex, and to try to compare the two societies in this regard is like comparing two three-dimensional structures which may or may not serve identical or similar purposes.

Two major problems emerging from the foregoing discussion need to be mentioned. First, there is the question of the authenticity and objectivity of the sources examined. With regard to the Yugoslav situation, for example, government publications tend to omit references to problems encountered in implementing multinational policies and to ignore criticism levelled by opponents. Conversely, accounts written by some emigres, more often than not, present a critical or plainly hostile interpretation of government actions, which may have prompted them to emigrate in the first place. In a similar vein, members of Canadian majority groups will assess the merits and demerits of multiculturalism differently from those of minority groups, and even among the latter disagreement might arise.

The second problem concerns the comparability of the functions of institutions or policies in countries with fundamentally different ideological orientations. Since multiculturalism is an integral part of the ideological apparatus serving the legitimization and maintenance of given socio-political structures, such as the Yugoslav and Canadian states, multicultural education has a distinctively political function. As a result, multicultural education in Canada and multi-national education in Yugoslavia have in common their supportive function of the political status quo, but they differ in their ideological objectives: in Canada, multiculturalism aims at diminishing potential conflict over an unequal distribution of resources, promising equal chances of access, regardless of traditional patterns of ethnic stratification. In Yugoslavia, the principle of social ownership assures equality of access, but the thrust of multiculturalism is more towards uniting traditionally antagonistic groups within a socialist order under the slogan "Brotherhood and Unity".

A few other points deserve mentioning. Achieving a multicultural society without linguistic equality appears to be possible only if multiculturalism is defined in very narrow, folkloristic terms. As a corollary, multicultural policies should benefit the individual as well as the group. Only if the individual can personally identify with such policies will he lend active support. While strengthening the group, the rights of the individual must also be safeguarded. Furthermore, the egalitarian thrust of multiculturalism has to be compatible not only with the dominant social philosophy of a given country, but also with its political and economic objectives and realities. If multiculturalism is merely appended to otherwise entrenched political and economic structures, the effects will be marginal, at best.

Yugoslavia's present multi-national policy is certainly more "seasoned" than Canadian multiculturalism. Not only has the former been in effect for more than three decades, but it has also undergone changes and refinement. One could also argue that the urgency of finding an adequate solution to the problem of national unity was by far more pressing there than in Canada. However, the fact that more and more countries perceivethe need to accommodate ethnic or national minorities within their boundaries cannot be ignored. Both the Yugoslav and the Canadian solutions have the potential of contributing significant insights. While the Yugoslav formula of multiculturalism has so far successfully weathered the test provided by the departure from the scene of its founder, President Tito, Canada's seems to be heading for turbulent waters under the dual pressure of continued inflow of immigrants and depressed economic conditions.

If an institution, including state or school system, wants to survive, it must satisfy the basic needs of its constituents.

> "...Human rights are not only a matter of justice for individuals and groups, but also a condition <u>sine qua non</u> for the continued survival of a national or a social system."[34]

NOTES AND REFERENCES

1. Young, J.C. "Education in a Multicultural Society: What Sort of Education? What Sort of Society? in **Canadian Journal of Education,** Vol.4, No.3, 1979.
2. **Debates,** House of Commons Ottowa 1971.
3. Reitz. J.G., **The Survival of Ethnic Groups.** McGraw-Hill Ryserson. Toronto 1980. p.12.
4. Avery. D., **Dangerous Foreigners.** McClelland and Stewart. Toronto 1979.
5. In the Canadian context, such "nations" would comprise the Indians and Metis, the Innuit, as well as the French and British groups. The term "nationalities" in Canada would designate the so-called ethnic groups. In Yugoslavia, the term "moslem" designates religious affiliation. "Moslem" designates the Moslem Slavs of Bosnia-Herzegovina. A "nation" is defined in terms of common territory, history, culture and language. "Nationalities" in Yugoslavia do not have their own territory or distinct common history, but only common culture and language, leaving the Albanian "nationality", for example, in an ambiguous position.
6. Topaloski, Ilija., "Language Rights in Yugoslavia" in **Language and Society,** No.8, Autumn 1982. p.13.
7. Dorotich,D., "Ethnic Diversity and National Unity in Yugoslav Education: The Socialist Autonomous Province of Vojvodina" in **Compare,** Vol.8, No.1, 1978, p.81.
8. Detailed sociological analyses are given in Porter, J., **The Vertical Mosaic,** University of Toronto Press, 1965, Clement, W.,**The Canadian Corporate Elite,** McClelland and

Stewart, Toronto, 1975, and Newmand P.C., **The Canadian Establishment,** McClelland and Stewart, Toronto 1975.

9. Anderson, A.B. and Frideres, J. **Ethnicity in Canada,** Butterworth, Toronto. 1981.

10. Werner, S. "Panem et Circenses? Ten Years of Multicultural Policy in Canada" in Dorotich, D., (Ed). **Education and Canadian Multiculturalism: Some Problems and Some Solutions.** Canadian Society for the Study of Education. Saskatoon. 1981.

11. Horvat, Branko., **An Essay on Yugoslav Society,** International Arts and Sciences Press, New York, 1969, p.150.

12. Ra'anan,G.D., **Yugoslavia after Tito,** Westview Press, Boulder, Colorado. 1977, pp.27-36.

13. Bicanic, R., **Economic Policy in Socialist Yugoslavia,** Cambridge University Press, 1973, p.181.

14. **ibid** p.183.

15. Varga, L., "National Equality in Education, Culture, Science and Other Social Activities" in Dragic, N., (Ed). **Nations and Nationalities of Yugoslavia,** Medjunarodna Politika, Beograd, 1974, p.332.

16. **Ustav Socijalisticka Federativne Republike Jugoslavije,** Savremena Administracija, Beograd, 1974.

17. Reitz. J.G., **loc. cit.**

18. Clement, W., **The Canadian Corporate Elite.** McClelland and Stewart, Toronto, 1975, pp.232-237.

19. Horvat, B., **loc.cit,** p.92.

20. Bicanic, R., **loc.cit,** pp.189-191.

21. Ra'anan, G.D., **loc.cit,** p.33.

22. Institute for Social Research. **Innovation in Higher Education: Reforms in Yugoslavia,** O.E.C.D., Paris, 1970, p.61.

23. Pervan, R., **Tito and the Students,** University of Western Australia press, Nedlands W.A., 1978, p.97.

24. Anderson A.B. and Frideres, J. **loc.cit,** pp.271-85.

25. Anderson A.B. and Frideres, J. **op.cit.,** p.293.

26. Anderson A.B. and Frideres, J. **op.cit.,** p.294.

27. Varga. L., **loc.cit.** pp.338-9. "Nation" here refers to neighbouring countries from which the nationalities originate.

28. Doder, D., **The Yugoslavs,** Random House, New York, 1978, p.207.

29. Dorotich, D., **loc.cit.** pp.81-90.

30. Varga. L., **loc.cit,** p.361.

31. Maruschak, L., "Impressions of Chernivtsi and Ukraine" in **The Green and White,** University of Saskatchewan Alumni Association, Fall, 1982, p.29.

32. Doder, D., **loc.cit.** p.40.

33. In Vojvodina, for example discussions in the parliament are held in five languages, with simultaneous interpretation provided for all.

34. Dorotich.D., "Education for Ethnic Minorities in Canada, with some implications for Canada" in **Second Banff Conference on Control and East European Studies, Education Presentations,** The University of Alberta, Edmonton 1978, p.19.

6 THE EMERGENCE OF CULTURAL DIVERSITY IN AUSTRALIA

DUDLEY HICK

"Dogs, horses and aboriginals possess perfect memories and have no need to forget; though perhaps it would be better to say that they have so little to remember that the task is simple".

On reading this statement now, one's reaction is astonishment at its artless naivety, and outrage at its offensive assumption that aborigines can be categorised with dogs and horses. Yet this was published in 1938 by the editor of the Victorian Historical Magazine in what he presumably thought was a learned article.[1] Numerous similar examples could be quoted, since such an attitude was not considered objectionable, nor even idiosyncratic at that time. The European settler simply did not understand the aborigine, did not want to understand him, and had no real awareness of his existence.

Following the establishment of the penal colony in New South Wales in 1788, the new society adopted the values of the old from whence they had come. Property ownership was sacrosanct, land grants were made, and on these lands sheep and cattle grazed. The aboriginal population had over many millenia developed a different kind of society, based on the tribal community. They were nomads, and hunters, and found the newly introduced domestic animals easier to hunt than kangaroos, and this brought them into conflict with the new arrivals. Many of these had been transported for the very offences which the aborigines assumed to be a natural condition of their existence, and were swift to retaliate with all the modern means that they possessed. This involved shooting on sight, expeditions to hunt down and destroy the poachers, and the poisoning of food and drinking places. In the course of time the threat to the new settlers was removed, but with it any possibility of an accommodation with the indigenous population, and certainly no understanding of their culture.

Henceforth the aborigines lived on the fringe of white society. Where they were starkly visible in the poorer

117

quarters of the large cities, they were in menial employment, if indeed they worked at all, and were seen to live ugly, squalid lives, evident proof, if one wished to think so, of their innate inferiority. Where they were seen by few in the remoteness of their vast continent, their image was romanticised. Missions were established and well-intentioned ministers and missionaries sought to civilise the pagans in their care. Christian values were carefully inculcated, and the way of life of the white man was offered as a superior model for emulation. A citizenry intent on keeping Australia white and racially pure - these were the days before the new political ideology of national socialism demonstrated with awesome reality the logical and terrifying conclusion of such a policy - felt embarrassed at a group, whose very presence highlighted the absurdity of the White Australia policy.

Aboriginal communities lived on reserves or outstations, away from public of foreign scrutiny. Here their civil rights were circumscribed in the name of their individual and corporate welfare. They were not considered capable of handling financial matters, beyond the spending of pocket money. They were housed, clothed and fed, and cared for in matters of health, along with the stock that grazed the properties. They were sometimes treated with affection, and often with kindness, but rarely with understanding. There was in some quarters a genuine concern for the education of the children, and schools were provided in the vain hope that they would be assimilated into white society, and there was disappointment and disillusion when they didn't. There are on record many instances of children being taken from their natural parents and placed with foster parents, and there must be very many more that are unrecorded. Cruel and heartless as it may seem, it must be conceded that the intentions were well meant. Wherever white Australians were in contact with aborigines in country towns, prejudice and hostility reigned, and the missions and reserves offered a haven. If little that was positive could be achieved in the matter of aboriginal advancement, at least the negative aspects of racial strife could be avoided, or at least minimised. Those who cared accepted with resignation that the aborigine was ill-equipped to survive in the modern world, and that his race was inevitably doomed to extinction.

> "Like most Australians of my generation, I accepted the prevailing dogma that Aborigines were doomed to become extinct and believed that, apart from behaving towards those we encountered with common humanity, there was nothing that we could usefully do."[2]

This prediction was totally inaccurate since it is now known that the aboriginal population was increasing with some rapidity. It is estimated that in 1788 there were some 300,000 aboriginal inhabitants of the continent, and that this number had been reduced to something like 40,000 in the early part of the century. The tide seems to have turned just before the second world war, and by 1970 there were between 120,000 and 150,000 people of aboriginal descent in Australia. More significantly more than half of these were under fifteen years of age, and of these half were under five.3   This ignorance however is not surprising, since no accurate demographic records were kept of the aboriginal population, and when the quinquennial census was taken the aborigines simply did not count.

In May 1967 a referendum was held to ask the people to agree to two proposals - to include the aboriginal population in the census record, and to empower the Federal government to legislate in regard to aborigines in any state.   Most referenda   in Australia have been defeated.   This one was carried with a 'Yes' vote of 91 per cent.   This overwhelming vote did not necessarily mean that the average Australian had undergone a dramatic change of heart.   The two proposals were reasonable and, it seemed, innocuous.   What is more the media explosion in the decades after the second world war had made Australia part of the 'global village', and its citizens were keenly aware of the racial issues in Africa and America. Those who were not in daily contact with aborigines, and this was the great majority, had become agonisingly conscious that all was not well in their own backyard,   and were not averse to some token adjustments.

The first positive result of the establishment of the Council for Aboriginal Affairs in 1967 was the collection of data on the aboriginal population. What had been suspected and ignored for generations was now officially documented. Housing, if this is the word that can properly be used to describe the accommodation, was generally sub-standard. This may not seem relevant or important to a tribal nomadic existence, but if the previous policy of assimilation had had any effect, it meant that aborigines had been incorporated into white society at the lowest socio-economic level.   Such a condition of abject poverty had serious consequences in every other sphere.   The health of aborigines was generally poor. Infant mortality rates were unacceptably high, malnutrition among children was practically endemic, and leprosy and venereal disease among adults was a serious and growing problem. In education the picture was equally gloomy. Hardly any had gained a tertiary qualification, less than 1 per cent had achieved the Leaving Certificate, and of those who had attended school at all, most had only a primary education, or at best an incomplete secondary. A study in 1968 revealed that no school in Central Australia could boast of a full-blood aboriginal child, who had reached secondary standard, and no teaching assistant had completed a full primary course. Moreover few white teachers had been trained for the task, and none could speak an aboriginal language, or claim to be fully

119

conversant with the culture.[4] The employment picture was just as bad. 7 per cent of aborigines in the work force were unemployed, compared with 1 per cent in the general population. Only a very few were in occupational categories above the lowest level of skill, and most were engaged in some kind of manual labour.

Once the magnitude of the problem had been exposed, the question of its resolution had to be faced. It so happened that an industrial dispute at Wave Hill Station in 1966 had been followed by the establishment of a camp at Wattie Creek, and the assertion of a claim for land rights by the Gurindji people. In the ensuing years further claims were made, and, aided and advised by influential white people, the aboriginal claims won a significant measure of public sympathy. The Federal government did not want to alienate public opinion, but was under pressure from powerful pastoral and mining groups. It equivocated. To accept that the traditional association of aborigines with the land was a proper basis for granting unconditional ownership would have opened a Pandora's box. Instead the government compromised by proposing general purpose leases, large enough to comprehend the tribal lands. But passive resistance by ministers, politicians and public servants thwarted all progress, and by 1972, when the government lost power, not one such lease had been granted.

Within days of assuming office in December 1972, the Australian Labor Party committed itself to the cause of Aborigines Land Rights, and Mr. Justice Woodward was appointed as a Royal Commissioner to advise on the means of implementation. His recommendations were accepted by all the major political parties, and legislation in accordance with them was introduced in 1976, shortly after the return to power of the Liberal Country Party Coalition. Its effect in the Northern Territory, the direct responsibility of the Federal government can only be described as dramatic. Indeed Coombs stated that the rights granted 'represented the biggest major advance in the status of Aborigines in Australian history since white colonisation.'[5]

In the States progress has been variable. Despite the massive 'Yes' vote in the 1967 referendum, which could be interpreted as a direction to the government to act, the conservative coalition parties have been timidly reluctant to usurp the sovereignty of the States. In South Australia, since the departure of the medieval Sir Thomas Playford, successive governments have acted in matters of social concern in an enlightened manner. At the other end of the scale there is Queensland. To describe its government as conservative or reactionary is insufficient and incomplete. Yet it does govern efficiently and effectively to meet the needs and demands of certain sections of its electorate. As these do not correspond with those of its aboriginal population, the granting of land rights has been repeatedly and resolutely refused. Indeed the government has even refused to allow the transfer of title of lands purchased for aborigines by the Federal Aboriginal Land Commission. When Charles Perkins, a well-known aboriginal activist, campaigned for an extension of land rights in New South Wales, his attack on the government equated it with Queensland, this being the most offensive comparison that can be made of any government in the Commonwealth.6

Yet a trend has been started. If governments, and more importantly the community at large, genuinely seek a multicultural society, in which all groups are equally served, land rights will no more be an issue of contention, but an accepted and unquestioned fact. In the meantime other urgent matters have to be faced. In the last decade there has been little real improvement in aboriginal housing. Aborigines do not wish to live on white charity, yet they cannot afford to provide for themselves. Many fall below the poverty line, even when employed in the humble occupations open to them. Large numbers are unemployed, the precise number cannot be known. How can one classify an aborigine living on a reserve or on lands that are now his? The rate of unemployment in Australia had now passed 7 per cent. The government no longer showed 'grave concern', but was alarmed, in panic. Faced with the threat of electoral defeat it reacted hysterically with plans and projects, and job creation schemes. How easy by comparison it would have been in the times of full employment, to have created jobs for aborigines, when their unemployment stood at the same level of 7 per cent. But few then cared.

The health of aborigines is directly related to the comparative poverty in which most of them live. Before 1973 health policy was concerned with the provision of therapeutic services, to cure illnesses and diseases that arose from the conditions in which they lived. As nothing was done to ameliorate these conditions, it is understandable that the health programmes were singularly unsuccessful. In recent years emphasis has been placed on preventive medicine. Health workers have an educational role, and have had some success in encouraging communities to help themselves, and to be aware of what needs to be done. In Sydney, and later in other large cities, the Aboriginal Medical Service has succeeded in developing worthwhile programmes in nutrition and general hygiene, and continues to do so despite the withdrawal of financial support by the government. This pettiness, presumably as a reprisal for political activities, makes one wonder whether the previous Federal government was sincere in its commitment to a multicultural society, in which the aborigines should have an equal and respected place. The recent change of government may seem more positive legislation come in to being, though its effectiveness will only be known after a number of years.

The educational field has seen changes too. In the days when it was the policy to assimilate aborigines into the mainstream of Australian society, they were placed in schools where they competed with white children, or in some cases in schools where the organisation and curriculum were the same. As has been shown, this left the aborigines at the bottom of the ladder as far as academic achievement and success went. In the interesting interregnum of the Whitlam Labor government, 1972 - 1975, a new policy was adopted. Children would, initially at least, receive their education in their own language, and would be taught by teachers recruited from their own communities. This has proved to some extent successful in facilitating the learning process, and in ensuring an appropriate cultural environment for the children. At the same time they were not denied access to the dominant culture, and thus opportunities to succeed in its terms. The introduction of the Aboriginal Secondary Grants Scheme and the Aboriginal Study Grants for tertiary education also encouraged urban children to continue their studies, and to gain qualifications that might enhance their prospects of employment above the level that had been the norm. Evidence as to the success of these schemes is scanty, but it may be noted that in New South Wales, in 1982, 89 children sat for the Higher School Certificate, as opposed to 31 ten years earlier. Of these, 14 scored above 50 per cent, whilst 55 were under 25 per cent. It would be hard to construe this as a major achievement, but at least it is an improvement, however slight.[7]

There is still a long path to follow before aborigines can truly assume their role as equal citizens in a multicultural Australia. On the one hand they must contend with active hostility and discrimination wherever they are in close contact with white society, despite the intention of the Racial Discrimination Act passed in the last phase of the Labor Government. On the other they had to endure smug condescension from people who should know better, such as Senator Baume. As Minister for Aboriginal affairs, he stated blandly that Aborigines and Torres Strait Islanders, representing 1.2 per cent of the population held 9.6 per cent of the land area of Australia.[8] This statement is probably true, but truth has many faces, and what deductions may be drawn from Baume's statement? Is it that already more than enough has been done for aborigines in the matter of land rights and equality of opportunity? If so it was but a sad commentary on the intelligence of his government, and the purpose in the Australian community to achieve a just and humane balance between all the groups that it comprises. Or should one equate the barren acres granted to the aborigines with the lush pastures of the eastern States and the priceless real estate in the great metropolises? Whatever view one takes, there is no escaping the fact that the original inhabitants of this country, the only ones who indeed are not recent migrants, are the most defenceless in the protection of their own culture, and the most injured in the process of acculturation.

It is for this reason that this chapter has begun with an

examination of the aborigines in Australian society. Numerically they compose little more than 1 per cent of the population, and could well be dismissed to a final paragraph. But their plight is desperate. They did not migrate here of their own free will, they were here when the English arrived, and they stayed when a European civilisatin was imposed on their continent. They had no say in the direction of events that followed, and their voice is but faintly heeded today. In this respect they were even worse situated than the convict who supplanted them, the unwilling arrivals to a land they made their own. In the first half of the nineteenth century the penal colony expanded and began to prosper. English and Irish culture fused, not without abrasion, into a fairly homogeneous society and the small percentage of other migrants were easily accommodated.

The first surge of migration on a large scale came with the discovery of gold in 1851. The population of Australia more than doubled in the following ten years. In Victoria, the main target of the gold seekers, more than 70 per cent of the population in 1861 had been born overseas, and the vast majority of these came from the British isles. Easily the largest non-British group came from China. Like the others they came to seek prosperity, and were prepared to work hard to achieve it. They expected to be allowed to live in peace under the protection of British law. In the event few prospered, most were reviled and many physically assaulted. Life on the goldfields was hard and primitive, law enforcement inadequate, and it is easy to understand that a group whose members were so physically different, whose customs were so strange, and whose culture so suspect, should be excluded. Government machinery could barely cope with the provision of services for the rapidly expanding population, let alone engage in the civilised refinement of encouraging and educating for racial harmony and cultural understanding.

At the 1861 census there were 38,300 Chinese in Australia, of whom only 11 were women.[9] Clearly it was the intention of men to make their fortunes and return home, and many did in fact go back to China. With such a disparity in the balance of the sexes, the problem was likely to disappear with time. But it had become an emotional one, almost a matter of principle. The gold rush was over within a decade or so, but the hatred and bitterness persisted, and permeated every quarter of the continent and each strata of society. In one sense it may be argued that the focus on the Chinese helped towards the creation of a homogeneous white society. The colonies had been granted self-government and were moving towards federation. Mutual suspicion between English and Irish was submerged in the need to agree on a form of constitution, under which Australians could enjoy freedom, security and opportunity, and develop a sense of national identity. It was difficult to agree on the form and composition of the new nation, but it was remarkably easy to agree on whom to exclude. The brief and cathartic experience with virtually uncontrolled Chinese migration had convinced almost every Australian that the society should be exclusively white. The British Empire had demonstrated its immense superiority in its expansion in Africa and Asia in the nineteenth century, and it seemed natural for the ordinary citizen to conclude that non-white races were intrinsically inferior, and that their presence in Australia would debase the quality of society. Edmund Barton, the first Prime Minister, expressed the common view in his categorical denunciation of the doctrine of racial equality, and ironically a Jew, Isaac Isaacs, later to become the first Australian-born Governor-General, urged the avoidance of 'the contamination and degrading influence of inferior races.'[10]

The Commonwealth of Australia came into existence on 1st January 1901, and one of the first Acts to be passed into law was the Immigration Restriction Act of 1901. It is significant that the Act itself did not specifically prohibit Asian immigration. This would have caused great offence to Japan, and embarrassment to Great Britain, supposed guarantor of the freedom and equality of the constituent races of its Empire. Successive Australian governments have become noted for the hypocrisy with which they conduct affairs of state. The first one set a splendid example of this art in prescribing the education test. Individual immigration officers were required and empowered to administer a dictation test in a European language, if they judged that the circumstances necessitated it. In practice English and European migrants were not usually tested, and Asians were. Moreover if the officer felt that someone whom he considered would be an undesirable migrant was likely to pass the English test, he was authorised to select any unlikely European language. In one case it is known that Transsylvanian dialect of Romanian was used.[11] The ostensible purpose of the Act was to keep out those whose education and skills were inadequate for adjustment to Australian society. Its effect was to admit many poorly educated and unskilled Europeans, and to exclude some highly skilled and well educated Asians. Its covert purpose was to keep Australia white, and in this it was remarkably successful.

It has often been claimed that the heroic fiasco at Gallipoli in 1915 somehow turned Australia into a nation in its own right. This dubious assumption obscures the complexity of what exactly an Australian is. The first world war exacerbated the latent hostility between those of Irish descent and those of English, and in keeping with this there were sharp religious differences in the society. But at least Australians **felt** that there was a common bond. They shared in the ' Anglo-Saxon' heritage, more properly now called Anglo-Celtic, in all its variety. They were governed by the principles of British law and in the Westminster tradition. Most importantly they spoke English as a common language, and were intolerant of those who did not. There was a time in the nineteenth century when an embryonic multiculturalism showed signs of flourishing. German settlers had formed their own schools and maintained their language through instruction in the vernacular. In 1916 they were forced to close or change to teaching in English.[12]

This marked the beginning of a deliberate attempt to make English the exclusive national language, and by implication, the Anglo-Australian culture the norm. When migrants arrived they were expected to conform, to speak English and to be like other Australians. Nearly all the migrants were of British stock and found little difficulty in meeting these requirements. The remainder simply had to adjust, and so the policy of assimilation was born. The pressure on them was enormous. if a child did not speak English he was regarded as handicapped.[13] There were no official services to provide for the non-English speaking migrant, little recognition of his cultural needs, or indeed of his existence. Tables of immigrants published in 1937 did not indicate the nationalities and relative percentages.[14] In fact the book in which they were published, assumed that the British isles were virtually the only source. Migrants from northern Europe were preferred, since their cultural pattern was similar to the Anglo-Australian. They tended to learn English quickly, to marry outside their cultural group, and thus appeared to assimilate easily. When southern Europeans came they generally did not have assisted passages and had to be sponsored by a friend or relative, and so a pattern of chain migration was gradually established. They were regarded as a source of cheap labour, and thus a threat to the Australian standard of living, and unsuited ever to become worthy citizens.[15]

In the 1930's another type of migrant emerged, the refugee from persecution in Germany. The Australian government was slow to respond at first to the pleas for entry, being more concerned with the preservation of a homogeneous society than with humanitarian considerations. Even when it did allow the refugees to enter, it was with the proviso that they brought funds with them and had a sponsor in Australia. Some 5,000 eventually came, and although few in number, they did add to the diversity of European settlement in Australia. It would be incorrect to say that any great change had been wrought by the outbreak of the second world war in 1939, but at least the stage had been set for the eventual recognition of the cultural contribution that could be made by the new arrivals, and their acceptance as worthy participants in society.

The war demonstrated that Australia was vulnerable and open to invasion in times of conflict, and that it could no longer rely on Great Britain for defence. Allied to the need to increase the population for this purpose, was the realisation that more manpower was required to extend the economic basis of the country by developing its rich resources. The government therefore decided to encourage large-scale but controlled migration. The natural preference was for British settlers, but Australia was under pressure to assist in the resettlement of the enormous number of displaced persons in Europe. In the decade after the cessation of hostilities more than 170,000 refugees from central and eastern Europe settled in Australia. They were required to enter employment for at least two years as directed by the Australian government, irrespective of their professional qualifications or skills.[16] This tarnished somewhat the reputation that Australia may have gained for an unselfish humanitarian act. But it was in line with the long tradition of encouraging migration that suited Australia. They were expected to assimilate into the Australian society without disturbing it unduly, and to stay in jobs where they were needed.

Once the refugees had been resettled the flow of migrants continued. Apart from the British, the major source was southern and south-eastern Europe. According to the 1971 census figures there were 283,705 migrants from Italy, 160,880 from Greece, and 118,730 from Yugoslavia.[17] A substantial minority of these received assisted passages, but the great influx can be attributed to the pattern of chain migration established before the war. In consequence, as they joined their friends and relatives, the Italians and Greeks particularly tended to congregate in specific suburbs in the large cities, forming cultural enclaves. Thus were sown the seeds of a multicultural society, but at the time unrecognised and unwanted. At a later date the Australian Ethnic Affairs Council stated its view that

> "a major aim of government policy in the 1950s and 1960s was to ensure that this kind of multiculturalism did **not** develop in Australia and many Australians still believe that the ethnic communities which it implies are a divisive force in the community and a threat to national cohesion. In their view ethnic communities are ghettoes, and they see no alternative to a common system of institutions for everyone, on the one hand, and destructive racial-ethnic, on the other.[18]

It is evident that the government, and indeed most Australians, wanted to perpetuate the dominant Anglo-Celtic culture, and it was hoped that the problem would go away as the new arrivals gradually adopted it. Yet there was a vocal minority who recognised that the society had changed, and was destined to change much more. It was impossible to defend the White Australia policy, even under the hypocritical guise of the education test, and public opinion forced the government to introduce a new immigration Act in 1958, in which there was no reference to race or nationality.[19] This did not at first result in the admission of a significant number of non-

Europeans, since the Minister and his officials retained the absolute discretion to issue entry permits. But opposition to the covert continuation of the White Australia policy did result in a gradual liberalisation, and towards the end of the 1960s, some 10,000 non-Europeans were being admitted each year.[20] This was just enough to prove that the White Australia policy was dead, but not enough to disturb the conformist tranquility of Australian society, nor to bring into serious question the idea that all new arrivals would eventually assimilate into the mainstream of society.

The assumption that migrants, if left alone, would quickly adjust to the modes of Australian society, had its effect on the educational provision for them. As most were of British origin and spoke English, it was felt that they needed no special attention. This was a popular fallacy of the period, and by extension to European migrants it was believed that the only obstacle to full assimilation was an inadequate command of the English language. In the days when migrants came by ship, English classes were held on board, but at best this would only have provided survival skills in their new country. In 1947 continuation classes were introduced in hostels and centres. In 1952 there were 28,000 enrolled and this number increased slowly each year.[21] As this was not a very large percentage of the annual arrivals, it could mean that the European migrants were exceedingly quick to acquire a command of English. It is much more likely though, that they were too busy working to establish themselves economically to attend classes, or that they found the tuition inadequate and ineffective. The important point is, that nobody seemed to know, and nobody really cared. Some provision had been made for the obvious migrant need, and if they were not availing themselves of it, that was their business.

Migrant children were even worse served than their parents. The formal school system provided a conservative curriculum geared to the traditional needs of Australian-born children. It was generally authoritarian, conformist and teacher-centred. Non-English speaking children were expected to attend school and normal classes, and to acquire proficiency in English painlessly. When they did not do so, and failed to make satisfactory progress in the various subjects, it was generally considered a problem of the teacher, rather than the child. Lack of comprehension interfered with 'normal' class teaching, was the lament. There was no suitable material for teaching English to migrants, and even if there had been, its application would have been frustrated by the inflexible school organization. In 1960 the Commonwealth Immigration Advisory Council published the results of an enquiry, which showed that migrant children had adjusted well, that problems of adjustment evaporated quickly when English was mastered, and that this happened fairly quickly. It recommended that parents should be encouraged to speak English at home, and that the formation of national groupings at school should be discouraged.[22] These conclusions have since been shown to be substantially untrue, but its bland satisfaction with the existing situation was certainly indicative of the views of the majority of Australians. They wanted migrants to assimilate unobtrusively and without reciprocity and this wish became irrationally, what was perceived to be the actuality.

During the 1960s more and more migrants entered from southern Europe and tended to settle in suburbs where their compatriots were already living. As they established and strengthened these cultural bridgeheads, they began to make their voices heard, and it was becoming increasingly difficult to believe that the policy of assimilation had worked, or would work. At the same time there was a trend in Australia to examine social problems, of every kind, and to seek solutions for them. A greater interest in education was leading to a shift away from a rigid teacher-centred system towards a consideration of the individual child and his needs. During 1968 and 1969 the New South Wales Department of education conducted a survey into migrant education. It was not a particularly good piece of research, and was of limited value for future planning, but it did admit that 'no definite policy had been formulated to meet the very special needs of these children as it was hoped that any problems encountered by the children would disappear with progression through school.'23 This succinctly summarised the official and popular attitude previously and marked the beginning, in this and other states, of a recognition that migrants had their own contribution to make to Australian society.

Integration now replaced assimilation as the slogan. It was never really clear precisely what this meant. It seems in retrospect to have acknowledged that migrants were never going to assimilate completely, to discard their old ways and to live as Australians had lived for generations. It implied that they could keep their customs, their eating habits, folk dancing and traditional celebrations, but that they should operate economically, politically, and socially according to the dominant culture in Australian society. To do this they needed to speak English well. As it had ecome plainly evident that the acquisition of a foreign language does not just easily happen, the policy of integration required a systematic planned approach to the teaching of English to migrants. The Commonwealth government introduced the Child Migrant Education Programme in 1970, and the state governments followed suit by developing their own programmes in conjunction. Training courses for teachers were inaugurated, and a start was made on the development of suitable teaching materials.

Just as it was arrogantly assumed that the best teachers for aboriginal children were white and English speaking, so it was with the teaching of migrant children. The teachers could have been selected from amongst those who taught foreign languages in the high schools, and who know what it was like to learn a foreign language. But they were not. The majority were, like most Australians, monolingual, with no direct experience of foreign language learning, however sympathetic and well-intentioned they may have been. The Commissioner for Community Relations drew attention to this as a major defect in the programme, but his remained a voice crying in the wilderness.[24] There are too many variables for it to be possible to assess how effective this teaching was, or whether skilled linguists could have done a better job. But the disregard for skills in languages other than English is symptomatic of an attitude towards migrants, and the languages they spoke, which had long existed and which had little changed under the policy of integration.

Perhaps the most important aspect of the new approach was the official concern for migrant welfare and the examination of their needs. The Henderson Commission of Inquiry into Poverty in Australia, 1970, had established the extent of poverty among the population at large, including those born overseas. Subsequently specific research studies were commissioned, and two of these dealt with migrants in considerable detail. It was revealed that there were over 100 ethnic groups in Australia, defined as 'a collection of persons who, for physical, geographical, political, religious, linguistic or other reasons, feel themselves, or are felt by others, to constitute a separate people.'[25] Thirteen of these were analysed carefully, presenting an accurate description of the settlement pattern of each group, its cultural development, and the situation in respect of health, education, housing and employment. In general migrants tended to have a greater incidence of mental illness than the average, their educational level was lower, accommodation poorer, and they were employed in occupations at or below the Australian mean, being under-represented in the professions and higher-status positions.

The complete integration of migrants in Australian society should require that all of these factors corresponded to the Australian pattern. To redress the balance it was not sufficient to provide equality of educational opportunity, but positive discrimination in favour of migrants, and aborigines too. A Federal government report in 1976 acknowledged this, and in addition conceded that the need for English language competence was not the only requirement, as had previously been thought. Cultural and socio-economic factors were often severe impediments to the ability of migrants to take advantage of educational opportunities, and consideration had to be given to this, in organising and integrating the total educational experience of migrant children.[26] Recognition was also, belatedly, given to the fact that integration is a two-way process. It was advocated that the curriculum for all Australian children should be adapted to include teaching about all the cultures that now composed society. It was also noted that ethnic schools had proliferated since 1970, and that these tended to isolate migrant children from the mainstream. In consequence it was proposed that these should be linked with the normal day schools, and that some migrant languages should be taught in the primary and secondary schools.27

Some moves were made in this direction, and an added impetus came following the publication of the Galbally report, whose major recommendations were accepted by the government. When the Prime Minister announced this in 1978, it represented a major change of direction, and heralded the acceptance of multiculturalism, and an equally worthy place for all groups in Australian society. The guiding principles were stated to be:

a) all members of our society must have equal opportunity to realise their full potential and must have equal access to programs and services;

b) every person should be able to maintain his or her culture without prejudice or disadvantage and should be encouraged to understand and embrace other cultures;

c) needs of migrants, should, in general, be met by programs and services available to the whole community but special services and programs are necessary at present to ensure equality of access and provision;

d) services and programs should be designed and operated in full consultation with clients, and self-help should be encouraged as much as possible with a view to helping migrants to become self-reliant quickly.28

The report identified areas of special need, such as the law, income security, employment and health, and made recommendations to ensure the removal of discriminatory practices, whether these were intentional or incidental. It regarded communication as the basic problem underlying all others, and proposed measures to ensure that children were not disadvantaged at school, and adults not restricted by language difficulties in their choice of employment. But what made this report truly significant in its commitment to a multicultural society, was the acknowledgement that some migrants did not speak English well, some would never do so, and that there were some situations where an inadequate command of the language placed an unjust stress on them. It therefore recommended that bilingual staff be recruited in government offices and agencies, where migrants were likely to come for help or advice, and that until this was complete the interpreter and translation services be extended.

Already some progress has been made in this regard. More funds have been made available for the teaching of English as a Second Language, and appropriate teaching kits have been produced.29 The Schools Commission suggested that provision should be made for the teaching of community languages. It sensibly warned that there was little prospect of Australia becoming a bilingual society, but nevertheless asserted that children should have the opportunity to attend a bilingual school, if they wished to do so.[30] The Australian Ethnic Affairs Council also stressed the desirability of language maintenance for migrant children, and for aborigines.[31] On educational grounds alone, it seems obvious that a child should receive his early education in his mother tongue, and until such time as his knowledge of English is sufficient to allow a transfer to be made. Until now the individual needs of the child had been subordinated to the assumed more important needs of society, and education in the vernacular had been condemned as divisive and undesirable. Multilingualism is the strongest component of a multicultural society, since language is the essence of culture. It is only when this is truly recognised and implemented that Australia can genuinely claim to have allowed its ethnic groups a proper place in its society.

It is heartening that the Commonwealth government should invite debate, in 1982, on the need for a national language policy. In a discussion paper it showed how more than one million Australians regularly used a language other than English in their private lives. The major languages spoken were Arabic, Dutch, French, German, Greek, Italian, Polish, Spanish, and the languages of Yugoslavia.[32] It was estimated that other languages spoken amounted to about one hundred. It was suggested that this plethora of languages was a valuable national resource. Valuable not only in terms of diplomacy and trade, but as an enriching factor in the general life of the community. The resolution of the problem of harnessing this linguistic resource is fraught with difficulties and is a task for the future. But if it is to be attempted, account must also be taken of the multiplicity of languages spoken by the aboriginal people. It is estimated that there are some 50,000 speakers of aboriginal languages, some spoken by only a handful of people, and that 16,000 speak aboriginal Kriol. These languages are not likely to be learnt and spoken by many white Australians, they have no utilitarian value in the international field, yet their preservation is an imperative if the aboriginal people are to be included as equaly partners with other ethnic groups in a multicultural society.

At present Australia is a multicultural society only in the sense that it includes large ethnic groups with their own languages and cultures, which have made their presence felt. The ideal society has been described the the Commonwealth government as one;

"where groups would co-exist harmoniously, free to maintain many of their distinctive religious, linguistic, or social customs, equal in their access to resources and services, civil rights and political power and sharing with the rest of society particular concerns and values, which have national significance. There would be diversity, equality and interaction through sharing. Ideally each group would have members distributed over the socio-economic range so tht each individual would have opportunities for both upward, downward, and lateral mobility. All of the groups would abide by a set of norms that stress tolerance of group differences and the belief that the interests of no one group would be placed ahead of the welfare of the total society."[33]

This is a noble goal, but doubts must be entertained whether it is realistic. In the same document, it is conceded that the present level of intolerance in Australia is remarkably high, with 83 per cent of the Australian-born population believing that 'having a lot of migrants has not been so good for this country.'

The elimination of such prejudice is a herculean task, and will take many many years to accomplish. It should of course start in the schools, and the New South Wales Department of Education has already issued its policy statement. This is a remarkable exercise in wishful thinking, and contains little of practical value for the classroom teacher, faced with the task of eradicating a long tradition of intolerance. Indeed it claims that its aims are inherent in the aims of primary and secondary education,[34] and as these had evidently not been achieved to date, the prospects of future success are not bright, without a complete overhaul of the existing school system.

In the heady rush towards a multicultural society little attention had been given to the precise definition of the term. It is currently popular to draw a distinction between cultural pluralism, the coexistence of different cultures, and structural pluralism, the coexistence of parallel ethnic group organisations. The various ethnic groups state that they favour the former, but the existence of so many sporting, social, religious, and even political organisations leads many in the dominant Anglo-Celtic culture to believe that the real preference is for the latter, and that this will accentuate divisions and disharmony in society.[35] This fear is not without foundation, since it is hard to imagine a flourishing cultural pluralism being based on anything but a strong ethnic identity, and the structural organisations in which it may be expressed. The paradox is of course that a culturally heterogeneous society depends on a vigorous homogeneity of its composite parts.

There will also be important decisions to be made regarding the intrinsic value of certain cultural customs, which are in conflict with the traditional values in Australian society. Is the vendetta an acceptable practice? Should bigamy be permitted, if undertaken in accordance with traditional religious beliefs? There are many more examples, and if a determination has to be made it will have to be by the dominant culture, which in itself implies the concept of superiority. There have already been instances where Australian magistrates have condoned punishments in accordance with aboriginal tribal law, but this is with a group who live together in relative isolation. One would think it could hardly be applied to another group living with and among other groups in a major city. Such issues have been raised by the Ethnic Affairs Council, and merit serious discussion and close attention.

In its study of the problems associated with multiculturalism the Council saw the question of the use in Australia of 'foreign' languages as being the most severe. Religious pluralism had always been tolerated, as had to some extent many other customs. But the use of languages other than English was an affront to most English speaking Australians. They did not like to hear strange languages being spoken in the streets, and were suspicious of foreign language newspapers. Officialdom supported the private view with its restrictions on the use of any language but English in radio broadcasting and in the schools.[36] Although such linguistic prejudice is less acute today, it could so easily be revived by the proposed introduction of bilingual programmes, which may well impose intolerable strains on the schools, and on other sub-systems in society.[37]

As the move towards making multiculturalism a reality in Australian society gains momentum, the catchphrase that cultural diversity is compatible with social cohesion will be severely tested. Barbara Falk, in an address to the Australian College of Education in 1978, posed the question whether cultures could indeed be integrated without being assimilated into a new composite of them all.[38] Her acute analysis of the situation suggested a transformation of individual and community attitudes that could lead to a genuine multicultural society. Yet the experience in other countries promotes scepticism. Australia has a long tradition of importing educational ideas from North America, and the current enthusiasm for multiculturalism is yet another example. Definitions of it abound, yet confuse rather than illuminate. Brian Bullivant goes so far as to call them a mixture of 'rhetoric, muddled thinking, special pleading and confused terminology.'[39] Moreover he argues that the claims made for multicultural education are not based on any worthwhile research evidence. Teaching about other cultures does not necessarily reduce prejudice and discrimination. Enhancing a child's ethnic sense of self-esteem does not automatically result in a better school performance, nor do culture-based programmes result in greater equality in education and consequently improved employment prospects.

Inequality is inherent in Australian society. If free enterprise is to be encouraged and individual effort rewarded, this must logically be so. The question of equal access to higher status occupations, or equal opportunity to accumulate wealth, the benchmark of a materialistic society, is one for society as a whole, and not to be treated ethnically on a group by group basis. Language maintenance and cultural preservation could in fact increase isolation and restrict such opportunities. Much is often made of the fact that about 20 per cent of the population were born overseas, in presenting a case for multiculturalism. But half of these came from Britain, so that 90 per cent may be said to living, working and achieving in Australia within the Anglo-Australian culture. Legal, political, economic, and educational institutions are part of this culture, and partial isolation from it is going to make success more difficult to achieve, not easier. No group willingly and readily surrenders power and privilege. Positive discrimination in favour of aborigines in respect of land rights, scholarships, housing and health, has already provoked resentment from disadvantaged white Australians in areas with a significant aboriginal population. The preferential treatment accorded Asian refugees has aroused a degree of envy, and a suspicion that racial prejudice is still dormant in the body politic, ready to emerge as the economic situation deteriorates. There is always the hope that education will cure the ills in society, but hope and fine words are a poor alternative to definitive programmes. These have yet to be introduced comprehensively and their evaluation lies in the future.

NOTES AND REFERENCES

1. A.S. Kenyon, History and memory, **The Australian Educational Review**, 9, 1938, pp. 7-8.
2. H.C. Coombs, **Kulinma - Listening to Aboriginal Australians,** Canberra: ANU Press, 1978,p.3.
   Coombs, a distinguished and compassionate Australian public servant, became the chairman of the Council for Aboriginal Affairs, when it was established in November 1967.
3. **Ibid.** 1978, pp.82-3.
4. T. Roper, **Aboriginal education - the teacher's role**, Melbourne: National Union of Australian University Students, 1969,p.181.
5. Coombs, 1978, p.222.
6. Charles Perkins was one of the few aborigines to gain a tertiary qualification and his remarks were reported in the New South Wales journal for aborigines, **Aboriginal Quarterly**, 4, (2), 1981,pp. 32-3.
7. **Aboriginal Quarterly**, 4 (3), 1982, p.9.
8. This is reported in the South Australian journal for Aborigines, **Aboriginal Affairs Newsletter**, 3 (2), 1981, p.6.

9. A. Huck, **The Chinese in Australia**, Croydon, Vic: Longmans, 1968, p.5.
10. A.T. Yarwood, **Asian Migration to Australia - the background to exclusion, 1896-1923,** Melbourne: MU Press, 1964, p.24. The Chinese were not the only Asian people in Australia, but they formed by far the largest group. This book provides an account of Asian migration and presence in general.
11. F.S. Stevens, (Ed), **Racism: the Australian experience,** Sydney: ANZ Book Co, 2nd ed., 1974, p.137.
12. M. Clyne, **Factors Promoting Migrant Languages Maintenance in Australia,**p.124, in P.R.de Lacey and M.E. Poole, (eds.), **Mosaic or Melting Pot - Cultural Evolution in Australia,** Sydney: Harcourt Brace Jovanovich, 1979.
13. A.J. Grassby, **It's time for migrant education to go,** in P.R. de Lacey and M.E. Poole, 1979, p.279.
14. W.G.K. Duncan and C.V.Janes (eds.), **The future of immigration into Australia and New Zealand,** Sydney: Angus and Robertson, 1937, p.123.
15. G. Sherington, **Australia's Immigrants - 1788-1978,** Sydney: George Allen and Unwin, 1980, p.118.
16. **Ibid.** 1980, p.134.
17. D. Cox, **The Role of Ethnic Groups in Migrant Welfare,** a research report for the Commission of Inquiry into Poverty, published by the Commonwealth Government as **Welfare of Migrants,** Canberra: Australian Government Publishing Service, 1975. p.145.
18. The Australian Ethnic Affairs Council, **Australia as a Multicultural Society,** Canberra: AGPS, 1977,pp.6-7.
19. The Immigration Reform Group, **Control or Colour Bar? - a proposal for change in Australia's immigration policy,** Melbourne: The Immigration Reform Group, 1960,p1.
20. B.M. Bullivant, **The Pluralist Dilemma in Education,** Sydney: George Allen & Unwin, 1981, p.176.
21. Commonwealth of Australia, **Adult Migrant Education Program,** Annual report to the Parliament 1977-8, Canberra: AGPS, 1979, p.2.
22. Bullivant, 1981, p.179.
23. New South Wales Department of Education Division of Research and Planning, **Migrant Education in New South Wales,** Sydney: Government Printer, 1971, p.6.
24. A.J. Grassby, Out of the melting-pot, **The Educational Magazine,** 32 (4), 1975, pp.33-5.
25. D. Cox, in **Welfare of Migrans,** 1975, p.125 see 17 above. 26. Commonwealth Department of Education, **Major Trends and Developments in Australian Education 1975-6,** Canberra: AGPS, 1978, p.40.
27. Commonwealth Department of Education, **Report of the Committee on the Teaching of Migrant Languages in Schools,** Canberra: AGPS, 1976,pp.111-8.

28. Commonwealth of Australia, **Report of the Review of Post-arrival programs and services for migrants,** Canberra: AGPS, 1978, p.4. It is interesting to note that this report was also published in Arabic, Dutch, German, Greek, Italian, Serbo-Croatian, Spanish, Turkish, and Vietnamese.

29. Commonwealth of Australia, **Child Migrant Education,** Annual report to the Parliament 1979-80, Canberra: AGPS, 1980, p.5.

30. Schools Commission, **Report for the Triennium 1982-4,** Canberra: Schools Commission, 1981, p.118.

31. Australian Ethnic Affairs Council Committee on Multicultural Education, **Perspectives on Multicultural Education,** Canberra: AGPS, 1981, p.8.

32. Commonwealth Department of Education, **Towards a National Language Policy,** Canberra: AGPS, 1982,p.1. These languages were defined as having more than 45,000 speakers. Chinese had 30,000 speakers according to the 1976 census, and so has probably acquired the status of a major language since then, with the arrival of many Indo-Chinese.

33. Commonwealth Education Portfolio, **Discussion Paper on Education in a Multicultural Australia,** Canberra: AGPS, 1979, p.18. The implications for teacher education and the school's curricula of this document The Galbally Report, and both federal and state reports, are discussed further in the subsequent chapter by James Lynch.

34. New South Wales Department of Education, **The Multicultural Education Policy Statement,** Sydney: Government Printer, 1979, p.3.

35. D.R. Cox, Pluralism in Australia, **ANZ Journal of Sociology,** 2 (2), 1976, p.113.

36. Australian Population and Immigration Council and Australian Ethnic Affairs Council, **Multiculturalism and its Implications for Immigration Policy,** Canberra: AGPS, 1979, p.9.

37. M. Skilbeck, Core curriculum for a multicultural society, **New Education,** 3 (2), 1981, p.52.

38. B. Falk, **Personal Identity in a Multi-cultural Australia,** Hawthorn Vic: ACER, 1978,p.3.

39. B. Bullivant, Multiculturalism - No, **Education News,** 17 (2), 1980, p.18.
    See also J.J. Smolicz, Multiculturalism - Yes, pp.12-16, in the same issue.

7 COMMUNITY RELATIONS AND MULTICULTURAL EDUCATION IN AUSTRALIA[1]

JAMES LYNCH

In the early post-war period, industrialized societies around the globe sought greater equality of educational opportunity by means of social and structural strategies. The ongoing and effective legitimation of those societies necessitated the ideological orientation inherent within such strategies if the commitment to democratization, awakened and tempered in the heat of war, was to be put into effect. The common school or comprehensive school was seen in those days as a kind of panacea for societies' ills which would herald the dawn of a new age of social, economic and educational harmony and equity.

Gradually, as new strategies were tried and found wanting, equality was sought in the pursuit of compensatory education and in additional reforms such as internal school re-structuring, curriculum renewal and development. With these latter developments the pursuit of educational equality had passed irrevocably from its structural into a cultural phase and a panoply of new organisations and writings emerged, committed to such goals as "a cultural perspective on the curriculum". The hidden and parallel curricula were discovered and gradually a reappraisal began of the cultural capital available as a base-line for the selection of valued knowledge called curriculum.

Parallel to this latter development, old monist orthodoxies began to be challenged by the presence in Western European societies such as Holland, France, West Germany, Sweden and the United Kingdom, of increasingly diverse cultural backgrounds and presuppositions. In 'older' countries of mass immigration such as the United States, Canada and Australia 'melting pots' were discarded and national policies of multiculturalism espoused.[2] The balancing act involved in the implementation of educational policies attuned to multicultural societies has been described as **The Pluralist Dilemma**[3] by Bullivant, and certainly education to preserve and foster cultural diversity, on the one hand, and to maintain the national cohesion of the policy,

137

on the other, has presented western democracies with massive
legitimation problems: and nowhere have these been more
acutely felt than in Australia.

Although geographically large and diverse, Australia has
still a relatively small population. The record shows that,
from a figure of 1.1 million in 1860, the Australian
population had increased to 8.3 million in 1950, 10.3 million
in 1960, 12.7 million in 1970, and by 1977 it was estimated to
be 14.2 million. Whilst estimates differ, at the 1976 Census,
161,000 or 1.2 per cent of the population described their
racial origin as Aboriginal or Torres Strait Islander, i.e.
the groups which occupied the land before European settlement.
The population as whole continues to be highly urbanised, a
concentration second only to city states such as Hong Kong and
Singapore with the bulk located in the capital cities and
major town, predominantly on the south and east coasts of the
continent.

Arrivals from overseas are classified on entry as
permanent, long-term or short-term indicated by the travellers
expressed intention on arrival. The former predominance of
settler arrivals in the late 1940's has now been replaced by a
situation where the majority of arrivals are tourists, with
almost 98 per cent arriving and departing by plane. Almost
four million immigrants have arrived in Australia in the post-
war period with approximately 80 per cent settling, accounting
for roughly 80 per cent of Australia's post-war population
growth, although numbers have declined in the most recent
decade from 185,000 in 1970 to 75,000 in 1977[4] by 1980,
approximately 40 per cent of the total population was of
migrant background, making Australia number two country after
Israel in terms of the proportion of immediate migrants and
children in the population.[5]

At the same time there has been a substantial change in
the composition of migrant entry. Whereas, previously,
roughly a quarter of migrants came from northern European
countries, this had declined by the late 1970's to
approximately 6 per cent, whilst migrants from Asia has substantially increased. Migrants from the U.K. and Eire
constituted approximately 35 per cent to 40 per cent
throughout the post-war period.

Educational provision is, according to Australia's federal
constitution, a responsibility of the state (and from 1st July
1979 Northern Territory) governments, and it is these
governments which administer their own primary, secondary and
technical education. Universities and Colleges of Advanced
Education are subject to Commonwealth (i.e. national)
legislation whilst retaining autonomy of different levels
granted them by appropriate state legislation. Education is
compulsory between the ages of 6 and 15 (16 in Tasmania) and
there is a strong, predominantly Catholic, denominational
school sector. The majority of schools are comprehensive and

co-educational although there are many single sex schools in the denominational sector. Teachers for both sectors are trained in universities and colleges with the latter institutions producing the majority.

The Commonwealth (National) Government has responsibility for migrant education and both migrant and multicultural education is funded by the Schools Commission in Canberra by means of payment to government and non-government education authorities in each state. There is also a national Adult Migrant Education Programme funded by the Commonwealth Government Department of Immigration and Ethnic Affairs, to help adult immigrants learn English and obtain essential information about Australian society. There is an extensive network of ethnic schools, run mainly on a part-time basis of from 2-8 hours per week and there may well be as many as 1,000 such schools with the Greek community alone having 350 schools catering for 25,000 pupils.[6]

Thus, with a small population of just over 14 million, 65 per cent of which is concentrated in a few urban areas, over 40 per cent of its population of migrant background and over a hundred language groups, Australia is **par excellence** a multicultural society. Economic difficulties and the arrival of large numbers of Indo-Chinese refugees appear to have sharpened the need for multicultural education, for such phenomena appear, in some cases, to have turned back the cloak under which racialist attitudes were slumbering and to have brought back echoes of the former "White Australia Policy". True, this policy has long since been discarded by all responsible political parties and all are now firmly - even enthusiastically - committed to the concept of Australia as a multicultural society. In spite of this, however, a report by the Commissioner for Community Relations pointed out that, although the Aborigines comprise only 1 per cent of Australia's population, 30 per cent of the cases of discrimination handled, since the Office of the Commissioner for Community Relations was established in 1975, have concerned Aborigines.[7] Then, too, the ongoing controversy over sacred Aboriginal sites, as at Noomkanbah in Western Australia, and exploitation of mineral resources have led to what one correspondent has described as "Australia's parallel to Wounded Knee".[8] The New Humanist Society also raised a storm and identified a genuine moral dilemma by raising the issue of clitoridectomies in Australia, and one newspaper in a major editorial on the issue, asserted that most discussion about migrants centred around the duties of the host country to the newcomers, rather than also vice versa in a mutual process. It hinted at the possibility of a backlash, arguing the responsibility of the various Ethnic Councils in this "Two-Way Street".[9] Then, during a strike over the employment of two Kampucheans at a Lidcombe factory, posters appeared outside the works, carrying messages such as "An Asian

Australia? Never", and "Jobs not refugees. White Australia or Asian Takeover".[10]

Australia is not helped either by its longer term record on community relations and pluralism. The early persecution and even extermination of some Aboriginal groups has left its heritage, and although Australia was a signatory to the United Nations Declaration on Human Rights in 1974, it was not until 1975 that legislation ratifying and legislating for implementation was passed by the Federal Parliament, in the form of the **Racial Discrimination Act,** and the Office of the Commissioner for Community Relations was established. That was in the heady days of idealism of the Whitlam Government. More recent steps aimed amongst other things at establishing a Human Rights Commission, have resulted in intense conflict between the Upper and Lower Houses of the Federal Parliament. They were seen by many, more-over, to be partly directed at bringing the independent Commissioner for Community Relations, under greater bureaucratic, perhaps even political, control, for the Commissioner's findings had been inconvenient, even embarrassing and devastating for many politicians.[11]

Then too, assimilationism, as the 'order of the day', has a long history in Australia as elsewhere. In the early post-war period, at a time of vigorous immigration to Australia for instance, the country was dominated by what has been called the "myth of homogeneity", and accordingly its educational system was tailored towards a blatantly assimilationist policy.[12] The assumption since Colonial times, and drawn from British cultural hegemony, had been that Anglo- British was the best, and that thus to 'pass muster', children had to be moulded to adopt this culture. The "White Australia Policy" too, whilst less explicitly than formerly, continued vigorous and active in that period.

But, if earlier waves of immigrants had accepted this cultural dominance with relative passivity, the post-war migrants, many of whom were displaced persons, and often of high academic achievement in their own cultures, were not to be of the same metal. Whereas the Commonwealth Government had sponsored a large-scale immigration programme at the end of the War on the assumption that the population would remain predominantly British, in the event, over half of the migrants who arrived were of non-British stock. (With mass immigration now ended the proportion of British immigrants has become even smaller). But in spite of this, until 1970 when a five-year Child Migrant Education Programme was commenced with a budget of some $A1m in the first year, special migrant education programmes were only considered relevant to adult learners, and Victoria was the only state prior to that date where attempts were being made to introduce special arrangements for the education of migrant children and particularly in schools with large numbers of children from non-English speaking backgrounds.[13] Similarly, bilingual education programmes, even for Australia's original inhabitants, are of comparatively recent origin with such provision for aboriginal children in the Northern Territory dating from 1972, and the establishment of a National Aboriginal Education Committee from 1976, although it must be said that Aboriginal Family Education Centres were established as early as 1969 in New South Wales with a grant from the Bernard van Leer Foundation.

As the 1970s progressed, however, there was a marked rejection of former chauvinism, and increasingly academics became more and more interested in the concept of a pluralist society, a multicultural society and gradually one served by a multicultural education system. To be sure, a number of distinguished Australian social scientists had laboured with little acknowledgement to contribute to the field of ethnic minorities and their problems over a number of years, including the late Dr. Jean Martin and Professor Jerzy Zubrzycki amongst many others. But it was only in the late 1970s that Australian educationists began to devote particular attention to the development of multicultural education for everyone in Australian society.

The exact take-off point for this interest is difficult to locate but certainly there was widespread dissatisfaction with the first five years of the Child Migrant Education Programme and its over-assimilationist orientation, in spite of the advance which it represented over previous positions on the education of migrants. The mid 1970s were bad years for Australian immigration as well with an approximately 25 per cent return rate of long-term immigrants.

The 1975 Schools Commission Report consequently suggested extensive changes, including the development of multicultural education. The Report epitomized the confluence in time of a whole series of political, social, economic and cultural influences which began progressively and relentlessly from that time to focus Australian educationists' attention on the concept of a multi-cultural education for a multicultural society, gaining in momentum until the pasing of the 1970s saw a veritable plethora of reports and other publications and writings addressing themselves to the task.

Foremost and seminal amongst these was a slender but important and influential document submitted by the Australian Ethnic Affairs Council, established in January 1977, to the Australian Population and Immigration Council concerning the 'Green Paper' on **Immigration Policies and Australia's Population** and entitled **Australia as a Multicultural Society.**[14] Its assertion that "...policies and programmes concerned with education for a multicultural society apply to all children, not just children of non-English-speaking background, and have ramifications throughout the curriculum" represented a . milestone in the development of an Australian philosophy of multicultural education.[15]

The proposals for policy which the document put forward

included the expansion of intensive English language centres, a review of the teaching of English as a second language, the development of bilingual education for students who enter the school system fluent solely in a language other than English, the development and fostering of community language education, the establishment of incentives to develop ethnic studies programmes with the object of giving all children a more authentic view of the nature of society than that of the current monocultural education and the encouragement of ethnic schools to improve their standards. Inherent within these proposals, the document saw the need to recruit teachers of non English-speaking background and to train all teachers to work in a multicultural and multilingual education system, and a review of materials production by the main national materials-producing bodies with a view to supporting the needs of the classroom teacher faced with students who knew little or no English. [16]

In the meantime a review group had been established in September 1977, to look at post-arrival programmes and services to migrants and to report back to the Commonwealth Government. In particular this review group was asked to examine and report on the effectiveness of Commonwealth Programmes and services for those who migrated to Australia, including programmes and services provided by non-government organisations which received government assistance, and to identify areas of need or duplication of programmes or services. The report of this group, or **Galbally Report** as it came to be known after the Chairman of the review group, found major gaps in provision, and in the field of multicultural education it proposed a major commonwealth initiative to ensure that greater priority was given to multicultural education for children in all schools, recommending the allocation of $A50m specifically for multicultural education in the ensuing three years. [17]

Further, it proposed the establishment of machinery at Commonwealth level to coordinate Commonwealth policies and programmes in relationships with schools and school systems in regard to multicultural education and an approach by the Tertiary Education Commission to all tertiary institutions with a view to the inclusion of elements on the cultural background of major ethnic groups within appropriate professional courses. It also recommended the establishment of an institute of multicultural affairs to be directed by a small group of experts in multicultural development and migrant issues with a budget of $A1.8m over the following three years.

The Report pointed to the way in which the pattern of migration to Australia had altered over the previous six yars with the proportion of migrants from Britain and other European countries declining from the previous 70 per cent to less than 40 per cent, at the same time as the proportion of migrants from the Middle East and Asia, including refugees, had increased significantly. It pointed out that there were more than 100 different languages and dialects spoken within Australia and that over 20 per cent of Australia's current population had been born overseas with over half of these coming from countries with very different languages and cultures.

It set out four guiding principles for policy: those of equality of opportunity, the right to the maintenance of personal culture without prejudice or disadvantage, the need for special services of programmes to ensure equality of access and provision for migrants, and client involvement in the design and operation of services and programmes with the encouragement of self help as much as possible.

The Report had the unique distinction of being tabled in Parliament simultaneously in English and nine other languages. It was immediately accepted by the Federal Government and an allocation of $A50m was made for the implementation of its recommendations over the first three years. A joint watchdog committee was established to oversee its implementation, comprising a Galbally Implementation Group and members from the Standing Committee of the Ethnic Affairs Council. Substantial funds were also made available for research and curriculum development through various bodies such as the Educational Research and Development Committee, the Curriculum Development Centre in Canberra, the Schools Commission and the State Education Departments.

The month before the publication of the Galbally report, that is in April 1978, a high level group was established with representation from the Commonwealth Department of Education, the Schools Commission, the Tertiary Education Commission, the Curriculum Development Centre, the (since disbanded) Education Research and Development Committee and the Australian Capital Territory Schools Authority with the task of clarifying the concept of multicultural education within the Commonwealth Education portfolio.

The need for such clarification had been recognised not only by the Galbally Report, but also by the 1978 Schools Commission Report and the work of the Portfolio Group was seen as a first step in implementing the Galbally recommendation for the establishment of formal machinery to coordinate Commonwealth policies and programmes in the field of multicultural education.[18] The group defined the term multiculturalism as an 'ideal' society where groups would co-exist harmoniously, free to maintain many of their distinctive religious, linguistic or social customs, equal in their access to resources and services, civil rights and political power, and sharing with the rest of society particular concerns and values which have national significance: or diversity and interaction through sharing.[19] Whilst embracing the concept of structural pluralism as a necessary prerequisite to multiculturalism, the group felt it incombent on them also to define the cohesive elements within Australian society which would need to be emphasized in order to avoid fragmentation. Amongst the major of these were the existence of national institutions, of language, of shared democratic values including egalitarianism.

The report defines four central aims for multiculturalism which emerged from its deliberations. These include, cultural identity, the need for fostering of interaction and positive attitudes toward cultural diversity, the encouragement of cohesion by means of shared values and structures, and, the need to promote equality of opportunity for all members of society.

The Committee identified the need for appropriately knowledgeable and sympathetic teachers to introduce multicultural education, implying pre- and inservice courses to sensitize all teachers and educational administrators to the multicultural reality of Australian society and to what it means to teach in a multicultural society. It underlined the need for courses at both levels aimed at language development, and in particular, at enabling all teachers to handle everyday language problems occurring in multilingual classrooms.[20] Finally, it pointed to the important role of ethnic aides and their inservice needs.

This relay was taken up by a committee of the Schools Commission in its report on multicultural education.[21] The Committee had been established in June 1978 by the Minister for Education to make recommendations to the Schools Commission on the distribution of the additional funds to be made available for multicultural education arising out of the Galbally report over the period 1979-81. The Committee recommended means to achieve greater coordination in the field of multicultural education at national and state levels, including the establishment of a National Standing Committee on Multiculturalism, appointed by the Commonwealth Minister of Education which would advise the Commonwealth Government through the Schools Commission on matters relating to education for a multicultural society. A system of information exchange was also proposed, to include the production and distribution of information bulletins and the convening of meetings.

In terms of finance it recommended that an amount of $A1,040,000 be set aside for the Schools Commission's multicultural education programme in 1980 and $A2,440,000 in 1981. Of these funds some were to be allocated to support the development and modification of curricula in schools. An amount of $A40,000 was allocated in 1980 to the National Curriculum Development Centre in Canberra in order to enable it to produce and distribute to schools in Australia, guidelines providing schools and school communities with essential information for the development of programmes for education for a multicultural society. $A0.5m had been set aside for 1979 for the Schools Commission's work in fostering the teaching of community languages and it was proposed that this would continue in 1980 and 1981. In 1980 and 1981 it was proposed that $A100,000 in each year be provided to the Curriculum Development Centre for the fostering of Curriculum Development covering initially the primary grades.

Amongst other recommendations were those concerned with relationships and support to be given to activities in the field of School/Community interaction with the objective of bringing the community closer to the school, the development of research and development activities by the National Educational Research and Development Committee. A sum of $A170,000 was suggested for the appointment of liaison officers to work with ethnic community schools.[22]

Meanwhile, the Curriculum Development Centre which had received approval for the development of project activities in the area of education for a multicultural society from the Ministry of Education in late 1977 had completed its exploratory phase and established in early 1978 an Interim Advisory Panel on education for a multicultural society. In a confidential report to the Curriculum Development Centre Council the committee attempted to pen-in the fine details of the high ideals and aspirations which had been described and enumerated in previous reports. It was particularly concerned with four areas of clarification: the concept of a multicultural society, the role of education, curriculum implications, and specific programmes and activities which the Centre might undertake.[23]

Conceptually the document was a great step forward and it introduced a much needed dose of academic rigour to thinking about multicultural education. It addressed itself to seven major areas: Australia as a multicultural society; the nature of ethnicity; value orientations towards cultural diversity; core and shared values; the role of the school in a plural society; and, education programmes and activities for a multicultural society.

Seeing the co-existence of several ethnic cultures and a stable and unified society and state as perfectly compatible, the document attempted to identify what it saw as shared values in Australia, including: western style parliamentary democracy, a relative degree of economic opportunity for each individual to improve himself financially according to his own ability and resourcefulness, the English language as the universal language for all Australians, the freedom of the individual to pursue his own private life, and equality before the Law.[24] Whilst these shared values were seen as mainly a derivative from the cultural heritage of the Anglo majority, the Interim Advisory Committee made a passionate plea for the retention of ethnic cultures within Austrlian society without detriment to these shared values; rather as an enhancement to them.

One of the major priorities identified by the advisory panel was that to be given funding for teacher education, implicit within which was continued support for multicultural education at the tertiary level. In detail, it recommended the development of a general multicultural perspective and orientation in educators and administrators, a research study, including empirical pre- and post-testing of teachers and students, together with the development of pre- and inservice courses and packages. It also propsed that teachers should undergo specialised training for specific tasks, such as those of ethnic and Aboriginal studies, community languages, bilingual education and English as a second language, and that the Tertiary Education Commission should be approached for financial support for such specialised training.

In tabular form it also recommended actual courses to be introduced in schools and other educational institutions for the purpose of furthering the objective of a multicultural society under six major headings: multicultural perspectives for educators and administrators, multicultural perspectives for curriculum, ethnic and aboriginal studies, community languages (ethnic and aboriginal), bilingual education, and English as a second language.[25]

Meanwhile initiatives and enthusiasm were percolating to other levels of government. Individual States were participating in the development of multicultural education in some cases building on Commonwealth initiatives, in some cases launching their own. In New South Wales, for instance, under the terms of the Ethnic Affairs Commission Act of 1976 the Commission was required to furnish a report concerning its constitution and function. In an extensive documentation which appeared in June 1978 the Commission looked at its own functions and its future role, under the headings: the immigrant and government, the immigrant and the education system, the immigrant in the work force, the immigrant in the welfare and health services, the immigrant in the legal system, the immigrant living outside Sydney, the immigrant and the quality of life and the immigrant woman. It attempted to look beyond the concept of multiculturalism, seen only as the need to preserve the cultural heritage of Australians, to the non-English speaking background and to envisage the fundamental issue as being the right of minority groups to achieve total participation in the Australian and New South Wales political and social systems.[26] The Report took its philosophy from a statement of the Right Honourable Mr. N.K. Wran QCMLA, at the time he was leader of the opposition, in a statement delivered before the state election in May 1976, where he said "It is a basic human right that no individual or group in the community should be discriminated against or excluded from the fullest participation in the social, economic and cultural life of the community or from the fullest share of the opportunity which the community offers."

Whilst its concern was much wider than education and its focus not yet fully multicultural, it dealt with such topics as: eduation for cultural interaction, community languages in schools, the use of overseas teachers, the training of teachers, teaching of English as a second language, ethnic aides, the involvement of parents, teaching adult immigrants, and ethnic schools.

The Report made a series of recommendations aimed at the development of further inservice programmes and movement towards the position where every teacher training institution has a compulsory course of multicultural education for all prospective teachers. It even suggested that the Department of Education consider the possibility of offering preference in employment to teachers who had completed a pre-service training course with a significant multicultural education component.[27] In addition to such issues as community languages in schools, ethnic schools (which already qualify for state aid), the use of overseas teachers, ethnic aides and the training of teachers were clearly identified as key elements. The role of ethnic aides is problematic in view of the fact that whereas the concept and theoretical base claimed for the role are exciting ones, full of promise, the funds available for implementation envisage that such aides will be employed on hourly rate roughly equivalent to that of a school cleaner.

State and Catholic Education Departments made a very real effort to encourage and facilitate the implementation of multicultural education policies, and this was enhanced by the establishment of independent action groups and committees such as those in New South Wales and Western Australia.

In Queensland the Council of Directors of the Department of Education set up a Working Party on Multicultural Education in January 1978, which eventuated in November of that same year in a discussion paper entitled **Education for a Multicultural Society.**[28] This document was distributed to all schools in Queensland and a number of school-based curriculum development exercises, funded by grants from the Commonwealth, were distributed by the Queensland Multicultural Co-ordinating Committee. The Report included a Departmental policy statement and visualized "the total curriculum permeated by multicultural objectives in which are embedded specific studies for and about different cultural groups...".[29]

A teacher was seconded full-time to the Education Department's Curriculum Branch to work in the area of 'education for a multicultural society' and several part-time staff were also engaged.

In New South Wales and as part of the state distribution of the Galbally curriculum development, the Education Department of New South Wales issued in November 1979, its

"Multicultural Education Policy Statement".[30]   Although a slender document, the policy statement is a model of clarity, envisaging the aims of multicultural education as being:

- the development in all students of an understanding and appreciation of the multicultural nature of Australian society;
- the development of awareness of the contributions of people of different ethnic backgrounds to the development of Australia;
- the development of intercultural understanding through the consideration of attitudes, beliefs and values related to multiculturalism;
- the fostering of behaviour that facilitates interethnic harmony; and
- an enhanced sense of personal worth in students through an acceptance and appreciation of their specific Australian ethnic identity as well as their Australian national identity in the context of a multicultural society.

Two basic aspects of multicultural education were seen as fundamental to the practices of all schools and for all students: multicultural perspectives to the curriculum and education for interncultural understanding. Additionally, however, it supported such aspects as ethnic studies, English as a second language, education and culture through language education.

In the second part of the document a guideline statement on multicultural education appears to assist schools in implementing multicultural education programmes. This includes identification and examination of multicultural dimensions in the history of Australia, the provision of experiences through Literature, Music, Singing, Dance, Arts, Crafts, Cooking, folk-tales, games and sports of various cultures, the study of poetry, stories and plays reflecting the experiences in Australia of people from various ethnic backgrounds, the incidental experiences of aspects of other languages and the selection and or development for classroom use of Australia-oriented materials.

A number of management practices are asserted to have already been successful in schools, including:

- the involvement of bilingual personnel in enrolment and orientation programmes;
- the employment of teachers aides and other auxiliary staff;
- the use of parents to read stories to children in languages appropriate to the school; and
- communications from school to home using appropriate community languages;
- allowing the use of school facilities for ethnic community groups and adult migrant education

- services classes;
- stocking through libraries of books and materials in various languages;
- use of multilingual signs on school property directing school visitors to significant places on the school site;
- the use of community people and parents as interpreters at parent organisation meetings;
- consultation with parents of the various ethnic groups;
- recognition of cultural diversity in the school population;
- undertaking school excursions to locations emphasizing the cultural diversity of the school community;
- developing a sensitive recognition of the cultural diversity of the Australian population and its celebrations of Australian National days, etc.;
- consideration of the cultural norms of the various ethnic groups;
- involvement of voluntary helpers who were familiar with culture and language of the school population, etc.

On the basis of this policy statement, in January 1980 the State Department of Education wrote to all schools seeking bids for funds, provided as a consequence of the Galbally report, for activities related to multicultural education. Funds were offered for two types of grants, small scale grants to a maximum value of $A2,000 to support local initiatives and programmes at the school level and special project grants to support more extnsive initiatives and programmes at the school, community, district and regional levels. Over 300 bids for projects were received by the Department by the deadline for submission at the end of March.

South Australia was early into the field with its "Ten Schools Project" incorporating about 30 primary schools in an attempt to change the organisation, curriculum, attitudes and communication of schools and teachers to more adequately reflect the multicultural nature of their communities. Community languages were already taught in both primary and secondary schools, and research was initiated, surveys conducted and excellent materials produced including an outstanding Multicultural Materials Kit.[31]

In Victoria an Advisory Committee on Migrant and Multicultural Education (VACMME) was established in 1979 with an important role in the encouragement and funding of projects in education for a multicultural society and over $A90,000 was allocated in small grants in the first year. A Greek Bilingual Pilot Project was launched including a joint Victoria/South Australia project to develop materials for Greek Community Language Teaching.[32]

Other States too set up mechansims for the distribution of small grants to schools and they and independent education bodies such as the Catholic Education Commissions were involved in publishing and refining policy statements.[33] In addition to the policy statements, materials and packages produced at State level, there has also been a prolific outpouring of material produced by Federal agencies and national organisations such as the former Curriculum Development Centre in Canberra.[34]

In terms of introducing courses responding to the growing ideology of multiculturalism, Australia moved quickly too. At the tertiary level, for instance, a survey found over 300 multicultural education courses on offer with some 28 of these at Colleges of Advance Education in New South Wales and 23 at universities – numbers probably far in excess of equivalent provision elsewhere.[35]   (See Table 1)

TABLE 1

MULTICULTURAL EDUCATION COURSES IN INSTITUTIONS AND EDUCATION AUTHORITIES IN AUSTRALIA (1979)

KIND OF INST	NSW	VIC	SA	WA	QLD	TAS	ACT	NT	TOTAL
C.A.E.	28	8	6	63	21	–	3	–	129
UNIV.	23	30	4	7	8	7	10	–	89
OTHER	24	64	8	6	6	–	–	9	117
TOTAL	75	102	18	76	35	7	13	9	335

In a sense, the incidents cited at the beginning are thus isolated and, on the whole, Australia has a relatively good record on community relations. Further, over the past four or five years it also has an enviable record of commitment to the concept of a multicultural society by a multicultural education system. For example, more or less at the same time as the incidents related at the beginning were taking place, advertisements were appearing for staff for the new Australian Institute of Multicultural Affairs, set up as a consequence of the Galbally Report, which envisaged that the new Institute would have a major role, **inter alia**, in providing advice to the Commonwealth Government, in conducting and commissioning research and studies and fostering promotional and educational activities.[36]

In October 1979 enabling legislation was passed to establish the Australian Institute of Multicultural Affairs, with major objectives: to develop an awareness of the diverse cultures that now exist in Australia as a result of migration and an appreciation of the contributions of those cultures to the enrichment of the community; to promote tolerance, understanding, harmonious relations and mutual esteem among the different cultural groups and ethnic communities; to promote a cohesive Australian society through the sharing of diverse cultures; to assist in promoting an environment that affords the members of the different cultural groups the opportunity to participate fully in Australian society and achieve their own potential.

It was seen as playing a major role in providing advice to the Commonwealth Government on all matters relating to the achievement of its objects, commissioning and conducting research and studies, furnishing reports to the Minister; making information available to members of the Australian community and to particular bodies, organisation or groups within that community, and, conducting promotional and community educational activities, including the establishment of a repository of literature and other material relating to the diverse cultures of members of the Australian community.[37]

Within a few months of its foundation the Australian Institute of Multicultural Affairs had undertaken an ambitious, national survey of activities in multicultural and migrant education, an assessment of programmes in the field and an indentification of areas for further research.[38] The review indicated the strong faith of ethnic minority communities in the role of education in multiculturalism, pinpointed the restricted availability of suitably trained teachers as an obstacle to the effective development of multicultural education (see the comment in note 27) and identified a considerable growth in ethnic schools over the previous five years. At the tertiary level the survey recommended a considerable expansion of the teaching of community languages, the introduction of some TESL training in all teacher pre-service courses, and the widespread incorporation of multicultural perspectives within existing general studies units. The study identified thirteen so-called multicultural centres in tertiary institutions, all of which had been established within the previous decade.

Thus, in spite of certain lamentable historical 'incidents' and, notwithstanding early post-war phases when the "Commos" and "Reffos" were blamed for everything, and there was continuing substantial discrimination and easily awakened prejudice against some ethnic and cultural groups (and on the basis of sex), and more recent setbacks such as the banning of the SEMP (Social Education Materials Project) in Queensland in 1977, Australia has made very substantial academic and practical contributions to a field which is of increasing world-wide interest.[39] Many of its strategies have been different from those of the United States, Canada and the

United Kingdom, and the momentum created by the hard and mostly unrecognised work of a few pioneers in this field has placed Australian aademic insitutions and Australian society in an enviable position to successfully launch and implement the concept of a multicultural society – a task which is being widely and enthusiastically tackled. In this respect, Australian society has a headstart towards greater social harmony and cultural enrichment on the basis of a pluralist cultural commitment than is available to many other countries, and they could well look to her example to inform their multicultural endeavours.

NOTES AND REFERENCES

1. An earlier version of this chapter first appeared as "Community Relations and Multicultual Education in Australia", **Comparative Education** (1982), 18 : 1 pp.15-24.

2. For a categorisation and explanation of this phenomenon, see Watson,K. (1979) "Educational Policies in Multicultural Societies", **Comparative Education**, 15 : 1, pp.17-31. An interesting categorization of the Australian development by an eminent expert in the field is Smolicz,J.J., "Multiculturalism: The Three Phases", **Education News** (1981), 17 : 8, pp.22-27.

3. Bullivant, B. (1981) **The Pluralist Dilemma in Education**, Sydney: George Allen & Unwin.

4. Details of these first two paragraphs taken from Australian Bureau of Statistics, 1979, **Year Book Australia 1979**, Canberra: Commonwealth of Australia, Australian Bureau of Statistics. An up-to-date and useful overview is: Department of Immigration and Ethnic Affairs, **Review of Australia's Demographic Trends**, Canberra: Australian Government Publishing Service, 1981.

5. Information given in a talk by Professor Jerzy Zubrzycki on 15th April, 1980 in Newcastle, New South Wales.

6. Information taken from draft report to the Australian Education Research and Development Committee, see Kringas, P. and Lewins, F., 1979, **Migrant Definitions of Ethnic Schools: Selected Case Studies**, Canberra: Department of Sociology, Australian National University, September, unpublished.

7. Quoted in publicity for Office of the Commissioner for Community Relations (1979) **Lets End the Slander: Combating Racial Prejudice in Teaching Materials.** Canberra: Australian Government Publishing Service.

8. **Newcastle Morning Herald** (1980), April 12, p.7 9. "A Two-Way Street", **The Sydney Morning Herald** (1980), Saturday, April 12, p.12.

10. "Kampucheans Keep Jobs as Factory Strikers Return to Work", **The Sydney Morning Herald** (1980), Saturday, April 19, p.2.
11. See Commonwealth of Australia, Commissioner for Community Relations, **First Annual Report 1979,** Canberra: Australian GovernmenrrPrinting Service, 1976: **Second Annual Report 1977**, Canberra: Australian Government Printing Service, 1977; **Third Annual Report 1978,** Canberra: Australian Government Printing Service, 1978; **Fourth Annual Report 1979,** Canberra: Australian Government Printing Service, 1979. The **Fourth** Report is particularly illuminating, for it gives an overview of race and community relations in Australia.
12. Claydon, L. et al. (1977), **Curriculum and Culture.** Sydney: George Allen and Unwin.
13. Price, C.A. and Martin, J.I. (1976) **Australian Immigration: A Bibliography and Digest.** Canberra: Australian National University, p.33.
14. The Australian Ethnic Affairs Council (1978) **Australia as a Multicultural Society.** Canberra: Australian Government Publishing Service.
15. **Ibid.,** p.11.
16. It is interesting to compare these recommendations with similar ones made by the Rampton Committee in the United Kingdom. See Committee of Inquiry into Education of Children from Ethnic Minority Groups (1981) **Interim Report: West Indian Children in Our Schools,** London: HMSO (Cmnd. 8273). See also recommendations 8.6 and 8.7 of the Australian National Inquiry into Teacher Education (1980). **Report.** Canberra: Australian Government Publishing Service.
17. Review Group on Post Arrival Programmes and Services to Migrants (1978) **Migrant Services and Programmes.,** Canberra: Australian Government Publishing Service, **passim.**
18. Commonwealth Education Portfolio, **Discussion Paper on Education in a Multicultural Australia.** Canberra: 1979.
19. **Ibid.,** p.18.
20. **Ibid.,** p.27.
21. Schools Commission, Committee on Multicultural Education, **Education for a Multicultural Society** (1979). Canberra: Schools Commission.
22. **Ibid.,** pp. 59-63.
23. Interim Advisory Panel to the Curriculum Development Centre Council (1979) **Education for a Multicultural Society: Concept and Implications.** Canberra: Curriculum Development Centre.
24. For purposes of comparison, see also Curriculum Development Centre (1980) **Core Curriculum for Australian Schools.** Canberra: Curriculum Development Centre.

25. **Ibid.**, p.53. For some undisclosed reason, the document appears to have remained confidential but see also an alternative version of the tabulation which appears in Smolicz, J.J. (1979),**Culture and Education in a Plural Scoiety.** Canberra: Curriculum Development Centre, pp.268–269. Dr. Smolicz was a leading member of the Interim Advisory Committee.

26. The Ethnic Affairs Commission of New South Wales (1978). **Report to the Premier: Participation.** Sydney, New South Wales: Ethnic Affairs Commission for New South Wales. See also Parliament of New South Wales (1979), **Action Status of Recommendations "Participation"**, Sydney: Ethnics Affairs Commission of New South Wales, June 30th.

27. The problem is that the relatively conservative and monist character of the main sources of Australian teacher education may not afford an intellectually very rich seed-bed for the introduction of such policies. For the inherent traditionalism and 'Angloid' culture of many such institutions does not easily provide a vehicle for the initiation of pluralist policies which are calculated to afford the ethnic community groups, not least the Aborigines, freedom from discrimination. See the results of empirical research conducted from mid 1979 and conveyed to the Auchmuty National Inquiry into Teacher Education in March 1980. See Beswick, D.G., et al., (1980) **Australian Teacher Educators and Education Policy.** Melbourne: University of Melbourne, Centre for the Study of Higher Education, p.55, **et passim.** For a cultural-historical 'explanation' of the aetiology of Australian teacher education, seey Hyams, B.K. (1979) **Teacher Preparation in Australia,** Hawthorn Victoria: Australian Council for Educational Research.

28. Queensland Department of Education, Working Party on Multicultural Education (1979) **Education for a Multicultural Society.** Brisbane: Department of Education (June).

29. **Ibid.,** p.2. As a practical example of the latter category could be cited the document drawn up by the Queensland Aboriginal and Torres Strait Islander Consultative Committee entitled **Guidelines for Studies about Aborigines in Queensland Schools.** Brisbane, February 1980.

30. New South Wales Department of Education (1979) **Multicultural Education Policy Statement.** Sydney, New South Wales: Cyclostyled manuscript.

31. Details taken from a paper by Deputy Director General of Education, in July 1980 given to the Second National Conference of the Ethnic Communities Council of Australia.

32. I am indebted to the Victorian Ethnic Education Services of the Education Department in Melbourne for the information contained in this paragraph.
33. See, for instance, "Education in a Multicultural Australia" **Catholic Education Circular** (1979), 79:9, p.57.
34. See, for example, Curriculum Development Centre, **Curriculum Resource Package: You've Got to Start Somewhere.** Melbourne: Trout Films, 1981. (Including a Teachers Handbook written by Catharina Koopman).
35. Commonwealth Department of Education (1979) **Bulletin.** Woden, ACT.
36. See, for instance, **The Weekend Australian** (1980), April 12-13, p.15 and **The Sydney Morning Herald** (1980), April 12, p.23.
37. Cited from **ibid.**
38. Commonwealth Department of Education (1979), **Bulletin 1979,** (Information on Courses in TEFL, TESL, Migrant and Multicultural Education and Ethnic Studies), Woden, ACT.
39. See, for example, recent contributions from the United States such as Banks, J.A. (1981) **Multiethnic Education: Theory and Practice.** Boston: Allyn and Bacon, Inc. and from the United Kingdom such as Jeffcoate, R. (1979) **Positive Image: Towards a Multiracial Curriculum.** London: Writers and Readers Publishing Co-operative.

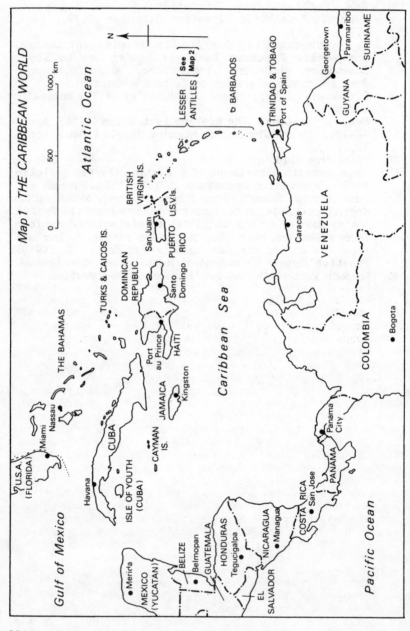

Map 1 THE CARIBBEAN WORLD

8 EDUCATION AND THE MULTICULTURAL CARIBBEAN

COLIN BROCK

> "Cultures cannot any longer be understood by contemplation of their navels. None is intelligible in isolation, apart from its adaptation to others in the world cultural net, ... it becomes commonsense and necessity to learn how to interpret cultures as much from the outside, from their environmental contexts, as from their inner values."[1]

Nowhere would the above quotation be more at home than in application to 'Caribbean Cultures'. The area has been variously described in terms ranging from 'cultural aridity' to 'rich cultural mix', and in that both are fair comment we come abruptly to the crux of the West Indian problem - an endemic concern with cultural identity. One could almost say that every West Indian is a multicultural microcosm.

Not surprisingly, formal educational provision has had a significant part to play in the processes whereby the forms of multiculturalism in the Caribbean have come about. It is obvious too that different degrees of multiculturalism, operating at a range of scales from individual to international, have implications for the recognition and possible solution of contemporary educational problems in the area.

This applies not only to the peoples of the Caribbean Region itself, but also to West Indian communities in metropolitan locations.[2] Indeed, in so far as familial links are maintained between Caribbean lands proper and Caribbean enclaves in European and North American cities, the latter may legitimately be considered part of the 'Caribbean World'. Nonetheless, there are many different and additional components in the urban multicultural context of the West Indian diaspora, not least the very high proportion of such communities born in their adopted locations, that takes them beyond the scope of this chapter. One must not forget, however, that their changing cultural characteristics and socio-economic fortunes do have some influence on the perceptions and attitudes of West Indians in the Caribbean.

157

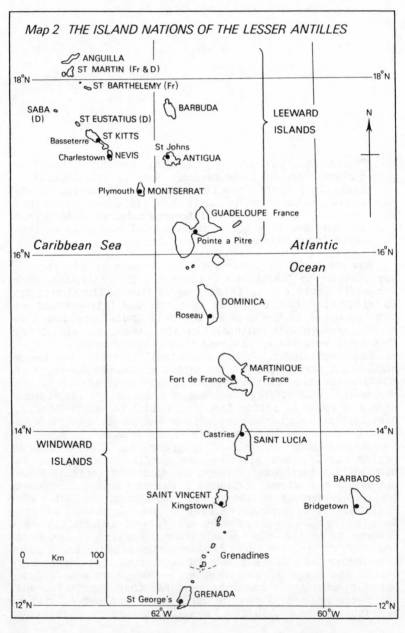

Map 2 THE ISLAND NATIONS OF THE LESSER ANTILLES

Such messages and images may engender either greater cultural disparity or greater cultural cohesion, according to their content and mode of transmission. Seemingly conflicting views of the educational prospects of pupils of West Indian origin in British schools illustrate this point[3], though more thorough-going analysis confirms the generality of disadvantage in respect of the educational experience of this group.[4] Disparities within this relate to the ongoing dynamics of the human ecology of multicultural British cities.

While West Indians in Dutch[5] and French cities are not without educational problems akin to those of their British counterparts, these problems appear to be less acute. This may have something to do with the mode of colonial administration, including educational provision, in the three groups of territories, as well as with contemporary social policy in the respective metropolitan motherlands. Certainly, due to the highly localised system of indirect rule, a greater degree of cultural diversity was enhanced within the British West Indies than within the Caribbean Departements of France D'Outre Mer, or the components of the Joint Kingdom of the Netherlands and The Netherlands Antilles. So, while we shall be concerned mainly with the Commonwealth Caribbean, there will be some discussion of the French and Dutch Antilles by way of contrast.

The Caribbean Region

The aforementioned 'European Affiliated Areas' of the Caribbean as Hauch[6] terms them, are also enmeshed with economic and educational networks within the New World, and in turn, the wider Caribbean Region itself.

The Caribbean Region comprises the West Indian Islands, adjacent islands (eg. The Bahamas), and the Circum-Caribbean Mainlands from French Guiana to Mexico (Yucatan Peninsula). Since Miami is a major central place in regional economic patterns, some would include Florida also. The West Indies divide conveniently into the Greater and Lesser Antilles. Within this region so defined are upwards of forty nations, with various degrees of political independence. Most of these nations are small in population total, in area, or in both. This is especially true of the islands:

"Smallness has condemned the islands to a history of tutelage and, in some cases, to microscopic versions of political dependence. A decade and a half ago only the three largest units - all in the Greater Antilles - were independent, and some of the smallest islands were dependencies of dependencies. Carriacou subordinate to Grenada, boasts it own fief, Petite Martinique." [7]

Some idea of the demographic and geographic scale of this area may be gained from Table 1, and from Maps 1 and 2.

Since educational provision is normally operated on a national basis, there are obviously many and varied systems present in the region. However, with many of the states so small and poor, the higher and even further education sectors have many crossnational connections, from bilateral to multilateral. United Nations and other international agencies are also involved in educational provision and projects in the area. We can therefore see a hierarchy of scales at which multicultural influences affect education, and certain political considerations operate. I have commented on the significance of smallness, and also old and new types of metropolitanism in another paper.[8]

Multiculturalism

The idea of multiculturalism is associated with that of pluralism in societies. Farrell [9] has investigated the relationship between education and pluralism in this part of the world, drawing on the work of M G Smith [10], and the concept of a continuum of societal types from the plural society at one pole to the heterogeneous society at the other. Despite the many qualifications placed by Farrell and others on the definition of a plural society, it would seem that most West Indian societies meet his major requirements for classification as such. Certainly, three of the main attributes of a plural society in Farrell's terms are commonly found in the Caribbean region. They are:

a. That the superordinate group is a distinct minority concerned with control, and discouraging acculturation of the subordinate majority.
b. That there is an urban minority, with separate institutions, which controls a rural majority.
c. That plural societies depend for their order on explicit or implicit force.

Such features, while being most strongly represented in the Latin Caribbean, are still evident in lesser degree and wide variety in the components of the British, Dutch and French West Indies. According to Henry, "human societies have tried repeatedly in their members of accomplish a completely predictable response system"[11], and in relation to the characteristics of plural societies outlined above, it would seem that educational systems, formal and non-formal, can be important instruments of political control and social manipulation. In this respect it is difficult to understand the multicultural context of education in the Caribbean without recourse to the legacies of colonialism.[12] Clearly then it is easier for formal education to be used in the maintenance of plurality than in its breakdown, even when the latter may be the objective. Whether it is unwilling or not, this may well be the effect in West Indian communities today, as well as in the islands. The position in both cases is politically and pedagogically delicate.

In such a situation, the significance of <u>language</u> is increased. In many West Indian states, the vernacular, itself subject to highly localised variation, is not the medium of formal education. The nature of the vernacular in any particular place will depend on the relative contribution of whatever European and African inputs there may have been, plus modifications arising from the relatively discrete evolution of social groups in plantocracies based on slavery. For example, on any one island there may have been a succession of colonial powers involved, a slave population deliberately derived from many different African tribes so as to minimise communication and potential rebellion, and further contributions from the languages of subsequent Asiatic immigrants. With particular reference to language, Henry states: "thus it is that though man has poured what he knows into his culture patterns, they have also frozen him round and held him fast"[13].

This takes on an added dimension when the semi-developed dialects and patois of small Caribbean communities are considered. So even where the desire of the superordinate group is for the acculturation of the majority, and the realisation of a heterogeneous society, very severe cognitive problems have to be overcome in the West Indian context. Acculturation involves the taking in not only of systems and institutions, but also values and orientations.

Language is patently the most telling cultural index and one of tremendous significance for education. It is also significant in respect of national identity, and, given the colonial legacy, places Caribbean administrations in a dilemma. To what extent should creole and patois be accepted in school, even encouraged? In general, socialist administrations in the region tend to encourage the utilisation of the mother tongue while more conservative regimes do not, preferring to maintain English as the medium of instruction. So there have sometimes been alternating policies of acceptance and rejection as administrations come and go. This can also be related to social class in that the professional middle classes may discourage their children from using non-standard English or patois, whatever their political position.

While language is a very special and significant feature in respect of educational disparity in the Caribbean, the distinctive cultures of sometimes very small states derive from the unique mix of valuables within each environmental and territorial context, usually insular. A number of selected groupings of variables as relating to education in this region should help in illustrating this: race, colour and class; economy and human ecology; religious and political factors.

In the Caribbean, and the 'British West Indies in particular, <u>race, colour and class</u> are closely intertwined, with human activities such as occupation and schooling among

TABLE 1   BASIC POPULATION FIGURES FOR CARIBBEAN COUNTRIES

Country	Surface area	Last Census	Population at last Census	UN Population estimate for 1980	%Growth of popl. 1975-80	Density of population (per km^2)
Antigua*	442	1970	65525	75000	1.0	170
The Bahamas*	13935	1970	175192	204000	3.1	17
Barbados*	431	1980	249000	253000	0.6	587
Belize	22965	1970	120936	162000	3.0	7
British Virgin Islands. *	153	1970	9825	13000	2.5	85
Cayman Is.*	259	1970	10460	12000	1.0	46
Colombia	1138914	1973	22551811	27520000	3.1	24
Costa Rica	50700	1973	1871781	2245000	2.7	44
Cuba	114524	1970	8569121	9833000	1.1	86
Dominica*	751	1970	70513	80000	1.3	107
Dom. Republic	48734	1970	4006405	5431000	2.9	111
El Salvador	21040	1971	3554648	4813000	3.7	229
French Guiana	91000	1974	55125	64000	1.4	1
Grenada*	344	1970	93858	98000	0.5	285
Guadeloupe	1779	1974	324530	334000	0.5	188
Guatemala	108889	1973	5160221	7262000	3.6	67
Guyana*	214969	1973	701885	884000	2.2	4
Haiti	27750	1971	4329991	5009000	1.8	180
Honduras	112088	1974	2656948	3691000	3.6	33
Jamaica*	10962	1970	1848512	2192000	1.4	199

Martinique*	1102	1974	324832	327000	0.1	297
Montserrat*	98	1970	11698	13000	1.3	133
Netherlands Antilles	961	1971	218390	266000	2.0	277
Nicaragua	130000	1971	1877952	2703000	4.6	21
Panama	77082	1980	1830175	1837000	3.0	24
St. Kitts-Nevis						
Anguilla*	357	1970	64000	67000	0.3	188
St. Lucia*	616	1970	100893	120000	1.5	195
St. Vincent*	388	1970	87305	122000	5.5	314
Suriname	163265	1980	352041	389000	1.3	2
Trinidad & Tobago*	5128	1970	940719	1139000	1.2	222
Turks & Caicos Is*	430	1970	5607	7000	4.4	17
U.S. Virgin Is.	344	1980	95214	95000	0.9	277
Venezuela	912050	1971	10721522	13913000	3.0	15

* = Commonwealth Caribbean Countries.

Abstracted from: United Nations Demographic Yearbook 1980, Statistical Office, Department of Economic and Social Affairs, United Nations Organisation, 1982.

the foremost threads. In as far as race, in strictly physical anthropological terms, may or may not have intrinsic significance for educational potential it would be a special factor, but not a cultural one. Nonetheless, concepts of race can be developed by dominant groups in a society in order to justify their socio-political status, and this has certainly happened in the West Indies. The very creation of a plural society based on slavery provides an endogenous dynamic of conflict that manifests itself in changing patterns of influence.

"To see any Caribbean society as nothing more than an ethnic or a racial collage is to confuse the shadow with the substance. But extreme caution is also necessary, for cultures never stand still and what may be a shadow today can be a substance tomorrow. Black power and negritude may owe their origins to social and economic inequalities butressed by racial mythologies, but that does not mean they can never act as independant influences on say, elections or political disputes"[14]

With such a caution in mind it is still instructive to consider classification of Caribbean Societies, such as that put forward by Lowenthal[15] and illustrated in Table 2.

TABLE 2

A Summary of Lowenthal's Classification of Caribbean Societies

Category	Type	Example
1	Homogenous societies without distinctions of colour or class	Turks and Caicos Is.
2	Societies differentiated by colour but not stratified by class	Anguilla
3	Societies stratified by both colour and class	Antigua Martinique Curacao
4	Societies stratified by colour and class, but with white Creole elites absent or insignificant	Haiti St. Lucia Nevis
5	Societies stratified by colour and class and containing sizeable ethnic groups mainly outside the colour-class hierarchy	Belize Trinidad Guyana

Abstracted from: Lowenthal D. (1972) **West Indian Societies,** pp. 78-79.

Fig. 1.   RACIAL/ETHNIC AND RELIGIOUS STRUCTURE

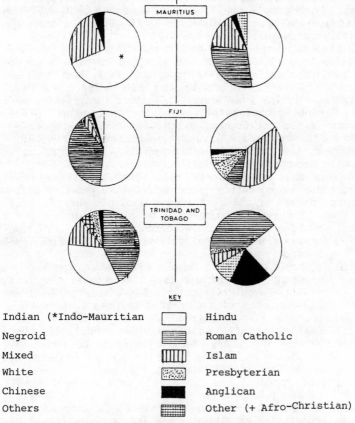

A Racial/Ethnic   B. Religious

MAURITIUS

FIJI

TRINIDAD AND
TOBAGO

KEY

Indian (*Indo-Mauritian		Hindu
Negroid		Roman Catholic
Mixed		Islam
White		Presbyterian
Chinese		Anglican
Others		Other (+ Afro-Christian)

Source: Brock, C. "Problems of Education and Human
          Ecology in Small Tropical Island Nations" in
          Brock C. and Ryba R. (eds) A Volume of Essays
          for Elizabeth Halsall: Aspects of Education
          No. 22, University of Hull, Institute of
          Education, 1980.

Such structures are results of differential colonisation and economy reflected in particular patterns of immigration and ethnicity, the main components in chronological sequence of arrival being: Amerindians; Europeans; Africans; Indians and East Indians; Chinese and Levantines. Detailed composition often reflects other colonial interests of the metropolitan powers. For example one finds Indo-chinese in the French territories and true East Indians in the Dutch islands and especially Suriname.

In respect of the Indian indentured diaspora, and Chinese minorities too, the Caribbean has examples comparable to the other small island zones of the tropics. Fiji, Mauritius and Trinidad are very comparable in this respect as Fig.1 illustrates. Tables 3 and 4 show how these immigrations were in the Caribbean case rather selective in time and place, with, as far as the Commonwealth Caribbean is concerned, little influence outside Guyana[16], Jamaica and Trinidad.[17] By contrast, the Indian element especially, is ubiquitous in the Indian Ocean and South Pacific nations.[18]

In general, the historic relationship between race, colour, class and education emerging from the peculiar socio-economic context of the West Indies was, not surprisingly, stratified. Three main groups could be identified:

- (i) a white/creole elite educated in metropolitan countries or in the local private and/or denominational secondary sector.
- (ii) a creole or mulatto 'middle class' which has emerged alongside the provision of public education systems, and is characteristically urban-based, professionally employed and interested in the maintenance of the selective principle.
- (iii) negro peasantry or proletariat subsisting on a ceiling of primary education (in some countries this stratum may include large numbers of Indians, eg. Guyana, or Amerindians, eg. Belize).

In recent decades, and especially in the more rapidly developing and urbanised areas, such as parts of Jamaica, Trinidad and Barbados, and not unrelated to increased and improved educational provision since Independence, there has been some adjustment to this simple stratification. In respect of Jamaica, for example, Miller[19], identifies an 'emerging middle stratum' which would fit between groups (ii) and (iii) above. He suggests a number of reasons for its emergence, namely: the return of Jamaicans from overseas having gained both experience and income; diversification of the urban economy and modernization; acculturation of the Chinese. He indicates that this stratum is still less educated than those above, and a strong retention of 'residual culture' is also characteristic, whether Black or Chinese.

In Trinidad the most striking adjustment is the emergence of significant sections of the Indian component into the

TABLE 3 : PERCENTAGE DISTRIBUTION OF POPULATION BY ETHNIC GROUP

Country	Ethnic group						
	African	Mixed	White	Chinese	East Indian	Other	Total
(a)							
Jamaica (1970)	91	6	0.5	0.5	2	0	100
Barbados (1970)	91	4	4	0	0.5	0.5	100
Belize (1970)	31	33	4	0	2	30	100
Trinidad and Tobago (1970)	43	14	1	1	40	1	100
Guyana (1970)	31	10	0.5	0.5	52	6	100
Surinam (1971)	(31)*	0	0	0	37	32	100
(b)							
Cuba	13	14	73	0	0	0	100
Dominican Republic	12	60	28	0	0	0	100
Haiti	90	7	3	0	0	0	100
Puerto Rico	(20)+	0	80	0	0	0	100

Sources: (a) Commonwealth Caribbean, 1970; Dew, 1976
(b) Rodriguez, 1965: Table 3 (1958 Estimates)

* Defined as 'Creoles'
+ Defined as 'no blancos'

n.b. Percentages have been rounded so that zero does not necessarily indicate total absence.

Source: Cross M (1979) Urbanization and Urban Growth in the Caribbean, Cambridge University Press, p.104.

TABLE 4 : MAJOR PHASES AND LOCATIONS OF INDIAN AND CHINESE IMMIGRATION IN THE CARIBBEAN

A. INDENTURED INDIANS

INTO	NUMBER	DATES
Guyana	239000	1846-1917
Trinidad	135000	1845-1917
Guadeloupe/ Martinique	80000	1862-1885
Surinam	35000	1846-1917
Jamaica	33500	1845-1917
St. Lucia	4400	1858-1883
Grenada	3000	1856-1878

B. CHINESE

INTO	NUMBER	DATES
Cuba	50000	1847-1860
Jamaica	5000	1860-1893
Trinidad	2600	1852-1872

Source: Brock C (1978) Caribbean World, Macmillan, p.11.

professional middle classes. This is paralleled by a markedly competitive drive on the part of this group through certain secondary schools, which has greatly enhanced achievement and the acquisition of qualifications.

The particular historical and geographical circumstances of Barbados which have enhanced the diversification of the economy, have also been conducive to early educational provision, access and development. Despite retaining clear features of colour/class stratification, the compactness and sophistication of the environment in general has meant that: "almost everyone is accessible to the dissemination of ideas as well as of goods and services"[20].

There are of course exceptions to the colour/class spectrum, such as the negro elite of Haiti and enclaves of poor whites in Antigua and Barbados. In Haiti, the only state in the region to have had black leadership for over 150 years, the nineteenth and twentieth centuries have seen a prolonged competition between negro and mulatto. Education has been involved in this power struggle, with both these priviliged urban minorities holding the negro peasantry in contempt and consequent poverty and illiteracy. But the vast majority of Caribbean countries do still exhibit the colour/class hierarcy of light to dark maintained in part by the correspondance of the educational systems to this legacy of colonialism whether of the British, French, Dutch or Spanish variety.

Differential permutations and combinations of the colour-/class kaleidoscope arise from particular patterns of economy and human economy that have evolved in each territory. The paternalism of the 'Bajan' plantocracy in respect of education was atypical of the West Indies. Yet even here slavery has left it mark. Whatever local differences there may have been between islands, the broad similarities of bondage have proved to be an enduring force in the emergence of the West Indian psyche. To the West Indian, the slave saga, and its sequel of economic dependence is the root cause of his alienation. Naipaul[21] refers to the West Indies as being 'manufactured societies' and 'labour camps'. He also portrays the deeply pessimistic feeling evident among some West Indians in respect of obstacles placed in the path of achievement:

"The history of the islands can never be satisfactorily told. Brutality is not the only difficulty. History is built around achievement and creation; and nothing was created in the West Indies".

Clearly such a feeling is enhanced by geographical insularity and smallness of economic scale. Possibilities for significant economic development in the small islands remain tenuous and dependent on outside investment and control. Some of the larger territories, however, have valuable non-renewable resources, notably bauxite in Jamaica and Guyana and petroleum in Trinidad. These three, together with the entrepreneurial Barbados comprise the "more developed countries" of the Caribbean Community, (CARICOM), the remaining members being officially termed the "less developed countries". Categorising CARICOM membership in this way relates to extra burdens being carried by the more developed countries which is commendable, but also carries with it some of the contempt in which the small island situation is held.

There has long been a feeling in the 'British West Indies' of 'Jamaica' versus 'The Rest'. This is understandable since Jamaica is physically and demographically much larger than the others, and is located in a different zone of the Caribbean. Jamaicans have long migrated for work in North and Central America and are inevitably the majority of West Indians in Britain. To many people outside the Caribbean, 'West Indies' comprizes only Jamaica in their perception of the region and its people. Jamaicans are well aware of this. Sharpley[22] reports one Jamaican's view of small islanders' likely identity problems in Britain:

"They're going to dream in London, they don't know where they're going to, but when they ask in London where them comes from, these yam and breadfruit little niggers, them's got to say Jamaica, 'cos nobody heard of dem islands"

Feelings of mutual resentment, even bitterness, between the larger and smaller islands, though probably subsiding somewhat, are a major product of slavery. The situation of bondage, where domination of one human group by another provided a formative framework of economic activity, has proved difficult to break out of, given the relative lack of physical resources and the severe limitations and costs of small scale insularity. According to Brookfield,[23] "Beckford[24] remarks that the most intractable problem of dependent societies is the 'colonised' condition of the minds of the people".

Beckford, a leading scholar of Caribbean economic history, clearly had the region in mind in respect of that judgement, and has highlighted the enormity of the attitudinal challenge facing those concerned with education in West Indian communities. The alienation deeply felt by many West Indians today in England derives from what they see as a confirmation of a long running pattern of betrayal. From the connivance of African chief and slave trader to the shanties of West Kingston[25] or the dole queue in Houndsworth or Harehills was the 'mixture as before' albeit in a new bottle.

Before the abolition of slavery and the emancipation resulting from this, the only educational provision was for the plantocracy. It took the form of private tutoring within the family, or boarding school in Britain. Miscegenous offspring, the beginnings of the creole sector, were sometimes envolved in this but the majority of the children of slaves received no formal education. The Established Church, as in England itself at that time, was interested only in the education of the elite and priests in the West Indies largely ingored the negro population, including the minority who had escaped from the plantations and set up subsistence farming communities.

With emancipation came, in theory, the opportunity for the negroes to free themselves from a dependent economy and develop an alternative livelihood. With some change of attitude on the part of the Anglican Church, and considerable interest of other churches, for the first time black West Indians came near to some limited form of educational opportunity. In addition, however, to the variety of religious attitudes to educational content there was also considerable variation between the islands in the relationship between the location of the free peasantry and access to productive land. It should be emphasised that the formal abolition of slavery did not mean the end of plantations or the plantocracy and their political power. What it did mean was a marked shift in the patterns of human ecology, making them even more particular to the island in question.

In Jamaica, the largest British island, there was a great deal of low and undulating land outside the plantations for a subsistence peasantry to develop into a relatively stable rural society, accessible to growing urban markets and influences, but attached to the land. We must remember that these people had no previous experience of the skills or the problems of subsistence farming. However, the gradual development of a public system of primary education[26] evolved slowly with the rural communities and belonged to them. So the rural population in Jamaica, with the exception of some minority mountain groups, has benefitted from education in the past, and sees it as on the whole relevant today despite disappointments with the situation of disadvantage as compared with most urban areas.

In Trinidad the establishment of plantations only just preceded emancipation. Consequently, at least in part, there appears to have been less of a divide between urban and rural society. In other words "In Trinidad rural is not so rural"[27]. Indeed, a higher proportion of rural school children achieve free places in the secondary sector than in Jamaica or Guyana. This is a result of both accessibility and attitude. Camacho sees the bulk of Trinidadian society as at least semi-urban, aware of economic and educational opportunities, and able to participate in their own development. As it happens, the 'East Indian' component of Trinidad's population is strongly represented in the small farming sector, where a combination of favourable physical context and cultural attitude to the land contrasts markedly with most other islands.

Nonetheless, this is possibly equally true of Barbados, where, the lack of any place of settlement for freed slaves contributed to the sharing of the social institutions as they developed. Very small in scale, but with a high degree of urbanisation based on a variety of entrepreneurial, servicing and manufacturing industries, Barbados has enjoyed the obvious benefits of good links between formal education and employment opportunities. In a situation of virtually no physical resources and hardly any space, Barbados has had to live by its wits, and clearly the long established education system has been a valuable asset in terms of human resource development. Urban and rural Barbados intertwine, for as Lowenthal[28] has described "Barbados is a city where sugar grows in the suburbs".

Smallness of scale in itself is, however, insufficient for the achievement of the degree of cohesion claimed for Barbados and Trinidad. Particular aspects of geography and history have played a vital part in each case. If we turn now to the Windward and Leeward islands, which have mostly experienced a much more unsettled political history, and are mostly mountainous, we find that escaped or emancipated slaves had stark choices of domicile.

"Families grouped together in places where they could best carry on the subsistence activities of farming and fishing. The best lands were, however, still used for plantations. So communities began to develop on the steep ridges between plantation valleys, and also at some places on the coast"[29]

There was and still is, a situation of very high population densities on the poorest land and in locations difficult of access. There was an almost total isolation of the peasantry from both the productive rural land, and also such urban development, and its attendant educational opportunities, as existed. Although primary schools were subsequently founded in these settlements, the chances of a rural child proceeding to secondary level in most of these islands is still poor in comparison with the urban child. The problem of urban/rural disparity in educational opportunity is apparent in most countries, and especially in the Third World, but in the West Indies numerous variations on this theme exist both between and within islands. With the possible exception of Barbados, the dichotomy remains and festers as the products of the rapidly expanding educational systems seek non-existent jobs in the towns.[30]

It is not surprising to find that in the Caribbean, where in view of its association with slavery, agriculture is a particularly unpopular occupation, urbanisation is rampant. Education is an important contributor to this process, since the bulk of its content is unrelated to rural life. As secondary education becomes available to rural populations, an upward drift in aspirations is enhanced. Foner[31] describes this with reference to part of Jamaica:

"The greater opportunity for rural children to attend secondary school has, paradoxically reduced the worth of such an achievement from an island-wide perspective. For example, white-collar workers in Coco Hill would be disappointed if their children entered occupations similar to those they follow. Instead, they want their children to attend private preparatory schools, prestigious high schools in Kingston, and university, and to enter professions such as engineering, architecture, and the law"

In some of the smaller islands it is not unusual now for the capital city to contain upwards of half the national population. They are, in effect, City States. This is acceptable provided that the economy of the island is urban based and buoyant, but this is rarely the case. Barbados, as we have already observed, now has a predominantly urban economy, but there is no room for more than one entrepot serving the Windwards and Leewards. Kingston, Jamaica, is of course a major commercial centre, but cannot employ the bulk of the output of the education system which in practice seems to disgorge there. In any case, in the larger cities there are already thousands of poor, and a complex zonation of enclaves of different groups from particular rural origins and religious/ethnic affiliations. Table 5, from Clarke[32], illustrates this in respect of Trinidad's second city, San Fernando. Elsewhere he attempts an analysis of relationships between race, colour and education in the same city.[33]

In some of the capital cities, notably Port of Spain, immigrants from other, normally smaller, islands further complicate the urban jig-saw. Distinctive national cultures lie juxtaposed to and only marginally linked with affinities within the structure of the host society. Between the Windward islands, especially St. Vincent and Grenada, and Trinidad there has developed a close yet volatile cultural relationship with intergenerational, occupational and even creative connotations.[34]

Goodenough has applied Clarke's mode of analysis to Port of Spain, and some educational aspects of this can be observed in the following comments:

"The social structure that emerges from the (1960) analysis is composed of a segmented Creole group with the Indian and other minorities aligning themselves with the upper portion or stratum of the Creoles. The Creole upper stratum is characterised by a division into two parts, the upper part being associated with professional status, university education and Presbyterianism; and the lower part correlating more closely with non-manual status, secondary levels of education, and Roman Catholicism, and reflecting the coloured middle class...The low status sub group is characterised by skilled or unskilled status, employment as domestics, the

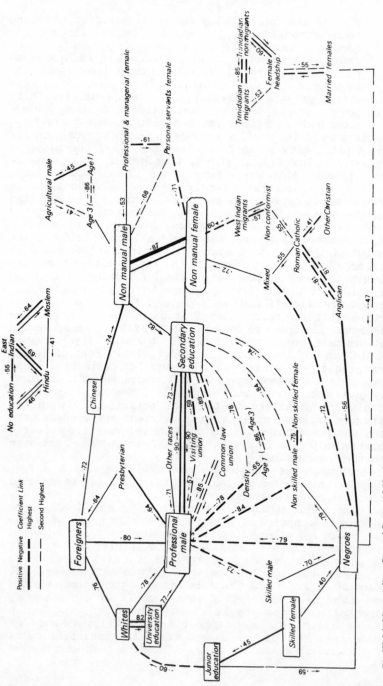

Fig.III-14. Metropolitan Port of Spain, 1960 : linkages between correlated census variables.

practice of common law and visiting unions, and achievement of low educational levels. It is also closely associated with the Anglican Church, and representative of the status of the majority of the Negro population".[35] There is clearly a very complex set of relationships between human ecology and education in the various parts of the West Indies. Education enters into this in various ways. Patterns of educational provision and attainment may seem merely to reflect other social and cultural indices. Viewed in a more dynamic way, however, and with the informal strand well in mind, education may be seen as the main process of cultural maintenance. In the plural societies of the Commonwealth Caribbean, given pronounced and continuing urbanisation but reduced international migration, national systems of education face new cultural challenges. It is not just a question of forging a national identity so much as of coming to terms with national realities. In some islands this may involve the resolution of inter-ethnic divergence in respect of a diversifying economy. Where occupational patterns are becoming racially/ethnically related in the modern sector, this is paralleled in the subject orientation and achievement in school. This problem is most acutely felt in Trinidad, and especially in the urban corridor extending eastwards from Port of Spain.

In the smaller island nations, degrees of discretion between urban and rural systems vary from place to place, but everywhere formal education is contributing towards the dominance of the urban system. If, as may well be, the long term survival economy of the bulk of the population is subsistence or at best small scale commercial farming, then some other form of education that is more in harmony with rural life will be needed. The spectre of slavery being what it is here will make it very difficult for people to accept a rural future, and an important factor in this will be a necessary redefinition of the role and nature of education. A start was made in Jamaica under Manley, using Cuban models and assistance and there have been some experiments with village polytechnics in Dominica, but the only significant and challenging response to date is that of the post - revolutionary reforms in Grenada.[36] Here an attempt is being made, though radical reform of both curriculum and teacher education to engender greater localisation and community orientation. A particularly welcome sign in this case is the prompt and real support being provided by the University of the West Indies School of Education to the scheme coalescing the initial and in-service training of teachers in Grenada.[37] The Grenadian experience illustrates the need for radical political change to back any thoroughgoing educational reform, and it is to the third group of variables that we must now turn.

The **political** **and** **religious** strands of Caribbean cultures have often been closely related in respect of education. Indeed, in most West Indian States, educational provision consists of some sort of cooperation between the Ministry of Education and one or more churches. Whereas, historically under the various colonial auspices the religious authorities were the more powerful, in the context of political independence the position has been reversed. Nonetheless, there is a very strong residual influence on educational attitudes as well as provision in respect of the religious factor.

Major religious influences in the Caribbean may be grouped to three categories:

    a.   Christian denominations
    b.   other World Religions
    c.   Afro-Caribbean developments.

Christian influences are predominant in most countries of the region. The Roman Catholic Church is most consistently represented, having been closely associated with the original European colonisation by the Spanish. Otherwise, Christian Churches vary considerably in their following, or even presence, from country to country, as indicated in Tables 5 and 6.

Christian denominations may be divided into three main groups. First there are the major sects, Catholic, Anglican and different Nonconformists. All of these have deep involvement in the evolution and contemporary operation of formal education systems. Obviously their different approaches contribute to multiculturalism intranationally and internationally. The Nonconformists showed considerable interest in the negro population, and were more popular with them than the major churches. As Bain[38] indicates in respect of Baptists and Methodists in the Bahama islands:

> "Their respective doctrines and modes of worship gave to the negro the opportunity to express some of the emotions which his social circumstances forced him to repress for most of the time, while the democratic organisation of both groups offered to individual members some scope for participation and self realisation essential to human dignity but normally denied to Africans in a slave society."

Most of the major Christian denominations were quick to seize opportunities arising from the emanciption of slaves in 1883 to influence the emerging societies. Education was seen as a priority concern, and within this, the training of teachers as a key area of conditioning. D'Oyley[39] neatly outlines the strategies of Anglicans, Baptists, Moravians, Presbyterians and Weslyians, a well as the Mico Chauty and the Church Missionary Society in Jamaica. Since this island remained for long the provider of teacher training for the 'British West Indies', interdenominational battles and influe-

TABLE 5.:   RACE AND RELIGION IN SAN FERNANDO, TRINIDAD

Race Name	Total and %	Religion Anglican	Methodist	Presbyt.	R.C.	Hindu	Moslem	Other*
Negro	18,784 46.9	8,639 45.8	878 4.7	37 0.2	7,199 38.2	6 0.03	11 0.06	2,014 10.7
White	1,306 3.3	422 32.5	21 1.6	64 4.9	649 50.0	0 0.0	0 0.0	150 11.6
Portuguese	140 0.4	1 0.7	0 0.0	7 5.0	131 93.0	0 0.0	0 0.0	1 0.7
East Indian	10,296 25.7	366 3.6	10 0.1	3,379 32.8	848 8.2	3,011 29.2	2,282 22.1	400 3.9
Chinese	705 1.8	166 23.2	0 0.0	11 1.5	473 66.2	1 0.1	0 0.0	54 7.6
Mixed	8,283 20.7	1,949 23.5	134 1.6	344 4.2	5,400 65.1	26 0.3	24 0.3	406 4.9
Carib	12 0.0	6 50.0	0 0.0	1 8.3	5 41.7	0 0.0	0 0.0	0 0.0
Syrians	152 0.4	10 6.6	0 0.0	0 0.0	135 88.8	0 0.0	0 0.0	7 4.6
Other	146 0.4	17 11.5	0 0.0	0 0.0	109 74.1	0 0.0	1 0.0	19 12.9
Not Stated	6 0.0	3 50.0	0 0.0	0 0.0	0 0.0	3 50.0	0 0.01	0 0.0
Total	39,830 100.0	11,579 50.0	1,043	3,843	14,949	3,047	2,318	3,051

*Comprising: Chirstian religious groups not listed separately in the table; other non-Christians; religion notstated; or with no religion. Source: Clarke C.G. Residential segregation and intermarriage in San Fernando, Trinidad, The Geographical Review, 61, 1971.

TABLE 6.: RELIGIONS AND DENOMINATIONS IN FIVE CARIBBEAN COUNTRIES (%)

Country Religion (%)	The Bahamas	Dominican Republic	Jamaica	Surinam	Trinidad/Tobago
R.C.	23	95	7	22	36
Anglican	23	0	20	0	21
Baptist	29	0	19	0	0
Methodist	7	0	7	0	0
Presbyterian	0	0	5	0	4
Church of God	6	0	12	0	0
Moravian	0	0	0	17	0
Dutch Ref.Ch.	0	0	0	4	0
Lutheran	0	0	0	2	0
Hindu	0	0	0	27	23
Islam	0	0	0	20	6
Others/None	12	5	30	8	10

Source: Brock C. Multiculturalism and Education in the Caribbean Region, Proc. of Thirteenth Annual Conference of the Comparative Education Society in Europe (British Section), University of Edinburgh, 1978.

nces these had repercussions elsewhere. His table, reproduced here as Table 7, charts the rise and in some cases fall of the various nineteenth century foundations, most of which operated along very traditional lines as far as method was concerned.

"But there were exceptions to the customary organisatio- nal patterns in the years before 1965: for instance, the stronger nonconformist groups, Baptists and Moravians, identified formal education as an integral part of village development. Such a pattern gave rise to many small, often cottage-type training centres which nurtured a close community spirit, benefitted from community labour for the building of the normal and day schools, and in turn educated the neighbours to better methods of planting and carpentry"[40]

Despite such examples which would probably fit well into today's radical Grenada, the formative period of the basic educational systems of the West Indies bequeathed a typically Victorian formality and a regard for formal schooling that in general survives.

Whereas in Jamaica, the Christian churches were involved after emancipation with a primarilly black population, in Trinidad there was a greater variety of clientele. As has been mentioned above, not only was the negro culture distin- ctive in the sense that a relatively short period of slave labour had obtained, but also there was the influx of East Indians as indentured labour throughout the second half of the nineteenth century and into the early twentieth. Most vigorous in their evangelising among the East Indians were the Canadian Presbyterians, who began their work in 1868 and concentrated in the centre and south of the country. From 1869 a Government Ordinance provided financial aid to mission school foundations, and later extended this to paying both fees and teachers salaries. The mission had 61 schools in Trinidad by 1911:"The school was the right arm of Presbyterian Evangelism and was instrumental in opening the door of many homes to the Gospel"[41] The Presbyterians in Trinidad were particularly instrumental in advancing the educational oppor- tunities of women and girls. By contrast the educational influence of the Anglican and Roman Catholic churches in respect of East Indians was minimal. In the latter case this was due in part to a multicultural educational policy which the East Indians feared might reduce their children's adherence to Indian culture.

The various North American sects of whom the Church of God and the Seventh Day Adventists are the most prominent in the Caribbean came into the eduational scene more recently. They seem to have grown in popularity with SDA secondary schools being sought after in some islands. The educational activi- ties of the other World Religions found in a few of the countries, especially Trinidad and Guyana where both Hinduism

TABLE 7 : SUMMARY OF NINETEENTH-CENTURY TEACHER TRAINING INSTITUTIONS IN JAMAICA*

DATES	NAME	SEX	DENOMINATION
1832-1848	Refuge	Women	Moravian
1835-1847	Airy Mount; to Villa de Medici (1836); to the Grove (1837)	Men	Anglican (CMS); Anglican/Mico (1842);
1836-present	Mico/Kingston	Men; women in early years and latterly	Anglican (1844) Mico Charity
1836-1837	Mico/Comfort Hall		
1836-1837	Mico/Somerton		
1836-1849	Kingston Central	Men, women	Anglican
1839-1900	Jamaica Metropolitan	Men, women	Baptist
1840-1900	Fairfield	Men	Moravian
1841-1843	Calabar	Men	Baptist
1841-1877	Kettering (Falmouth)	Women	Baptist
	Bonham Spring; to Montego Bay Academy (1844); to Ebenezer (1871)	Men	Presbyterian
1842-1843	(Auld's school)	Men, women	Wesleyan
1847-1851	Villa; to Croydon Lodge (1850)	Men	Board of Education
1859-1861	Brownsville	Women	Presbyterian
1861-present	Bethabara; to Salem (1899); to Bethlehem (1891)	Women	Moravian
1868-1871	Falmouth Model School	Men, women	Board of Education
1868-1876	Bath		
1869-1870	Montego Bay		
1869	Port Maria		
1870-1874	Port Antonio		

1872–1875	Charlestown	Men	Government
1870–1890	Stony Hill; to East Branch, Kingston; to Spanish Town		
1878–1890	St. Mary's	Women	Anglican/SPCK
1885–present	Shortwood	Women	Government
1897–present	St. Joseph's	Women	Roman Catholic

* In the case of some of the earlier endeavours, the assigning of dates must be somewhat arbitrary in view of the tentative nature of the operations.

After: D'Oyley V. (1979), 'Plans and Progress in Nineteenth-Century Jamaican Teacher Education', in D'Oyley V and Murray R (eds), Development and Disillusion in Third World Education, Ontario Institute for Studies in Education, p.10.

and islam are well represented, tend to be of the non-formal variety. That is to say, they are organised, but not normally in the form of general schooling, relating rather to community based religious instruction.

Afro-Caribbean religious developments of course have their roots in the slave populations who for a long period were almost untouched by christian evangelism. Not surprisingly they developed most strongly and with greatest variety in Jamaica. Revivalism, as these movements are collectively known, has its origin in an African anti-sorcery cult called 'myal', "now almost forgotten, with a wild dance, a death-and-resurrection ritual and a supposed power of making its votaries invulnerable to bullets"[42] but was also able to direct its effort towards confronting the European cultural as well as political colonialism evident in the post-emancipation development of West Indian, and especially Jamaican, society. In contemporary terms: "the Revivalists and Pentecostals alike share strong feelings agains established denominations and the ruling class"[43].

Barrett also indicates clear differences between them, in that:

"True Revivalists are nonfundamentalists; that is, the forbidden things taught by Pentecostals seem very strange to them. Abstention from liquor and tobacco, and such things as dancing and a little romancing now and then are very wholesome practices for Revivalists. Sin to them is not what you do but the spirit in which you do things"[44]

The capacity of African religious traditions to cater for the emotions has clearly survived the barbarism of the slave experience. These traditions include an aggressive, retaliatory element capable of successfully invoking demons against others, and combined with recent developments in the long standing traditions of Ethiopianism in Black American society, have produced the most significant protest movement in contemporary West-Indian society, Rastafarianism:

"At present, there is an increased availability of education, but most young Jamaicans are choosing to associate with the Revivalists and the Pentecostals, and a large body have opted for the Rastafarian religious expressions. They are finding these religious groups considerably more satisfying and relevant to their spiritual needs. In the last election, the present prime minister - born to the elite- took on the role of a Revival shepherd, calling himself Joshua and carrying a shepherd's staff. He won a landslide victory!"[45]

Rastafarianism in various forms has spread throughout the youth cultures of the West Indians in British and North American cities. Together with its recent association with reggae music it is the most potent force for a cultural convergence among young West Indians. However, Rastafarianism also has disruptive effects. Being of Jamaican origin, it can be unwelcome in other islands on that basis alone, particularly among the middle and older generations. Some of them see it a encouraging idleness, and running counter to their intense faith in the grinding process of formal education as a virtuous escape route from the land for their children. Others are uneasy about its apparent challenge, through reggae, to their particular local musical traditions.

The evolution of Rastafarianism as something beyond the range and character of other Afro-Christian movements in the West Indies is too large a theme to pursue further in this paper, but a number of texts in addition to Barratt's excellent book can be recommended.[46] However, the symbolic strength of the movement, in its various forms, at once the repudiation of white religious domination and a focus for a new West Indian identity, clearly has significant educational as well as political implications. Rastafarianism, at any rate in its urban manifestations is both anti-formal schooling and also anti-feminist. This puts considerable peer group pressure on West Indian pupils both in the Caribbean and in Britain.

Turning now to the political dimension and its relationship to multiculturalism and education, we must consider both the national and the international scales of reference. As has been illustrated, the earlier Colonial period saw educational responsibilities left to the whim of the various religious interests. During the nineteenth century, however, the British West Indian territories moved into a system of Crown Colony government. That is to say, each colony had a Governor as a direct representative of the Crown who, though subject to colonial regulations, in practice ruled over his fiefdom. In general, Governors did not remain long in any one posting and so each island was subject to a long succession of chief administrators with individual attitudes to education. Some were neglectful of it, others were obsessively interested in particular 'hobby horses'. The result of this phase of colonialism was to increase disparities within the region so that while at a broad level comparable, in detail the emerging educational systems of individual colonies were very distinctive. During this period which comes right through to the achievement of internal self-government, the local products of these individual systems of schooling took over their day-to-day administration, given the ongoing influence of the churches a distinctive interweaving of the legacies of religious inertia and political and social idiosyncracy.

This kaleidoscope of educational patterns and practices was regulated by the style and content of the metropolitan external examinations (the Cambridge and London 'Overseas'), in that the entire raison d'etre of the whole operation seemed to be to select and service the tiny minority of pupils who would sit these papers. There is indeed a formidable legacy of colonial education in the Commonwealth Caribbean, both structural and attitudinal.[47] Given the small scale of all the nations involved, there had to be some sort of regional cooperation post-independence, and it is here that problems of distinctive national cultures and economies emerge.

In 1948 the West Indian territories acquired their own University College, with campuses developing in Jamaica, Trinidad and Barbados. Ten years later they gained their independence from Britain in the form of one political unit, the West Indies Federation. By 1962 this Federation had collapsed beneath the strain of Caribbean geopolitics. It was a 'non-starter', born of a total misconception on the part of the British Colonial Office of the reality of West Indian island-scale nationality. The more powerful units became independent nations, including the three with the university campuses. Guyana founded its own university. The small cislands reverted initially to the status of colonies, and a few microstates remain as such. The others, beginning with Grenada in 1974 successively achieved individual independence. Within the Commonwealth Caribbean there is in reality though, a political hierarchy and a regional multiculturalism in both of which education plays a maintenance role.

Looking at the French, Dutch and British Antilles we can see different degrees of unification in respect of education, as well as distinctive inter as well as intra group variations associated with religion.

In the French Caribbean, the components of which eventually became, and still remain, Departements of France, the regulations and the opportunities of the French system were fully applied. While this involved the obvious dominance of French culture over such indigenous varieties as had emerged, it had clear advantages in other respects over the less centralised policies of the British and Dutch. As early as 1840 an ordinance proclaimed that free schools were to be established in towns and boroughs of the colonies so that: "moral and religous education could be given to slave children of both sexes".[48]

This led to a relatively equitable provision of primary and secondary schools throughout the French Antilles, which, together with close economic ties with Metropolitan France, has had a salutory effect on human resource development. Unimpeded migration to the mainland has provided access to employment opportunities beyond those feasible, qualitatively and quantitatively, in the island context. The same applies to access to higher education.

In his comparison of educational opportunities and facilities as between the French Antilles and the British West Indies, Murch[49] was able to show a clear advantage to the former, as indicated in Table 8.

Of course, since 1964 there has been a considerable

increase in educational interest by B.W.I. governments
following independence or internal self-government, but this
has been more than matched by recent reforms in the French
system. Currently and proportionally, about twice as many
Antilleans as West Indians are entering tertiary education.
However there have been signs, especially in Martinique, of
political and social stress occasioned by the presence of a
growing young stratum of qualified unemployed. This together
with the awareness of an affinity with other black West
Indians has led to some demand for independence.

TABLE 8

SOME EDUCATIONAL COMPARISONS AS BETWEEN THE FRENCH ANTILLES AND BRITISH WEST INDIES

	French Antilles 1964	B.W.I. 1964
School enrolment ratio (%enrolled of the est. population 5-19, adjust. for duration of the school year.	103	82
Pupil/Teacher Ratio (primary and secondary)	32	39
Public Spending on Education ($US per cap)	48	17

The Dutch Antilles are much more varied in their educational, religious and linguistic patterns. With Suriname now
independent, this group now comprises:
   a.   Leewards (Aruba, Bonaire, Curacao), population about
        250,000
   b.   Windwards (Saba, St. Eustatius, St. Maarten-part)
        population about 7,000.
The official language of both groups is Dutch, but the vernacular of the Leewards is Papiamentu, a Spanish based creole,
while English is the lingua franca of the Windwards. While
the Leewards are predominantly Catholic, and the Windwards
Protestant, the opportunities for separate schooling to small
group demand allowed under the Netherlands system leads to
some variation within each group of islands. Indeed even
official metropolitan comment questions the wholesale
implantation of all aspects of the Dutch system in the
Antilles:

"Afterall, the backgrounds of the Dutch and the Antillean
child being quite different, there is a great difference
too between cultural and behavioural patterns in these
countries. For fear that an educational system other
than the Dutch one would be harmful to the quality of
education, the Antilles have carefully copied the Dutch
example and did not see to it that a linking up was
realized between school and home. This obliged the children to live in two different worlds at the same time,
which was not favourable for their achievements at
school, nor for streaming, especially in the junior
classes of primary school."[50]

There is also considerable economic disparity between the
affluent Leewards and the poor Windwards. All this makes for
difficulty in reaching the declared policy of equal
educational opportunities within the Netherlands Antilles.

The language problem is proving particularly difficult.
According to Frank[51] there is a strong movement in the Leewards for the introduction of Papiamentu as the medium for
schooling. She indicates that "Papiamentu is unique among
creole languages in being a language of high social prestige".
The need for an international second language is accepted, but
there is a difference of opinion as to which of Dutch, English
and Spanish should be officially favoured in the curriculum.
Some support Dutch on traditional grounds, while others would
prefer to see it discarded a a gesture against colonialism.
Although itself a minority language in world terms, Dutch is
at least the natural second or first language of most teachers
in these islands. Proximity to Venezuela, and other connections with South and Central America, make Spanish a sensible
choice, especially as Papiamentu is related to it anyway.
English, as the normal language of the Dutch Windwards, and
important in the Netherlands itself can also claim support.
This problem clearly has educational implications, but as
Frank indicates, the final decision will be made on political
grounds.

Despite the cultural differences within the Netherlands
Antilles there has at least been consistent interest and
support for educational provision and development from the
Netherlands itself. The same goes for the French Caribbean.
By contrast the Commonwealth Caribbean contains a much more
varied set of cultural patterns and educational systems. This
is largely a result of the political history of these
territories, as outlined above.[52] Within this group, education has to contend not only with intra-national multiculturalism based on a mix of variables unique to each island, but
also the plurality of national cultures. It is in this
context that the following selected problems of educational
development in the Commonwealth Caribbean must be viewed.

Some Educational Implications of Independence

Independence, even self-government of internal affairs, carries an obligation to provide what have come historically and culturally to be regarded as normal educational services. It also carries a need to produce its own civil servants and teachers. Not surprisingly then, in most of the islands the last decade has seen both reapraisal and an expansion of education. In no two cases has the pattern been the same, though there are some regional trends, discussed further below. In general, however, the trend has been towards a greater difference between systems. Each government is at liberty to invite or accept educational aid from sources other than Britain, and responses to this have inevitably influenced both the degree of multiculturalism, and the complexity of its implications for education. At this stage, continued economic weakness and dependence encourages old and new metropolitan influences.[53] In addition to traditional British and Canadian links, and well established UN agencies, Latin American aid is now a significant factor. Notable in this respect was Cuban support in certain aspects of Jamaican educational reform during the Government of Michael Manley especially in respect of rural communities. Since the Grenadian revolution of 1979, Cuba has also been actively involved in educational reform, especially in providing printed materials in English for the adult education and literacy campaigns. Indeed, the educational dimension of the Cuban revolution itself provided a stimulus and inspiration for those responsible for educational planning in the new Grenada. For a socialist revolution to have taken place in one of the Windward Islands is somewhat ironic in that nearby Venezuala has long had designs in this area, and had been quietly increasing its influence inter alia by schemes of educational aid.

With all these forces leading towards expansion of educational provision the manifestation of at least physical evidence of development in the form of buildings carries with it considerable kudos for the local politicians and administrators. It has been known for these educational goodies to be disparately bestowed in accordance with regional differences in voting patterns. This is not of course peculiar to the West Indies, but in that it is a recent feature, it has sometimes deepened disparities and widened ethnic divides.

Developments and Problems in the Compulsory Sector

Most West Indians do not have the opportunity to partake of further or higher education. This terminal characteristic of schooling, together with the increased demand for it occasioned by both demographic and aspirationsl forces, has a squeezing and intensifying effect.

Taking the analaysis of the 1960 Caribbean Census by Roberts and Abdulah[54] as a pre-independence picture, we find that a ceiling of primary educational attainment was the norm (Table 9). The figures also show considerable variation within the Commonwealth Caribbean as to secondary education provision, and the proportion of the adult population having had no formal education at all. Comments made above as to the differential input of cultural variables, even within the ex-British islands, help to explain these disparities: varied environmental contexts for freed slaves, educational attitudes of plantocracies and churches, and idiosyncratic political and educational histories have all played their part. Relatively high figures for lack of education may be explained by linguistic and ethnic factors. Certainly the use of a French based patois in Dominica and Saint Lucia, and the ethnic diversity of Trinidad have influenced educational take-up if not provision. The case of Jamaica is less clear but may relate to isolation of some rural areas in a large island, and also the extensive development of shanty suburbs, especially West Kingston.[55]

Table 9

Educational Attainment 1960: Selected Islands

Figures are % of population aged 15 years and over.

Island	No Education	Primary Education	Secondary Education	University
Barbados	1.8	83.1	15.9	0.6
Dominica	13.4	79.0	6.4	0.5
Jamaica	16.8	74.4	6.7	0.3
St.Kitts/Nevis	3.8	89.1	5.9	0.4
St.Lucia	26.2	69.7	3.3	0.3
Trinidad and Tobago	11.3	72.9	13.6	0.7

After: Roberts G.W. and Abdullah N. (1965) 'Some Observations on the Educational Position of the British Caribbean, **Social and Economic Studies,** 14.

Such was the basis from which newly independent Governments set about building new educational opportunities, and it also reflects the relative educational disadvantage with which many West Indian immigrants entered Britain in the 1950's and 1960's. Despite many difficulties and constraints these governments, like many others in the 'developing world' made educational investment a priority. Partly due to a manageable smallness of scale, and also the competitive vigour of the churches, universal primary education had long since been a reality. With some influence from trends towards non-selective secondary education in Britain and elsewhere, the objective in some of the islands has been to raise the level of general education beyond the primary ceiling still in the 1960 census.

We are reminded by Jervier[56] that the regional trend is often set by Jamaica, and it was there that the attempt to infuse a Junior Secondary sector began. This was seen by some as a way of delaying selection and utilising the structural wedge to infuse new curricular orientations that could begin to cope with the Eurocentric legacy of the colonial era. But as King[57] reports, the initial thrust was appropriated.

"In the years after 1967 a number of junior secondary schools have been built to provide three years of secondary education for children in the age group 12+ to 15+. Formerly a small percentage of these children were selected on the basis of the Grade Nine Achievement Test to receive a second cycle of secondary education in the traditional high schools. Since September 1974 these junior secondary schools have been extended to provide five years of secondary schooling and are now designated secondary schools. Three comprehensive high schools have also been established"

Most of the smaller Eastern Caribbean states also followed the junior secondary route but here again, the infusion of this sector presented an opportunity for a radical curricular reorientation that has largely been already lost.[58] That there was a need for such a change has been clear for some time from the dysfunctionality of existing systems in respect of the societies and economies of which they are supposedly an integral part[59]. The problem is most acute in the smaller islands, where economic constraints and political vaccilations have rendered the evolution of the junior secondary schools a very piecemeal affair. Consequently the new sector, being incomplete, becomes of necessity selective. Pressures from the senior secondary schools often dictate the character or even content of the new curricula. Of course, the image of schooling, and expectations from it of most parents, supports this conservatism, especially as the radical alternative, in as far as they are aware of its nature, is urging a rural and community context which a colonial culture finds difficult to accept.

With the movement towards universal secondary education within discrete national systems comes the need for an examination alternative to that used by the grammar schools - normally the GCE Cambridge Overseas. Local secondary certificates vary considerably in content and standard, and are not normally recognised outside their home island. Inter island differences and even suspicions also hamper the progress of the successor to the Cambridge Overseas, currently emerging under the auspices of the Caribbean Examinations Council (CXC). On the basis that an essential component of independence was freedom from external control of examinations, and therefore of syllabusus, the Second Conference of Heads of Government of Commonwealth Caribbean Countries (1964) decided that the CXC would be established. In the event it took eight further years of negotiation before the Agreement setting CXC in motion was signed. Since 1972 the Council has experienced all the vicissitudes common to any federal enterprise in the Caribbean, but so far it has survived. The first papers were taken in a limited number of subjects in 1979, and now the full range is operative.

The main problems again are symptomatic of fundamental features of West Indian culture. Firstly, there was a great deal of suspicion in some islands as to the likelihood of their candidates being marked fairly by examiners from elsewhere in the Caribbean. A similar problem is apparent in some of the syllabus panels where the balance of content as between the West Indies as a whole and one's own island is vigorously and sometimes acrimoniously contested. In other words, the insularity characteristic is strongly evident. Secondly, there is the nature and style of the examination. It is very close indeed to the examination it is designed to replace. It perpetutes a formal style, and this is in keeping with the need to acquire a status equivalent to the Cambridge Overseas, not only from the University of the West Indies but from employers and parents also. From the balance of subjective evaluations, it would seem in many area to be more difficult than its predecessor, and if this is so then it is bound to intensify the individual struggle for educational success, without helping to provide the expected employment opportunities. In other words the style of the examination reflects Beckford's concern already quoted, for 'the colonised condition of the minds of the people'.

Such problems were apparently aggravated by the paucity of information issued by CXC to member Ministries of Education, and in turn to the teachers, parents and pupils to be involved in the first years of its operation. A few Governments decided not to participate, and in response to growing demand CXC produced a 'Fact Sheet' in April 1978 designed to allay public apprehension on the issue. It is an extremely formal document that in its conclusion states:

"The Council, mindful of the magnitude of its task, has consequently sought, received and continues to benefit from the active support of specialists. It looks forward to authorising syllabuses, conducting examinations and issuing certificates which will reflect and satisfy the needs and aspirations of the vast majority of the English-speaking Caribbean public"[60]

There is no doubt that these sentiments were sincerely expressed, but it is difficult to see them being realised through such an educational instrument as CXC. It is likely instead to be a dysfunctional influence in that, though only a minority of any age group will sit the examination, the ramifications of preparation will spread throughout primary and secondary schooling. The opportunity for a really new indigenous alternative educational philosophy would seem to have been lost because of continued cultural dependence on the part of educated West Indians. Indeed, in response to the parlous financial state of CXC arising partly from its style of operation and partly from the compounded costs of any regional enterprise in the Caribbean, the U.S.A. has for a limited period come to the rescue with a USAID project to sustain it. However, not surprisingly, this support carries with it certain cultural and ideological implications and constraints.

Since the majority of West Indians do not, as yet, proceed to Higher Education, this sector will not be considered here. Suffice it to say however that its evolution and maintenance are subject to the conflict between local, national, regional and metropolitan scales of consciousness and interdependence, as in the compulsory sector.[61] It is characteristic of the problem of education in a multicultural Caribbean, that politicians party to setting up the Caribbean Examinations Council with its continued cultural dependence should be major contributors to a publication entitled: 'Caribbean Education: Impasse and Dilemma'[62]. Introducing this book, in sharp contrast to the guarded confidence of the CXC quotation above, is the following statement:

"Like other Western-trained specialists West Indian educational planners and administrators have often been guilty of uncritical imitation. The colonialist perspective has clouded our horizons so that institutions designed for temperate climates, European cultures and metropolitan capitalist economies have been imposed upon a tropical, multi-cultural and exploited amalgam of peoples. Our own imprisoned consciousness and the threatening impasse and breakdown of our total societyis forcing our politicians and thinkers to asess the weakness of the present situation and to indicate possible choices for the way forward"

This is indeed ironical in view of the opportunities for radical reappraisal afforded by local control over educational policies for at least two decades now. It is of course likely that a more appropriate education for the majority of West

Indians would be relatively informal with strong community involvement and locale specific content. This would conflict with the capacity of formal education provision to assist the convergence of attitudes and responses, a capacity appreciated and encouraged by politicians in most countries of the world!

Nevertheless, misgivings about the efficacy of formal odels of a traditional kind for the West Indian situation were being voiced nearly half a century ago, even before the Moyne Commission. In his book 'Warning from the West Indies' Macmillan[63] describes education in the region a being stagnant in comparison with African developments, yet 'more advanced'. He indicated that it suffered from a confusion of counsel rather than neglect. Of schools in particular he stated: "as far as they cater for the blacks...they do it mainly for the already strong 'middle class', very little for the masses.... If deepening and sharpening social distinctions". Such a comment is commonplace today with reference to selective schooling and streaming in England. But whereas we have the resources to seek solutions through expensive experiments and re-organisation, West Indian states have not. More than that, however, metropolitan cultural dependence, with its version of 'education' still prevails over the fragmented cultural patterns of the Caribbean. A strong indigenous alternative has yet to emerge, but may be in the process of doing so. As yet, one can still go along with another of Macmillan's 1935 observations that: "The West Indian, in searching for an identity, is expressing one"[64] In this education is playing its part, and responding with various degrees of success to the particular multiculturalism obtaining. The pluralities with which it has to contend are not merely those which have become the conventional stock in trade of yet another field of educational studies, 'multicultual education', namely the problems of minority groups. Deeper than this lie the continued striving for the emergence of a realistic socio-economic strategy that will carry with it the new identities of each Commonwealth Caribbean State. The colonial bogey will not be laid to rest in its cultural form, until the economic system to which it relates is radically changed. Plantation agriculture and dependency on primary exports is as strong as ever. Slavery may have been abolished, but the system is served, with its cultural implications, remains. Within the Commonwealth Caribbean, Grenada has struck out and is attempting a radical alternative. Its education system undergoing radical reform is still uncomfortably straddling the old elitisim and the new collectivism.

Grenada's path with its Cuban backing is a matter of acute interest and concern to the USA, and herein lies another multi-cultural dimension within which the Commonwealth countries have to resolve their identity and their educational problems, namely the wider 'Caribbean World'. Some mention has also been made of the French and Dutch Antilles, of Cuba, Venezuala and the U.S.A., but as Map 1 illustrates there are many other components, including Association of Caribbean Universities, though its activities and its journal,[65] does provide one regional and educational network for highlighting and researching problems of common or complementary interest. Whether it is a disinterested body or a CIA cover is the sort of question to which the mostly small Commonwealth Caribbean countries address themselves as they seek an indigenous/regional alternative to the colonial educational legacies of the Old World.

Notes and References

1. Sahlins M.D. 'Culture and Environment: The study of cultural ecology' in Manners R.A. and Kaplan D. **Theory in Anthropology** Routledge and Kegan Paul, 1968, p.373.
2. Lowenthal D. 'West Indians Emigrants Overseas' in Clarke C.G. (Ed) **Caribbean Social Relations**, University of Liverpool, Centre for Latin American Studies, 1978, pp.82-94.
3. For example: (a) Coard B. **How the West Indian Child is made Educationally Sub-Normal in the British School System**, New Beacon Books, 1971. (b) Driver G. **Beyond Underachievement: Case Studies of English, West Indian and Asian School-leavers at Sixteen plus**, Commission for Racial Equality, 1980.
4. For example: (a) Giles R. **The West Indian Experience in British Schools**, Heinemann, 1977. (b) Taylor M. **Caught Between: A Review of Research into the Education of Pupils of West Indian Origin**, NFER/Nelson, 1981.
5. Bagley C. **The Dutch Plural Society: A Comparative Study of Race Relations**, Oxford University Press, 1973.
6. Hauch C. **Educational Trends in the Caribbean,** United States Department of Health, Education and Welfare, 1960.
7. Clarke C.G. 'Insularity and Identity in the Caribbean', **Geography,** Vol 61, Part 1, 1976, p.8.
8. Brock C. 'Problems of Education and Human Ecology in small Tropical Island Nations', in Brock C. and Ryba, R. (Eds) **A Volume of Essays for Elizabeth Halsall: Aspects of Education No.22,** University of Hull, Institute of Education, 1980, pp. 71-83.
9. Farrell J, 'Education and Pluralism in Selected Caribbean Societies', **Comparative Education Review,** Vol 11 No 2 , 1967 .
10. Smith M.G. **The Plural Society in the British West Indies,** University of California Press, 1965.
11. Henry, G. 'A Cross-Cultural Outline of Education', in Jennings J.D. and Hoebel, E.A. (Eds) **Readings in Anthropology,** McGraw Hill, 2nd ed. 1966.

12. Brock C. 'The Legacy of Colonialism in West Indian Education', in Watson J.K.P. (Ed) **Education in the Third World,** Croom Helm, 1982, pp. 119-140.
13. **op.cit**
14. Cross M. **Urbanisation and Urban Growth in the Caribbean,** Cambridge University Press, 1979, pp.102-103.
15. Lowenthal D. **West Indian Societies,** Oxford University Press, 1972, pp.78-79.
16. Cross M. **The East Indians of Guyana and Trinidad,** Minority Rights Group, 1973.
17. La Guerre J.G. (Ed) **Calcutta to Caroni: the East Indians of Trinidad,** Longman, 1974.
18. Crocombe R. (Ed) **Pacific Indians: profiles in 20 countries,** Institute of Pacific Studies, University of the South Pacific, 1981.
19. Miller E. 'Education and Society in Jamaica', in Figueroa P.M.E. and Persand G. (Eds) **Sociology of Education: A Caribbean Reader,** Oxford University Press, 1976, pp.47-66.
20. Lowenthal D. 'The Population of Barbados', **Social and Economic Studies,** Vol 6, No 4, 1957, p.495.
21. Naipaul V.S. **The Middle Passage,** Andre Deutsch, 1962.
22. Sharpley A. 'The Night the Knives Came Out', **London Evening Standard,** 26.10.1961.
23. Brookfield H.C. **Interdependent Development,** Methuen, 1975, p.161.
24. Beckford G.L. **Persistant Poverty: underdevelopment in plantation economies of the Third World,** Oxford University Press, 1972, p.235.
25. Clarke C.G. 'The Slums of Kingston', in Lowenthal D. and Comitas L. **Work and Family Life: West Indian Perspectives,** Anchor Boks, 1973, pp.174-187.
26. Whyte M. **A Short History of Education in Jamaica,** Hodder and Stoughton, 1977.
27. Camacho A. 'Education and Educational Opportunity', in Cross M. (Ed) **West Indian Social Problems,** Columbus, pp.99-117.
28. Lowenthal D. (1957) **op.cit.** p.472.
29. Brock C. **Saint Lucia,** Macmillan, 1976, p.9.
30. Cross M. 'Education and Job Opportunities' in Moss R. (Ed) **The Stability of the Caribbean,** Institute for the Study of Conflict, 1973, pp.51-76.
31. Foner N. **Status and Power in Rural Jamaica** Teachers College Press, Columbia University New York, 1973, p.59.
32. Clarke C.G. 'Residential segregation and intermarriage in San Fernando, Trinidad', **The Geographical Review,** Vol 61, No 2, 1971, pp.198-218.
33. Clarke C.G. 'Pluralism and Stratification in San Fernando, Trinidad', in Clark B.D. and Gleave M.B. **Social Patterns in Cities,** Institute of British Geographers, 1973, pp.53-70.

34. Keens-Douglas P. 'Tanti at de Oval', **"Tim Tim": The Dialect Poetry of Paul Keens-Douglas**, 1976, pp.26-32.
35. Goodenough S. 'Race, Status and Ecology in Port of Spain, Trinidad', in Clarke C.G. (Ed) 1978) **op.cit.** pp.33-34.
36. Jacobs W.R. and Jacobs I. **Grenada: The Route to Revolution**, Casa de las Americas, 1979.
37. Parker R.S. 'Small Island States', in Thompson A.R. (Ed) **In-Service Education of Teachers in the Commonwealth**, Commonwealth Secretariat, 1982, pp.144-187.
38. Bain R.E. 'Missionary Activity in the Bahamas 1700-1830' in Holmes B. (Ed) **Educational Policy and the Mission Schools**, Routledge and Kegan Paul, 1967, p.61.
39. D'Oyley V. 'Plans and Progress in Nineteenth-Century Jamaican Teacher Education' in D'Oyley V. and Murray R. (Eds) **Development and Disillusion in Third World Education**, Ontario Institute for Studies in Education, 1979, pp.5-32.
40. **ibid** p.6.
41. Harricharan J.T. **The Work of the Christian Churches among the East Indians in Trinidad: 1847-1917**, Artcraft, pp.25-26.
42. Jacobs H.P. 'Dialect, Magic and Religion' in Cargill M. (Ed) **Ian Fleming introduces Jamaica**, Andre Deutsch, pp.92-93.
43. Barrett L.E. **The Rastafarians**, Heinemann, 1977, p.26.
44. **ibid.** pp.26-27.
45. **ibid.** p.28.
46. For example: (a) Dalrymple H. **Bob Marley: Music Myth and the Rastas**, Carib-Arawak Publishing Ltd., 1976.
    (b) Garrison L. **Black Youth, Rastafarianism, and the Identity Crisis in Britain**, Afro-Caribbean Education Resource Project, 1979.
    (c) Nicholas T. and Sparrow B. **Rastafari: A Way of Life**, Anchor Books, 1979.
47. Brock C. (1982) **op.cit.**
48. Murch A. **Black Frenchmen: the political integration of the French Antilles**, Schenkman Publishing Company, 1971, p.34.
49. **ibid**, p.37.
50. Ministerie van Onderwijsen Wetenschappen, **Education in the Netherlands Antilles**, 1967, p.4.
51. Frank F.W. 'Language and Education in the Leewards Netherlands Antilles', **Caribbean Studies**, Vol 13, No 4, 1974, pp.111-117.
52. For record and analysis of the development of education in the 'British West Indies', see for example:
    (a) Gordon S.C. **A Century of West Indian Education**
    (b) D'Oyley V. and Murray R. (Eds) **Development and Disillusion in Third World Education**, Ontario Institute for Studies, Pergamon, 1971.
    (c) Williams E. **Education in the British West Indies**, University Place Bookshop, 1951.

53. Brock C. (1980). **op.cit.**
54. Roberts G.W. and Abdulah N. 'Some Observations on the Educational Position of the British Caribbean', **Social and Economic Studies,** Vol. 14, No1, 1965, pp.144-154.
55. Clarke C.G. (1967) **op.cit.**
56. Jervier W.S. **Educational Change in Postcolonial Jamaica,** Vantage Press, 1977.
57. King R. 'The Jamaica Schools Commission and the Development of Secondary Schooling', in D'Oyley V. and Murray R. (Eds) **op.cit.** p.52.
58. Brock C. 'Structural and Curricular Developments at the Junior Secondary level on the Caribbean Island of Saint Lucia', paper presented to the Biannual Conference of the Comparative Education Society in Europe, University of Valencia, 1979, **mimeo** p.11.
59. Ruscoe G.C. **Dysfunctionality in Jamaican Education,** University of Michigan Press, 1963.
60. Caribbean Examinations Council, **Fact Sheet,** April 1978.
61. Brock C. (1980) **op.cit.**
62. Mitchell D.I. (Ed) **Caribbean Education: Impasse and Dilemma,** C.C.C. Publishing House, 1974.
63. Macmillan W.M. **Warning from the West Indies,** Faber and Faber, 1935, p.145.
64. **ibid.**
65. **Caribbean Educational Bulletin/Boletin Educacional del Caribe,** Association of Caribbean Universities and Research Institutes (UNICA).

9 CULTURAL PLURALISM, EDUCATION AND NATIONAL IDENTITY IN THE ASEAN COUNTRIES OF SOUTH-EAST ASIA. [1]

KEITH WATSON

During the thirty years or so since the end of World War II, or since the granting of independence to the countries of the South East Asian region, there have been enormous changes and, in some cases, there has been enormous socio-economic progress. Unfortunately, however, the countries of South East Asia usually only figure in the European press if there is some crisis or other, although the picture is rather different if viewed from Australia, Japan and the USA. The truth is, that as the years have passed since independence was granted by the colonial powers[2] their interests have turned elsewhere. Thus, since the end of the Vietnam war in the early 1970s, Western awareness has been more concerned with the Middle East and, more recently, central Latin America as potential flashpoints for global conflict.

Yet there remain underlying tensions in all the countries of South East Asia. There are tribal conflicts in Burma. The recent massacre of Bangladeshi refugees in Assam is an indirect result of the Burmese expulsion of Bangladeshis from their territory during the late 1970s and early 1980s. Thailand is suffering from a "refugee problem" created by thousands of Laotians, Kampucheans and Vietnamese fleeing across the borders in the aftermath of Vietnamese invasion and are now living in refugee settlements along the Thai-Laos and Thai-Kampuchean borders.[3] Australia, Canada, France, the UK and the USA are amongst the Western powers that have been affected by the huge influx of Vietnamese refugees expelled from, or fleeing from, Vietnam since June 1978. Thousands more have settled in Hong Kong. Others are in refugee camps in Malaysia. Yet others are raped, pillaged or even murdered by Thai pirates in the Gulf of Thailand as they flee from their homeland in 'leaky' vessels. In the Southern Philippines and in Southern Thailand there are irredentist movements amongst the Muslim groups. In the Philippines opposition is directed against Christian control; in Thailand against Buddhist control. There are border disputes between China and Vietnam, Vietnam and Kampuchea and between Kampuchea

197

Cultural Pluralism in South-East Asia

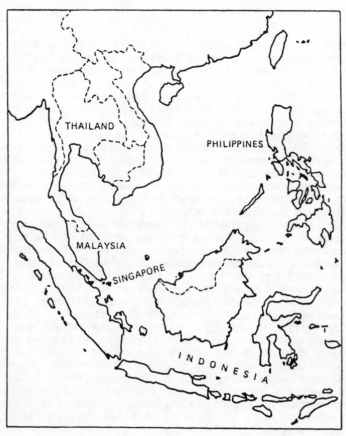

The Association of Southeast Asian Nations (ASEAN)

and Thailand. The 1981 census results in Malaysia have not yet been released, it is argued, because they are politically unpalatable showing a declining population birth rate amongst the Malays and an increasing birth rate amongst the non-Malays, the Chinese and Indians. Whatever the truth in these allegations, they serve to highlight the sensitivity of racial issues in this multicultural society.

The point is that, of all the geographical religions of the world, South East Asia must lay claim to being one of the most complex in terms of ethnicity and race, religion and culture, language and political relationships. As such it defies easy, pragmatic, western analysis. As a result, and, as several observers have commented, one of the tragedies of South East Asia is that it is generally not understood by most Westerners.[4] It is hoped therefore that this paper may serve to illuminate some of the region's complexities especially as they affect education. It is also hoped to show (1) that educational policies in culturally plural societies differ according to the threat felt by the dominant group; (2) that tensions are often **increased** in a multi-racial society as a result of educational policies; and (3) that the use of a national language as a medium of instruction and as a means of creating a sense of national unity **can** be successful, but equally it can bring about resentment and even resistance from different ethnic groups, which feel that their group identity is being threatened.

While reference will be made to the whole of South East Asia emphasis will be placed on those countries of ASEAN (The Association of South East Asian Nations), - Indonesia, Malaysia, Philippines, Singapore and Thailand - since not only is there relative political stability amongst them; not only has there been considerable progress in socio-economic development since about 1960, but because all five countries have most positively committed themselves, in word and deed, to educational expansion, to developing a national identity and to regional cooperation through SEAMEO (the South East Asian Ministers of Education Organization); and since information and statistics relating to educational expansion and development are most readily obtainable. Because the other countries, most notably Kampuchea, Laos and Vietnam, have been ravaged by war for much of the past two decades, it is not possible to ascertain an accurate picture of what is happening nor to acquire any meaningful information relating to educational development; Vietnam is perhaps the one exception to this picture.[5]

From the above paragraphs it will be obvious that one of the underlying factors of the region is that of conflict. Contrary to the widely held belief that all the uprisings in South East Asia since the end of World War II, whether communist or nationalist, have been as a direct result of colonial involvement, the history of the region is one of almost constant conflict within and between nations - conflict between Thais and Burmese, Thais and Khmers, Khmers and Vietnamese, Chinese and Malays.[6] As Osbourne has shown in his study on South East Asia "Region of Revolt" all the countries of the region "are states rather than nations, seldom providing the opportunities for citizenship to all within their boundaries."[7] As a result this inherent instability arises from a lack of ethnic and regional unity and a lack of national cohesion. Not surprisingly of the four types of revolt that have broken out during the past 2000 years, three of them have arisen as a result of "an ethnic diffusion not predisposed to unity". In any study of cultural pluralism and national identity, therefore, this overriding fact can never be overlooked.

Before turning to explore the South East Asian context in greater detail, however, it is worth examining the concept of cultural pluralism and the policy options available to governments.

Cultural Pluralism and Educational Policies

During the 1970s comparative educators became aware of, and increasingly concerned with, the phenomenon of educational and cultural diversity within a framework of national unity.[8] The interest comes as much from the resurgence of nationalism amongst minority groups in the advanced nations of the world, much of which has been associated with demands for separate and/or mother-tongue education, as it does from the very diverse nations of the Third World.[9] Indeed one German comparativist has stressed that there is a "growing necessity for taking into consideration the concerns of ethnic cultural groups in society from an educational point of view" because

"the idea of linguistic and cultural pluralism as something not merely tolerated, but as an acknowledged and promoted expression of the multiplicity within a political community has far-reaching consequences for the internal and also the external form of the school system.... The school is given the task of combatting a possible disintegration, and strengthening the notion of the unity of the State."[10]

Concern for cultural pluralism is nothing new, however, and the concept of a plural society is generally attributed to an American writer, J.S. Furnivall, in his observations of Burma and Java under British and Dutch rule. In the 1940's he made the following observations:

"In Burma, as in Java, probably the first thing that strikes the visitor is the medley of people - European, Chinese, Indian and native. It is in the strictest sense a medley, for they mix but do not combine. Each group holds to its own religion, its own culture and language, its own ideas and ways. As individuals they meet, but only in the marketplace, in buying and selling. There is a plural society, with different sections of the community living side by side, but separately, within the same political unit. Even in the economic sphere, there is a division along racial lines."[11]

Furnivall went on to argue that the mixing of racial and cultural groups in colonial societies was not a voluntary process but was one imposed, for economic reasons, by colonial powers and that nationalism in plural societies, far from being a unifying force, was instead a disruptive and dangerous one.

A more recent attempt at defining a plural society distinguishes between cultural pluralism and social pluralism. "Cultural pluralism usually develops from the presence in a given society of several ethnic or racial groups with different cultural traditions. Social pluralism is found where the society is structurally divided into analagous and duplicatory but culturally similar groups of institutions and the corporate groups are differentiated on a basis other than culture."[12]

The following attributes are then listed as typifying a plural society: the relative absence of a value consensus; the relative presence of conflict between corporate groups; the relative autonomy between parts of the social system; the relative political domination by one of the corporate groups over the others; tension and racial conflict resulting from perceived rather than actual differences and a belief that prejudice and discrimination are exerted by the majority group against minorities. The exponent of these views, a Chinese Malay, has based his observations on the Malaysian scene.[13]

Given the cultural and racial complexity of a plural society, whether this has come about as a result of conquest, migration or boundary changes, certain important questions about policy arise. Does governmental policy in general, and educational policy in particular, seek to eliminate, modify or encourage cultural diversity within a framework of national unity? Formal education in all societies is perceived as a transmitter of knowledge, customs and social values. In developing countries in particular, it is still regarded as one of the key instruments for bringing about social change, economic development and political modernisation through human resource development. Education is also seen as a weapon for breaking down the rural/urban gap by creating equality of opportunity for social mobility, at the same time as providing openings for greater economic involvement. In culturally plural societies it is seen by governments as a neutral means of redressing ethnic imbalances and of creating a sense of national identity where none existed before. It is often linked with economic policies designed to redress economic imbalances which might or might not coincide with race. It is argued that by helping to create a scientific, rational outlook and new approaches towards political modernisation, modern education will weaken tribal and ethnic loyalties by creating new allegiances, attitudes, loyalties and values. If job mobility and economic advancement are linked to education there will also be a social realignment, not along ethnic or racial lines, but along occupational and class lines. While it is accepted that these arguments may be justified in certain societies their validity for culturally/ethnically plural societies has been challenged because racial tensions can be exacerbated if one ethnic group apparently gains economic or political advantages as a result of education, or conversely if one ethnic group feels its values, culture and economic potential are challenged or considerably diminished as a result of educational policies. Moreover because educational and economic developments tend to take place faster in the urban areas than the rural areas

"where the rural-urban dichotomy happens to coincide with a racial or ethnic split, economic imbalances are apt to be seen as racial inequalities. In this way the usual social tensions may be charged with racial antagonisms to the point where they become politically explosive."[14]

Further difficulties arise in culturally plural societies because minority groups (ie. those without political power) may perceive the education system as transmitting majority values, whether religious, cultural or linguistic, which they fear or reject as being subversive of their own culture, religion and language. Many groups (eg. the Chinese) fear a loss of group identity if a school system does not recognise this language or culture as either equal to that of the majority or worthy of recognition in its own right. In some societies the majority may be prepared to allow a degree of cultural and educational autonomy for minority groups because it is politically expedient so to do. In other countries however, as for example in France in Europe, in Indonesia and Thailand in South East Asia, the majority finds it most expedient to impose a common education system, using a common language of instruction and centrally prescribed text-books and curricula.

The educational policies pursued depend, therefore, on a whole range of interrelated factors, economic, administrative, cultural, social and religious. Ultimately, however, they depend upon the way the **majority** ethnic group perceives its economic, political or cultural position in society vis a vis the minority. How minority groups react depends very much upon how threatened **they** feel within the social framework. If they become concerned about preserving their cultural and ethnic identity the three areas that are usually regarded as of vital importance are those of religion, language and a curriculum that recognises their historical and cultural traditions. Likewise the weapons most used by governments in culturally plural societies to achieve a sense of national identity and conformity to 'the good of the whole' are language, a common curriculum and economic policies. As will be seen, it is the interplay of these different factors that has created so many problems in South East Asia.

Finally, what policy options are open to governments in culturally plural societies?[15] These can range from extermination (eg. of intellecutals and minority groups in Kampuchea), expulsion (eg. of overseas Chinese from Vietnam and Bangladeshis from Burma), through separate development for different groups, (as in South Africa) the assimilation of minority groups into the values and social norms of the majority or host group, to the integration of different groups with the host society, with recognition being granted for the cultural, linguistic and religious rights of all groups or to synthesis, whereby all the different cultures present in society are welded together into a new hybrid mix containing elements of all. More recently there has been discussion of cultural pluralism whereby each group maintains its own identity and has legal, educational and constitutional rights. Within the parameters cultural pluralism there can be separation, in the Furnivall sense, or multiculturalism whereby each group adjusts and accomodates to each other. As will be seen Thailand, and to a lesser extent Indonesia, have pursued policies of assimilation; Malaysia is pursuing a policy of integration leading ultimately to synthesis, although officially it is argued that it is pursuing a policy of cultural pluralism; while Singapore is pursuing a policy of multiculturalism within a framework of cultural pluralism. Let us now turn to see how far the label of 'culturally plural societies' can be applied to South East Asia.

The South East Asian Context

What is South East Asia and how best can it be described? Is it a cohesive unit, geographically or politically, or is it more simply a "seemingly unrelated miscellany of states" lying between India to the West and China to the North and looking "like nothing so much as a man leaning out of the ballooning continent of Asia to fling a large armful of litter into the sea"?[16]

One thing is certain, South East Asia defies easy definition and it is not a unity. Although the Chinese and the Japanese referred to the region for centuries as 'Nanyang' or 'Nampo' respectively - 'lands of the southern seas', a not unreasonable definition given the fact that it is united and linked by water (see Map) - it was not until the creation of South East Asia Command during the Second World War that it came to be anything more than a geographical expression. In the immediate post war period the South East Asia Treaty Organisation (SEATO), was established as a defensive grouping with its headquarters in Bangkok. Its successor, ASEAN (Association of South East Asian Nations) is as much concerned with regional socio-economic coperation as it is with mutual defense agreements. In educational terms there is regional cooperation through SEAMEO. It is significant that although these groupings are not specifically concerned with cultural pluralism they are concerned with creating a sense of unity, national and regional, within a region of diversity.

If one looks at a map, South East Asia can be viewed from a variety of perspectives. It can be divided along ethnic lines - the Malay world of Malaysia, Indonesia and the Philippines; the Thai world of Thailand, Laos and the Shan states of northern Burma; and the Chinese world of Singapore, Burma with its links with Tibet, Cambodia and Vietnam with their direct links with southern China. It can be divided along political lines, either according to the former colonial rulers, British (Burma, Malaya, Singapore, North Borneo, Sarawak, Brunei), French (Laos, Kampuchea, Vietnam), Dutch (Indonesia) and Spanish and American (the Philippines) with Thailand as the one exception, or it can be divided according to the present politico-economic distribution ranging from the members of ASEAN (Indonesia, Peninsular Malaysia, and East Malaysia, Philippines, Singapore and Thailand) through the socialist society of Burma ('Socialism the Burmese way') to the communist societies of Laos, Kampuchea and Vietnam. It could equally be divided on religious grounds - the Buddhist mainland, the Islamic Malay world, Christian Luzon and the animist hill tribe areas. It could also equally be divided along cultural lines with Vietnam being the most strongly influenced by China in forms of dress, rice cultivation, social organisation and urban living; the rest of the mainland South East Asia and the Indonesian archipalegio being most strongly influenced by India in terms of kinship, cultivation, social customs, religion and dress; and the Philippines being most strongly influenced by Catholic Spain and later by democratic America.

If one examines some of the World Bank data on the region (Table 1) it can be seen that not only is there a clear divide between the ASEAN countries, which all fit into the Middle Income Country brackets, and the other countries of mainland South East Asia, Kampuchea, Laos, Burma and Vietnam, which are amongst the dozen poorest countries in the world, but between the ASEAN countries themselves there are enormous differences. Thus at one extreme is the small island republic of Singapore covering approximately 1,000 square miles and with a population of 2.4 millions while at the other is the giant island republic of Indonesia, made up of over 3000 islands, covering almost two million square miles, and with a population of 146.6 millions. In between are more 'average sized' countries: Malaysia with a population of 13.2 millions, Thailand and the Philippines with populations in the

TABLE 1

BASIC INDICATORS OF SOUTH EAST ASIAN NATIONS (1982)

1.1	Country	World Bank Ranking	Population (Millions) 1980	Area (1000sq. km)	GNP 1980($m)
MICs	(ASEAN)				
	Indonesia	(38)	146.6	1,919	61,770
	Thailand	(51)	47.0	514	31,140
	Philippines	(52)	49.0	300	34,350
	Malaysia	(76)	13.9	330	22,410
	Singapore	(95)	2.4	1	10,700
LICs.	Kampuchea	(1)	6.9	181	-
	Laos	(2)	3.4	237	-
	Burma	(9)	34.8	677	-
	Vietnam	(11)	54.2	330	-

1.2	Country	GNP per Capita	GNP Growth (1960-1980)	Infla-tion (%) 1970-1980	Pop'n Growth (%) 1970-1979	Life Expt.
MICs	(ASEAN)					
	Indonesia	430	4.0	20.5	2.3	53
	Thailand	670	4.7	9.9	2.5	63
	Philippines	690	2.8	13.2	2.7	64
	Malaysia	1,670	4.3	7.5	2.3	64
	Singapore	4,480	7.5	5.1	1.4	72
LICs	Kampuchea	80	-	-	-	-
	Laos	80	-	-	-	-
	Burma	170	1.2	11.2	-	63
	Vietnam	-	-	-	-	-

Source: World Bank (1981) World Bank Atlas
         World Bank (1982) World Development Report

high 40 millions. Population growth, however, implies serious problems for all the countries of the region (Table 2) and could undermine the pursuit for national unity if too many strains are placed on the economy.[17] Currently about 45 per cent of the populations of the ASEAN countries are of school age (ie. under 15). 60 per cent are below the age of 19. At current growth rates this means that by the end of the century 60 per cent could be of school age, with all that that implies.

Already there are considerable variations in GNP and per capita income between the countries (Table 1). What these figures do not reveal, however, are the differences within countries, Singapore excepted, between the urban populations and the rural population. Since this divide is frequently along racial lines tensions can be exacerbated, as has been the case in Malaysia. As Table 3 shows, while there has been a gradual move away from agriculture in all the ASEAN countries the majority of the labour force, again with the exception of Singapore, earns its living from agriculture. If educational provision is largely geared to an urban setting and favours only certain ethnic groups who happen to live in the urban areas it can become dysfunctional not only in educational terms but also as a means of creating national identity.

Undoubtedly the most complex facet of the region, however, is the ethnic, linguistic, religious and cultural variety which affects each individual country as well as the region as a whole. The two chief causes of ethnic diversity within the region

"have been population isolation and migration. By population isolation we mean that such physical barriers as seas or high mountains have prevented easy interaction between peoples so that tribal groups have evolved their own cultures - their own languages, artistic endeavours, modes of governance, objects of respect, occupational styles and the like. By migration patterns we mean the movement of large numbers of one ethnic group into a territory already occupied by other ethnic strains." [18]

The Proto Malay (or Indonesia) came overland from Assam and Burma between 2000-1500 BC, the Paroean (or South Mongoloid) came from Tibet and South China several thousand years later, and the Melanesoids came from the south and east Pacific region and today make up the primitive hill tribes scattered amongst islands or jungle hills. [19] The Indo-Dravidians and the Indo-Europeans are relative newcomers, only having penetrated the region during the past four centuries or so. Obviously there has been considerable racial inter-mixing during periods of migration but these ethnic differences are still apparent, and in some areas, most notably northern Thailand and Burma, Indonesia and the Philippines they are very striking.

TABLE 2

POPULATION GROWTH IN ASEAN (1960 - 2000)

2.1

Country	Population in		Growth Rate (%)		
	1960	1980	1960-70	1970-80	1980-2000
	(ooos)				
Indonesia	94.2	146.6	2.0	2.3	2.0
Thailand	26.2	47.0	3.0	2.5	1.9
Philippines	27.7	49.0	3.0	2.7	2.3
Malaysia	8.1	13.9	2.8	2.4	2.0
Singapore	1.6	2.4	2.4	1.5	1.3

2.2

Country	Projected Population		Static By
	1990	2000	
	(ooos)		
Indonesia	180	216	2110
Thailand	58	68	2070
Philippines	63	77	2075
Malaysia	17	21	2120
Singapore	3	3	2030

Source: World Bank Atlas 1981: Unesco Statistical
                                Yearbook 1977.

        World Bank: World Development Report 1982.

TABLE 3   DISTRIBUTION OF LABOUR FORCE IN ASEAN COUNTRIES (%)

Country		Agriculture		Industry		Services	
		1960	1980	1960	1980	1960	1980
Indonesia	(38	75	58	8	12	17	30
Thailand	(51)	84	76	4	9	12	15
Philippines	(52)	61	46	15	17	24	37
Malaysia	(76)	63	50	12	16	25	34
Singapore	(95)	8	2	23	39	69	59

Source: World Bank: World Development Report, 1982.

Thus if we use the criterion of <u>ethnicity</u> (Table 4) it can be seen that there are at least five major ethnic groups within the region and in individual countries in the region.

Table 4

Ethnic Divisions in South East Asia

<u>Proto-Malay</u>		<u>Paroean</u>	<u>Melanesoid</u>	
Malays	Burmese	<u>Thais</u>	<u>Hill tribes</u>	
Indonesians	Bajans	Laos	e.gKaren	Murut
Javanese	Kadazans	Khmers	Liso	Huiong
Sumatrans	Dayaks	Vietnamese	Yao	Meithai
Moluccans	Melanese	Chinese	Lahu	Semai
Bataks	Mireks	Mons	Miao	etc

<u>Indo-Dravidian</u>	<u>Indo-European</u>	
Tamils	British	Americans
Singhalese	French	Australians
	Dutch	Eurasians etc.

If we use the criterion of <u>race</u> we find that every country of the region has, to some extent, a diverse racial mixture. (See Table 5).

At one extreme Indonesia has over 300 different indigenous racial groups, each with distinct and strong cultural boundaries. This is not surprising when one considers that the country consists of over 3000 islands, many of them covered by dense jungle undergrowth, much of it inaccesible from different points of any given island. The result is that each group speaks its own distinct language or dialect, frequently mutually incomprehensible, and each has its own customs, culture and social patterns. The Javanese are by far the largest ethno-linguistic group comprising well over 40 per cent (or over 60 million) of the Indonesian population. The Sundanese between 20 and 30 millions are the next largest group. The other diverse and geographically scattered groups can be numbered in their thousands and have been classified as Coastal-Islamic and non-Islamic peoples [20] who dominate Sumatra, the Moluccas, the Celebes and Borneo. Interspersed amongst the urban groups are overseas Chinese settlers and Eurasians of Dutch-Malay descent.

The Philippines are likewise exceedingly diverse. Although consisting of 7,100 islands and coral islets, only a handful of them are occupied. Nevertheless there are at least 43 distinct ethnic groups speaking almost 20 languages and dialects. The two largest groups are those that speak Tagalog and Cebuano, but there are also Chinese speakers and bilingual groups speaking Tagalog and American-English. Because of the long period of commercial and cultural contact with Japan,

Cultural Pluralism in South-East Asia

TABLE 5   RACIAL COMPOSITION OF ASEAN STATES

Thailand

Thai	85.0%
Chinese	10.0%
Malay	2.5%
Indian	0.3%
Khmer	0.7%
Hill tribes	0.3%
Others	0.8%
	100.0%

Singapore

Chinese	76.2%
Malay	15.0%
Indian	7.0%
European/Eureasian	1.8%
	100.0%

Indonesia

Javanese	45.8%
Sundanese	14.1%
Madurese	7.1%
Coastal Islamic Peoples (Bugis, Batavians, Malays, Banjarese, Achenese , Palembangs, Sasaks, Makassars etc)	16.8%
Minangkabaus	3.3%
Mandailings	0.6%
Non-Islamic (Batak, Balinese, Dayak, Toraja, etc)	9.6%
Immigrants (Chinese, Europeans, Eurasians, etc)	2.7%
	100.0%

Philippines

Filipino	
Malay-Filipino	
Chinese	
Euro-Filipino	
Maranat	
Tasaday	

Peninsular Malaysia

Malay	53.0%
Chinese	35.5%
Indian	10.6%
Hill tribes / Europeans	0.9%
	100.0%

East Malaysia

Sabah

Kadazan	28.3%
Chinese	21.4%
Indigenous tribes	35.9%
Malay	2.8%
Others	11.7%
	100.0%

Sarawak

Iban	31.0%
Land Dayak	8.5%
Melanaus	5.5%
Chinese	30.1%
Malay	18.7%
Indigenous tribes	5.1%
	100.0%

China and other Asian nations and with westerners through three and a half centuries of Spanish colonial rule, followed by four decades of American control most Filipinos today are a cultural and ethnic mixture of East and West, but still tracing their origins to Malay ancestors. [21]

At the other extreme is Thailand where approximately 85 per-cent of the population is made up of Thais, but even here there are other racial distinctions. In the cities and smaller urban areas there are Chinese, Chinese-Thai who make up 10 per cent of the population, Indians and Vietnamese, excluding refugees from the recent Indo/China War. In the North of the country there are large numbers of indigenous tribes, each with its own language, customs and culture, and the north east is predominantly Laotian or made up of Thai-Lao. The major problem area, however, lies in the south of the country where 80 per cent of the population of the four southern provinces is Malay in language, custom and religion. Singapore is also clearly dominated by one racial group, the Chinese (76.2%), though both Malays (15%) and Indians (79%) make up sizeable minorities. Peninsular Malaysia has the most delicately balanced racial composition of the region with Malays making up only just over half the population (53%) and non-Malays, Chinese and Indians, making up almost 47%. East Malaysia is even more complex with Malays in both Sabah and Sarawak forming a noticeable minority of the total population structure. How far the 1981 census will reveal changes in the racial composition remains to be seen.

If we use the criterion of economic structure we find that in Indonesia, Thailand and Malaysia, it is the non-indigenous groups who predominate in the modern sector although changes are taking place. Chinese control the major businesses, import and export firms, banking, insurance, transportation, rice milling etc; Indians largely control the cloth market; and both groups dominate the professions - lawyers, doctors, accountants etc. Farming, especially small holder farming, is largely in the hands of Malays and Thais. In Singapore, the most industrialised country in the region and hence the one with the largest modern sector the contrast in employment of different groups is less marked.

If the criterion of religion is used we find that although Indonesia professes to be 88 per cent Muslim, there are over 150 different branches of Islam, many of them superimposed on animist beliefs or on earlier mystical abangan philosophy. In addition, there are Christians (7 per cent), Hindus (2 per cent), and Buddhist-Confucianists (2 per cent). In Malaysia, Islam is the state religion although only half the population is Muslim. The remainder of the population is divided amongst Buddhists (25.5 per cent), Hindus (7.4 per cent), Christians (5.3 per cent) and others (11.7 per cent). 94 per cent of Thailand's population belong to the Theravada branch of Buddhism, while Muslims, Christians, Daoists, Hindus and

TABLE 6   MAJOR LANGUAGES SPOKEN IN THE ASEAN COUNTRIES

Indonesia: Bahasa Indonesia, Malay, Javanese, Batak, (Dutch)
Malaysia: Bahasa Malaysia, Malay, Chinese, Tamil, English
Philippines: Tagalog, Cebuano, Iloko, Panay-Hiligaynon, Bikol, Chinese, English
Singapore: Bahasa Malaysia, Chinese, English, Tamil
Thailand: Thai, Chinese, English, Malay, Thai-Laos.

CHART I

PRESSURES AFFECTING EDUCATION IN CULTURALLY PLURAL SOCIETIES

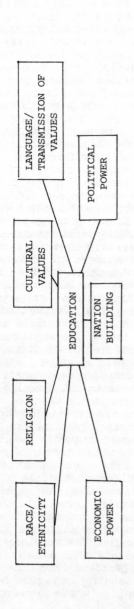

animists make up the remaining 6 per cent. Almost 85 per cent of Filipinos are Roman Catholics and 8.3 per cent are Protestant. At least 4 per cent are Muslims. Singapore has all the major religions of the world represented.

If one thinks of **linguistic** diversity the problems are even more striking since not only is there diversity along racial lines but **within** the major languages used there are also considerable variations. Thus Malaysia, Singapore and the Philippines are what Joshua Fishman calls "multi-modal nations," [22] typical examples of countries with "a variety of unrelated languages each with its own literacy tradition." [23] In the Philippines, whilst almost half the population is almost equally divided amongst Tagalog and Cebuano speakers, over 4 million people speak Ikoke, 3.8 millions speak Panay-Hiligaynon and 2.5 millions speak Bikol. There are at least four other major languages and numerous dialects [24]. In Malaysia and Singapore, although there are four main languages within each country - Malay, Chinese, Tamil and English - such a statement conceals the true picture since these languages cover numerous variations. In Malaysia for example bazaar Malay, rural Malay and Bahasa Malaysia are all widely used [25]. The Indian languages includes Telegu and Bengali as well as Tamil. Amongst the Chinese speakers throughout the region but especially in Thailand [26] and Singapore [27] it is possible to find speakers of Mandarin, Cantonese, Hakka, Hokkien, Teochiu and Hananese. Even in Thailand, which superficially would appear to be mono-lingual, there are at least three dialects within the Thai language, central Thai, Thai Korat and Thai Yuan. Lao is spoken widely in the north-east of the country and Malay, both rural and bazaar is spoken in the southern provinces. Indonesia's position would appear to have been simplified by the use of Bahasa Indonesian as the national language and **lingua franca** but not only are there other languages spoken which are related to Malay, but there are also numerous dialects and tribal languages spoken throughout the Indonesian archapelago. With the exception of Singapore, there are numerous tribes in all the countries of the region each speaking its own language or dialect [28]. Table 6 indicates the major languages spoken in the region as well as the national language.

It can be seen, therefore, that using any one, or combination, of the above criteria of ethnicity, race, religion, language, culture not only are the countries of the region culturally complex but education's role in the societies, especially in the context of nation-building, must take into consideration the interplay of the following forces, indicated by Chart 1.

Table 7 summarises the ethnic, cultural and linguistic composition of the ASEAN societies and the policies pursued with regard to language and ethnic diversity.

TABLE 7 ETHNIC, CULTURAL AND LINGUISTIC COMPOSITION OF ASEAN COUNTRIES

	INDONESIA	PENINSULAR MALAYSIA	SINGAPORE	THAILAND	PHILIPPINES
Population	146.6m	11.25m	2.4m	47m	49m
Government	Republic/ Military	Monarchy/ Democracy	Republic/ Democracy	Monarchy/ Military	Republic/ Democracy
Main Racial Groups	Javanese Sundanese Madurese Batak	Malay Chinese Tamil	Chinese Malay Tamil	Thai Chinese Malay	Filipino Malay-Filipino Chinese
Dominant ethnic group	Javanese (45.8%)	Malay (53.1%)	Chinese (76%)	Thai (85%)	Filipino (48.6%)
Religious beliefs	Islam Christianity Animism	Islam Hinduism Christianity Daoism	Christianity Islam Hinduism Daoism Buddhism	Buddhism Islam Daoism Animism	Christianity Islam Animism
Main cultural influences	Indian Dutch	Indian British	Chinese Indian British Japanese	Chinese Indian American	Spanish American Chinese

Major languages	Javanese Balinese Malay	Malay Chinese Tamil English	Malay Chinese Tamil English	Thai Chinese Malay English	Tagalog Cebuano Ikako Panay-Hiligaynon
National language	Bahasa Indonesia	Bahasa Malaysia	Bahasa Malaysia	Thai	Tagalog
Recognition of separate ethnic schools	No	Yes (but private only after primary level)	Yes	No (except a few private institutions)	Yes
Language policy in Education	Vernacular until Grade 3 thereafter the national language	Vernacular until Grade 6 thereafter the national language	Bilingualism Chinese and English schools*	Thai throughout	Bilingual
Education policies towards different racial groups	Assimilation	Integration	Cultural Pluralism	Assimilation	Integration

* until 1979 there were Tamil medium and Malay medium primary schools. (See Table 8)

Education and Nation Building

<u>National Unity</u>

All governments of the region have been concerned to use their education systems to foster a sense of national unity from their diverse populations. As a former Minister of Education in Singapore observed, "our ability to survive and prosper as individuals depends on our ability to survive as a nation and on our readiness to promote the collective interests of our people as a whole".[29] As a result a major objective of Singapore's education policy is "to inculcate attitudes of social discipline and responsibility, racial harmony and loyalty to the Republic."

Apart from the syllabi and textbooks, which stress the unity of Singapore and the need to pull together harmoniously, and the civics courses, which are designed 'to foster social discipline and national identity, to develop in the students an appreciation of moral and cultural values', a variety of extra-curricular activities are designed to develop a similar outlook. For example, at the morning flag-raising ceremony pupils repeat the pledge

"We the citizens of Singapore, pledge ourselves as one united people, regardless of race, language or religion, to build a democratic society based on justice and equality so as to achieve happiness, prosperity and progress for our nation."

The measure of Singapore's success can be seen from the frequently cited epithet that it is a 'multi-racial success story'. National unity in the Philippines has been forged over the centuries as a result of, first, Spanish, and then American Colonial rule. During the period of American domination especially, and in the years following independence, great stress was placed on a policy of 'bi-nationalism' (joint American-Filipino nationalism) as well as national unity. There has been opposition to the autocratic rule of President Ferdinand Marcos, but only amongst the small Muslim minority of southern Philippines has there been opposition to national unity.

Thailand's education aims are stated in more philosophical language.

"The Thai people shall be educated according to their individual capacities so they shall be moral and cultured citizens with discipline and responsibility, mentally and physically healthy, and with a democratic outlook."

The 'Thai people' referred to, however include ethnic Chinese, Laos, Malays and hill tribe people all of whom pursue the same centrally set examinations and all of whom study through the medium of the central Thai dialect. Since the revolution of 1976 there have been moves towards greater regionalisation of syllabus content and textbooks, but the underlying philosophy of the Buddhist Thai elite and the centrality of the Thai language prevails and each morning Thai pupils also pledge allegiance to their monarch and to their country. [30]

In Malaysia, likewise, "all aspects of the government's policy are geared towards the achievement of national unity. All projects (including education) are meaningless if the people are not united." [31]

The philosophy and aims of education in Malaysia are enshrined in the "Rukunegara" (the fundamental principles of the nation).[32] This aims at bringing about the ideal Malaysian, of whatever racial origin, who believes in God, is loyal to the king and country, upholds the constitution, abides by the rule of law and professes upright behaviour and morality.

Policy statements are one thing, but amongst the most effective longterm practical educational measures to help bring about a sense of national identity are the curriculum and syllabuses of individual subjects taught, reinforced through state control of the examination system. This approach applies throughout the region, though nowhere has it been a more consistent part of educational policy than in Malaysia since the Razak Committee of 1956 recommended bringing together the different language media schools into a common national system of education, and stated that:

"We cannot overemphasize our conviction that the introduction of a syllabus common to all schools in the Federation is the crucial requirement of educational policy in Malaya. It is an essential element in the development of a united Malayan nation. It is the key which will unlock the gates hitherto standing locked and barred against the establishment of an educational system acceptable to the people of Malaya as a whole." [33]

The idea of an education system acceptable to the people as a whole is an integral part of official policy which has been

"to establish a national system of education acceptable to the people as a whole, which will satisfy their needs and promote their cultural, social, economic and political development as a nation, with the intention of making the Malay language the national language of the country whilst preserving and sustaining the growth of the language and culture of people other than Malays living in the country."[34]

As one writer has said this policy is "ultimately aimed at destroying the distinct cultural elements of the immigrant communities and at replacing them by something which is distinctly Malaysian"[35] and as we shall see below, when we examine language and economic policies, it has not been without serious misgivings and resentments on the part of all the racial groups in the country.

It is language policies however, that have been used most positively to bring about a sense of national identity. The importance of language cannot be overstressed, especially in multi-racial societies, because it can become a barrier to integration if different ethnic or racial groups insist on maintaining their own languages as a means of transmitting cultural and social values, and if as a result, they resist the concept of a national language. As Francis Wong pointed out a few years ago,

"Language is an essential means of communication and when the language in question is also the mother tongue, it is one of the most important formative influences in moulding the intellect as well as the character of the child. Indeed it is a powerful instrument by which not only individuals may express their personality, but groups may also identify their collective consciousness."[36]

Indeed no immigrant group in the developing countries which has kept or tried to keep its own language exclusively has been assimilated into the host society.[37] This is certainly true of the overseas Chinese in South East Asia who have used their language as a means of defending their cultural identity and as a result have frequently remained foreigners in their country of adoption.[38]

It is precisely because of the dangers inherent in the linguistically plural societies of South East Asia that governments have sought to develop a national language as a means of fostering a national identity and of unifying heterogenous populations. A national language has become synonymous with the development of nationhood and nowhere is this more true than in Malaysia where the first Prime Minister, Tungku Abdul Rahman said,

"It is only right that as a developing nation we should want to have a language of our own...... If the national language is not introduced our country will be devoid of a unified character and personality - as I could put it, a nation without a soul and without life."[39]

However, this view applies equally in other parts of South East Asia.

Amongst developing countries generally, let alone in South East Asia, Indonesia is perhaps the most successful plural society to use a national language to weld together such diverse peoples. The reasons given for its success have been a unique combination of historical forces, the use of the national language in mass communications as well as in education, and the charisma of Sukarno in the early days of independence.[40]

The movement to develop a national language began in the 1920s. In an All Indonesia Youth Congress held in Djakarta in October 1928, Bahasa Indonesia was proclaimed the national language as part of a proclamation calling for "one country, one nation, one language." The Japanese occupation gave added impetus to the national language movement and the Declaration of Independence of 17 August, 1945, reaffirmed this. The Constitution simply states, "The Language of the State shall be the Indonesian language", while the valuable role of other languages (eg. Javanese, Batak) in the cultural diversity of Indonesia is recognised to such an extent that for the first three years of schooling the local vernacular is accepted as the medium of instruction wherever it is most widely spoken. The language is either Indonesian or Bahasa Indonesia. Thereafter all education is conducted through Bahasa Indonesian so as to give the whole education system a national character. It is significant also, that of all the ASEAN countries Indonesia allows no opportunities for its Chinese inhabitants to learn through the medium of any of the Chinese languages or dialects. [41]

Thailand has no stated official language policy, although it has pursued a consistent and successful one of using Thai as the national language and as the medium of instruction in all schools since state education began in the early 1920s. [42] The situation in Thailand is complicated by the fact that in the four southern provinces which border Malaysia there are making up 80 per cent of the population of the region; in the urban areas there are over 14 million ethnic Chinese, and 90,000 Indians and Pakistanis; while in the north and north east are hill tribes and Lao speaking peoples.

The Chinese had migrated from the southern provinces of China in considerable numbers during the eighteenth and nineteenth centuries. They were encouraged to settle and intermarry with Thais because of the valuable skills that they brought. Many, however, were simply birds of passage. Those who did settle were easily assimilated into Thai society, but at the turn of this century, Chinese immigrants came in ever increasing numbers and for the first time they brought wives with them. More importantly they began to develop their own schools, at a time when the monarchy was trying to create a state system of education, and as such revealed themselves as a distinctly alien group.

The real reason for the antagonism felt by the Thai leadership, however, was the economic stranglehold of the Chinese and the fear that this would increase. The Chinese general strike of 1910 had paralysed Bangkok and King Vajiravudh (1910-25) never forgave them, calling the Chinese, "the Jews of the East".

Beginning with the Private Schools Act of 1919 there began a series of measures aimed at suppressing the growth of Chinese schools. Official registration; the appointment of Thai principals; the insistence that all alien teachers had to pass a Thai language examination; central control of the curriculum and all textbooks used; the reduction in the number of hours that Chinese could be used as a medium of instruction first to 10 then to 6 and then to 3 hours a week; and finally forced closure of Chinese schools, often on the flimiest pretext, were all measures taken by successive Thai governments during the 1940s and 1950s to ensure that Chinese schools could not become subversive entities within the nation.[43] Economic restrictions were also imposed and certain jobs and professions were banned to aliens, most notably the Chinese. Gradually, therefore, the Chinese were forced to accept the supremacy of the Thai language. Since the 1950s Chinese schools have continued to close or be closed and by 1973 only 25 could be found operating outside Bangkok.[44] All of these were primary schools. At secondary level Chinese was not permitted in the regular curriculum though in at least one school in south East Thailand, Teochiu was introduced as a language elective in the session 1975/6 because of its usefulness as a business language [45] and more recently other Chinese dialects have been encouraged as options within state schools. In addition the government tolerates a few private language schools.

The 1940s and 1950s were marked by resistance of the part of the Chinese but this became   far less noticeable during the 1960s and 1970s. Perhaps the most compelling reason for this has been the importance of Thai in the state examinations and the need to pass these to gain entry to the universities as well as for advancement in public sector employment. Moreover it has been shown that the majority of Chinese students not only tend to favour either government of missionary schools but they have no real desire to expand separate Chinese schools again. [46] On the other hand they eagerly preserve their own cultural identity through informal meetings and teaching groups using their own ethnic teachers.

The Thai-Laos of the north east and the hill tribe peoples have posed a different problem since it has been amongst these groups that communist guerillas have been most active. Too frequently in the past these ethnic groups were ignored by the central government. They were regarded as socially inferior to the Thais of the central plain and of little value economically. However, as fears of political subversion have increased, the central government has been at great pains to initiate rural development programmes to develop static villages and to extend state education to the tribal areas using Thai as the medium of instruction in the schools at the same time as using centrally prescribed materials. How far these groups feel they identify with Thailand, however, is hard to tell, since traditionally they have migrated across the borders of Burma and Laos.

The real problem confronting the government, lies with the Malays in the south of the country since here ethnic differences are compounded by religion, culture and politics as well as by language. The Malays of this region are Muslims, speak Malay in preference to Thai and on several occasions have sought to secede from Thailand. The Thai authorities have sought to use the schools as the main instruments by which they win over the allegiance of the Thai Malays. The standard Thai curriculum using Thai as the medium of instruction has been imposed on schools in the area. Although there are those who think that within a generation or two the government will achieve its goal - "the creation in the south of full citizens of the Kingdom of Thailand, no longer Malay residents in Thailand but Muslim Thais,"[47] there are others who are less optimistic,[48] especially since to reach a position of responsibility they must accept the social, political and even cultural norms of the Thais, which might involve embracing the outward symbols of Buddhism. Apart from the continuing uncertainties of the southern Malays, now further compounded by communist guerilla activities in the region, there is little doubt that the Thais' use of Thai as the unifying language of instruction has led to the widespread assimilation of different groups within the country. Whether they will have the same success with the refugees from Laos and Kampuchea remains to be seen.

Singapore's policy of creating a harmonious multi-cultural society by encouraging bilingualism, even bi - or multi-culturalism, in schools has been interesting. Singapore inherited from the British colonial authorities a pattern of primary schooling in four language media - English, Tamil, Malay and Chinese - and secondary schooling in two, English and Chinese. Consistent with its policy of equality for all racial groups it has pursued a policy of bilingualism - even trilingualism - within its schools. Although 76 per cent of the population is Chinese (See Table 5), the government decided to adopt Bahasa Malaysia as the national language, as much for political reasons as for purposes of national unity, with English, the language of science and technology, being the major second language. In the early 1970s Malay was the most comprehensible language to most people (57.1 per cent in 1972), largely because there were so many different Chinese language groups, but English, which was only understood by 22.6 per cent in 1957 and by 46.6 per cent in 1972, has rapidly caught up and is now understood by well over half the population.[49] This is largely as a result of Singapore's educational policy. In order to provide equality of opportunity for all groups each of the 4 language streams was treated equally. However, because of Singapore's strategic location making it as dependent on its industrial capacity as on its entrepot trade, great stress has been placed on English as the language of technology and engineering. There is little doubt therefore, that, as a result, for educational and professional purposes, parents of Singapore pupils have opted for English medium schooling. This can most dramatically be seen from the table of enrolments for Singapore's primary schools during the past twenty years. (Table 8)

Tamil medium and Malay medium education is no longer available because of decline in demand. It must be stressed that parents have opted for English medium education on economic grounds. There have been no political pressures to bring this about. Indeed the government is at pains to encourage the learning of Mandarin Chinese amongst its majority Chinese citizens [50] to counter-balance the educational stress on English, but the merging of the Chinese medium Nanyang University with the existing English medium University of Singapore has ended much of the demand for Chinese education at secondary and tertiary levels and it is quite possible that by the end of the 1980s Singapore will have an almost entirely English medium education system with other languages being taught as major second languages. The political decision to allow equality of language media and to let market forces prevail has obviously paid off because no one language group, for example the Chinese, has been able to dominate, and the Indians and Tamils have been able to share equally in the building of the new Singaporean nation. In the context of Singapore, English, the essential language of commerce and technology, has proved sufficiently neutral not to threaten any one racial group.

Unfortunately this has not been true of Malaysia, where to the Malays "English came to be regarded not only as the language of colonial domination but also, after independence, as an obstacle to the educational, social and economic advance of the majority of Malays."[51] As a result the determination of Malay nationalists to replace the dominant position of English by Malay has been fraught with racial and political overtones that have threatened the very fabric of society, to such an extent that one observer has described language "as the Scylla and Charbidis of Malaysian multi-communal politics."[52] It is in Malaysia, especially peninsular Malaysia, that the greatest educational changes have taken place.[53]

Malaysia is undoubtedly the most complex and difficult country of the region to examine, for although in Peninsular Malaysia, Malays now form the majority of the population (53.1 per cent, see Table 5), this was not always so. In fact at the time of the Second World War Chinese outnumbered Malays by 43%:41%. Although there were Chinese settlers in the country before the British arrived on the scene, the British colonial authorities encouraged Chinese settlers into the Federated Malay State to develop commerce and industry, particularly the tin industry. At the same time they brought indentured Indian labourers from Madras and Southern India to work in the rubber plantations. The Malays, whose homeland it was, were left largely undisturbed, and there were numerous treaty rights preserving their "special status". As a result by the time of the Second World War, economic control of the country was largely in the hands of Europeans, Chinese and Tamils who

TABLE 8

TREND TOWARDS ENGLISH MEDIUM PRIMARY EDUCATION IN SINGAPORE
(1960 - 1980)

% enrolled in different language streams

Year	English	Chinese	Malay	Tamil
1960	57.9	39.3	8.6	0.2
1965	62.3	28.6	8.9	0.2
1970	69.3	29.0	1.6	0.1
1975	79.3	20.5	0.3	-
1979	88.8	11.2	-	-
1980	92.3	7.7	-	-

Source: Ministry of Education, Singapore.

TABLE 9

URBANIZATION BY ETHNIC GROUP IN PENINSULAR MALAYSIA
(Percentages)

Ethnic Group	1947		1957		1970	
	Urban	Rural	Urban	Rural	Urban	Rural
Malays	7.3	92.7	11.2	88.8	14.9	85.1
Chinese	31.1	68.9	44.7	55.3	47.4	52.6
Indians	25.8	74.2	30.6	69.4	34.7	65.3

formed the bulk of the population in urban areas. (see Table 9).

Part of the agreements reached between the British authorities and the Malay rulers was that Malay custom (adat) and religion (Islam) would not be interfered with. This was to have far-reaching educational and economic implications since the Christian missionaries, who were largely responsible for establishing modern, secular education in the country, were debarred from proselytising amongst the Malays and thus from establishing schools amongst them. Since the English medium schools that they established were principally in the urban areas where less than 20% of Malays lived, they were largely attended by Chinese and Indians, and by those urban Malays who sought an English medium education. While the motives of the British were intended to preserve the Malays from European 'contamination' "the effect was to keep the vast majority of Malays in a social and economically depressed position.[54] In fact the seeds of separatism[55] were sown as a result of colonial educational policies which allowed four parallel school systems to develop.

How these came about has been examined elsewhere[56]. The educational legacy left to the independent government of Malaya provides a classic example of social and cultural pluralism being reinforced through education. The British authorities had allowed mission societies to develop English medium schools, predominantly in the towns, and gradually became involved in their support through grants-in-aid. The needs of the civil service and commercial organisations for English speaking employees meant that these institutions had both high economic and social value. The only compulsory education was for four or six years of vernacular education at elementary level for Malays. This was government supported and underlined the special status accorded to the Malays. The authorities felt no particular responsibility towards educating the immigrant Chinese until the 1920s[57] and the immigrant Indians until the 1930s when grants-in-aid were made available. The only secondary education available was in aided English medium schools and private Chinese medium schools. Thus at the time of the Second World War, while primary education was available in four language media and secondary education in two, English and Chinese, for the bulk of the rural Malays and Indians on the rubber estates their primary schooling led to a dead end.

The result of this arrangement was that three forms of pluralism were created, social pluralism, cultural pluralism and economic pluralism. Social pluralism came about because English medium education, leading to the most prestigious social positions, was available for the Malay aristocracy and urban dwellers only; Malay education was available for the subject, and largely rural, classes. There was an assumption that the Malays were inferior academically or simply lacked interest, but it would appear that the real problem facing rural Malays was access to secondary school and not motivation[58] since once into the secondary school system Malays fared as well as, if not better than, Chinese or Indians. Cultural pluralism came about because the four language media schools reinforced the ethnic identity and cultural separation of the different groups. Only the English medium schools were 'neutral', but they helped create the third kind of pluralism - economic, because they conferred socio-economic advantage on those who attended them. Thus the language media of education became intricately bound up with cultural separation and economic advantage, and the even sharper division between the rural and urban educated which was largely on racial grounds.

Policies since the War have been concerned with how to bring the races more closely together in a national system of education, how to raise the status of Malays and how to bring about a sense of national identity, especially with the diverse peoples of Sabah and Sarawak joining the Malaysian Federation in 1963. The evolution of these policies makes a fascinating study,though there is not scope in this chapter to deal with the complications of the East Malaysian territories.

In the immediate postwar years the British authorities were particularly concerned with the need to reconcile the different racial groups, especially since the communist Emergency of 1948-60 revealed how few Chinese settlers identified themselves with the country of their adoption. Two educational reports of this period revealed how difficult such reconciliation was going to be. In 1951 the Barnes Report proposed the introduction of bilingual schools and the gradual abolition of all non-Malay schools. Opposition from the Chinese, who feared that their language and culture were under attack, came in the form of the Fenn-Wu Report, which while recognising the need for a national language, was bitterly opposed to the abolition of Chinese medium schools. Nevertheless the seeds of policy for future governments had been sown, for in 1956, the Razak Report, perhaps the most famous of Malaya's education reports, proposed the gradual abolition of English medium primary schools and their replacement by Malay medium schools (to be called National schools); the creation or official recognition of National-type Chinese or Tamil medium primary schools provided fifteen or more parents demanded such schools; the abolition of Chinese medium secondary schols and the introduction of Malay as well as English medium secondary schools. English and Malay were to be compulsory languages throughout the system and there was to be a common syllabus. These proposals, together with others initiated as a result of the Rahman Talib Report of 1960, were incorporated in the Education Act of 1961 and have served as the basis of educational policy ever since.

Following independence in 1957 the first step towards creating a national education system was the creation of a common syllabus to be adopted in all schools, regardless of their language media, designed to create a common outlook, common loyalty to the country and a common basis for the examination system. The second step was to develop a national language policy. This became enshrined in the Constitution of 1957 (article 152) and the National Language Act (1957)[59] which stated that Malay was to replace English as the national language - Bahasa Kebangsaan. The process was to be gradual until 1967. The official statement was that

> "for a period of ten years after Merdeka (Independence) Day and thereafter until Parliament otherwise provides, the English language may be used in both Houses of Parliament, in the Legislative Assembly of every State and for all other official purposes."[60]

The immigrant groups, the Chinese and Indians, were prepared to accept the development of Malay as a national language precisely because it was to be a gradual change and because English medium education, the passport to university and to the best jobs, was to remain. Even though in 1961/2 Chinese medium secondary schools were forced to go independent or to become English or Malay medium assisted schools the change was accepted, though not without some protest, because the Chinese perceived an alternative route via English medium schooling.[61] As a result there was a sudden dramatic increase in enrolments in English medium secondary schools, much to the concern of the Malay nationalists. Table 10 highlights this dramatic change.

Malays benefitted from the introduction of the first Malay secondary schools in 1957 and from the extension of compulsory schooling into a 3-year comprehensive lower secondary school in 1963. The creation of the **Dewan Bahasa dan Pustaka** (Language and Literature Agency) in 1959 to translate thousands of scientific and technical words into Malay and to develop Malaysian textbooks for use in schools also furthered the development of the national language as did slogans, posters, shop and road signs. Since 1967 when Malay became both the national and official language every opportunity has been taken to extend its use and to convert all secondary schools into Malay medium. As Chai Hon-Chan has said,

> "The underlying rationale of Malaysia's educational policy is that education with a common content syllabus, reinforced by a common language, would promote the growth of a **nationally homogeneous** outlook and the development of a core of **shared values** leading eventually to the evolution of a common culture which would then provide the basis for social cohesion and national unity."[62]

Unfortunately social cohesion and national unity were shattered in 1969 by two events that were to change the whole political and educational complexion of the country and to

TABLE 10   ENROLLMENTS IN ASSISTED SECONDARY SCHOOLS IN WEST MALAYSIA
(According to medium of instruction).

Year	English		Chinese		Malay	
1947	12510	82.3%	2692	17.7%		
1957	48235	59.8%	30052	37.3%	2315	2.9%
1960	72499	62.3%	38828	33.4%	4953	4.3%
1962	119219	90.0%			13224	10.0%
1965	208363	75.5%			67484	24.5%
1969	333927	71.2%			134889	28.8%
1971	349121	69.7%			151413	30.3%
1973	375090	63.5%			215686	36.5%
1975	425543	58.9%			296936	41.1%

(Source: Ministry of Education Statistics)

change the relationships between the Malays and Chinese even more markedly. The 1969 general election led to serious reverses for the ruling Alliance Party, largely composed of the Malay UMNO (United Malay National Organisation), and to fears amongst the Malays that political as well as economic power was in danger of being taken over by non-Malays. Several days later on 13 May, 1969 serious racial disturbances broke out between Chinese and Malays[63]. For some time Malay extremists had felt frustrated at the slowness of the moves towards Malayanisation in the education system, which they regarded as still favouring non-Malays, since the number of Malays in upper secondary school and at tertiary level was low, compared with other groups. In 1970 Malays for example, only accounted for 39.7% of degree enrolments. Now extremist views became listened to and from 1970 onwards there has been a major shift in emphasis in both educational and linguistic policy designed to discriminate positively in favour of Malays.

In 1969 Bahasa Malaysia was officially declared the national language and the language of government. In 1970 the Rukunegara or National Ideology, a set of principles to guide Malaysians in their relationships with each other, was proclaimed. In 1971 the Constitutional Amendment Act was passed. This forbade discussion of such sensitive issues as citizenship, the national language, the special position of the Malays and the sovereignty of the rulers. The Second Malaysia Plan (1971-1975) also clearly indicated that the Malays were going to press for their rights in language, education and economic development. From 1971 Bahasa Malaysia was to replace English as the medium of instruction in all English medium primary schools beginning in Grade 1. By 1978 all national secondary schools, by 1982 all upper secondary schools and by 1983 all university education was to be conducted through the medium of Bahasa Malaysia. Examinations were likewise to be changed to Bahasa Malaysia and a credit pass was to be a prerequisite for entry into teacher training institutions, higher education and government service. Even more disturbing for the non-Malays was that there were to be two levels set for the Bahasa Malaysia papers, one for native speakers and one for non-Malays. The heavy failure rate of almost 50% in the English medium sector, followed by a public outcry,led the government to introduce a common paper[64] though there are still widespread criticisms that Malay students are granted "concession marks". Understandably, the non-Malay groups, especially the Chinese, were initially most affected by these moves since they had always done so well in the English medium schools and since they dominated most of the university faculties. It was precisely this fact that angered the Malay extremists who argued that Malays were economically disadvantaged precisely because they were educationally under-represented at the tertiary level. They argued that there should be positive discrimination in favour of the Malays to redress both the economic and the educational imbalance. For most of the 1970s and early 1980s therefore, government policy has been directed at redressing the inferior position of the Malays, though the Fourth Malaysian Plan (1982-86) does acknowledge that poverty is not confined to the Malays. The twin pillars of this policy have been economic redress and positive educational discrimination, especially at higher education level.

Much help has been given to the Malays through rural development programmes, though the creation of a National Trading Corporation (PERNAS) designed to encourage Malay entrepreneurship, through urban development schemes, through special banking facilities and through special science and technology courses,[65] even though it has become increasingly apparent that there are socio-economic divisions within all the ethnic groups.[66] The New Economic Policy (NEP) aimed at reducing and eventually eradicating poverty among all races and at restructuring society so as to reduce and eventually eliminate the identification of race with economic function. The government's aim is to increase Malay participation in manufacturing industry during the twenty year period 1970 to 1990 from 16% to 40% and in commerce and construction from 28% to 50%. It is also planned for Malays to own at least a 30% share in commerce and industry by the 1990s. As the mid-term review of the Second Malaysia Plan stated in 1973, "The reconstruction of the racial employment problem envisaged in the Perspective Plan is indeed sizeable." That there has been resentment, suspicion and apprehension amongst the non-Malay communities has not led the government to waver in its policy.

The most striking discrimination in favour of Malays, however, has taken place at tertiary level. Until 1969 the University of Malay was the only tertiary level institution offering degree courses. It was dominated by the Chinese, and to a lesser extent, Indians, especially in the science faculties and in core courses leading to high professional status. Since the early 1970s, therefore, the government has sought to redress this trend by creating new universities and tertiary level institutions for Malays only, while at the same time refusing the Chinese to open their own Chinese medium university; by awarding a large number of public scholarships to Malays: and by increasing the numbers of Malays enrolled at tertiary level.

A report issued in 1971,[67] argued that overall enrolments at university, as well as on a faculty by faculty basis should, as far as possible, reflect the racial composition of the country as a whole; that in faculties under-represented by Malays every effort should be made to attract Malays; that criteria "other than academic criteria" should be used to admit rural Malays; and that public scholarships should be used to alter the racial imbalance in the science faculties.

The acceptance of the Majid Report and the implementaion of many of its recommendations has had a dramatic effect on the racial balance of university enrolments. Almost 90% of Malays at university are on public scholarships, compared with 22% of Chinese and 20% of Indians, and whereas in 1970 Malays accounted for only 49.7% of tertiary enrolments, by 1975 they accounted for 65.1% and by 1980 for 73.2%. As one observer has put it:

> "The redefinition of the national school system to give prominence to the Malay medium of instruction and the recent efforts at engineering student enrolments represents the most comphrensive and direct attempts by the Malay governing elites to raise the social and economic status of Malays through education."[68]

Inevitably non-Malays resent what they see as the progressive whittling away of what they believe are their educational rights. Provided that employment opportunities have not been too difficult, tensions have not risen too much, but with employment in the public service based on a 4:1 quota in favour of Malays and with pressures for Malays to enter the private sector in increasing numbers under the NEP, there is bound to be increased competition for scarce jobs, with Malays being the most favoured group, and tensions and frustrations could again spill out along racial lines.

Although discrimination in favour of Malays in education and employment continues, recognition that poverty is not confined to any one racial group and that Malaysia will only survive if all the races can live harmoniously together has led the government, at least publicly, to say that its policies are aimed at "the well being of all races, from all walks of life and in all religions of the country." Certainly a note of caution has crept into the discussions about ethnic policies and there are some observers[69] who already see a glimmer of hope that a new Malaysian value system is beginning to develop as future ruling elites become increasingly Malay-educated and Malay-speaking. In urban areas there is evidence to show that this is happening. Whether or not harmonious relations will become the norm, however, will depend on whether the gulf between privately educated Chinese and publicly educated Malays grows: whether the socio-economic gap between the bumipu-tras (rural Malays or "sons of the soil") and those Malaysians living in urban areas can be bridged: and how far Malays will be prepared to recognise Malay-educated, Malay-speaking non-Malays (ethnically) as partners in citizenship. Two further complications in the equation must also be taken into account. Will increased enrolments in private Chinese-medium schools lead to further divisions in the Chinese ranks - between the Chinese-educated and the Malay-educated? And will the resurgence of Islamic fundamentalism in this Islamic country, where almost half the population are <u>not</u> Muslims, exacerbate religious differences? Time alone will show.

Conclusions

It can be seen from this survey of the ASEAN countries that the use of education to create a sense of national identity is far from easy, that it can produce unexpected results, as in the case of Singapore, and that it can heighten racial tensions in <u>certain</u> contexts, as for example in Malaysia or in Southern Thailand. It can also be seen that educational policies differ considerably according to the position perceived by the real dominant elite. Thus the Thais, who felt economically threatened by the Chinese, took action, both educational and economic, to curb the Chinese power. The Malays, feeling both economically and politically threatened by the Chinese, and to a lesser extent, the Indians, are pursuing policies of positive discrimination in favour of their own kind. The Chinese in Singapore, feeling threatened neither economically nor politically, nor ethnically, have been able to pursue a generous policy towards all races.

It can also be seen that the use of a national language to create a sense of national identity can have quite different outcomes. Thus, while in Indonesia, the Philippines and Thailand, with the exceptions of the Muslim minorities in the last two countries, national language policies have been largely successful, in Singapore the national language has been bypassed for educational purposes. Instead parents, and pupils, have opted to use an international language, English, the language of science and commerce, as their educational <u>lingua franca</u>. In Malaysia, on the other hand, there has been undoubted resistance to the extension of Bahasa Malaysia because in the minds of many non-Malays it has been too readily associated with policies of positive discrimination favouring one ethnic group at the expense of others. Nevertheless, in the ASEAN region as a whole, governments are conscious of the need to maintain a delicate balance between the different ethnic groups within their borders, if for no other reason than national security, and during the 1980s national identity/unity will continue to be as important an aspect of policy as socio-economic development.

NOTES AND REFERENCES

1. This paper is based upon one that appeared in the Proceedings of the British Comparative Education Society's Annual Conference, 1978 and a modified version of which appeared under the title 'Education and Cultural Pluralism in South East Asia', in **Comparative Education**, vol. 16, No.2, June 1980, pp139-158.

2. Philippines (1946), Burma (1948), Laos, Kampuchea, Vietnam (1954), Malaya (1957), Singapore (1959), Indonesia (1945 but realistically 1959), Sarawak and North Borneo (1963).

3. **Time**, 18 October, 1982.

4. e.g. Bloodworth D, **An Eye for the Dragon. South East Asia Observed**, 1954-1970, (Farren, Strauss and Giroux 1970); Osborne N: **Region of Revolt; Focus on South East Asia** (Penguin Books 1971).

5. Hick, D. (1982): "Colonisation and Education - Vietnam" in Watson, K, (ed.) **Education in the Third World**, Croom Helm,London,(1982) pp.108-118.

6. Bastin, J. and Benda, H.J., **A History of Modern South East Asia** (Prentice Hall 1968, 2nd ed.); Hall DE: **A History of South East Asia**, (Macmillan, 1964).

7. Osborne **op.cit** p.17.

8. e.g. The theme of the Third World Congress of Comparative Education Societies held in London in June 1977 was on "Unity and Diversity"; the April 1978 issue of **Compare** Vol.8 No.1, was devoted to Linguistic Minorities and National Unity. See alsow Watson, K. "Educational Policies in Multi-Racial Societies", **Comparative Education** February, 1979. The World Yearbook of Education, 1981; the 1983 Conference Proccedings of the Comparative Education Society in Europe, etc.

9. Watson, K. **ibid.**

10. Anweiler: "Comparative Education and the Internationalization of Education", in **Comparative Education**, Vol. 13, No 2, June 1977, p.112.

11. Furnivall J.S., **Colonial Policy and Practice.** (New York Univ. Press 1956), p.313.

12. Chai Hon-Chan: **"Planning education for a plural society"**. (UNESCO, IIEP, Paris 1971), p.18.

13. **ibid,**

14. **ibid**, p.13.

15. See Smolicz, J.J. (1981), "Culture, ethnicity and education: multi-culturalism in a plural society" in McGarry J, et al (eds.): **Education of Minorities**, World Yearbook of Education 1981, London, Kogan Page, pp.17-36. Watson, K. (1982), "Educational Policies in a Multicultural Society", **Spectrum**, 14,2, pp.13-19.

16. Bloodworth, **op. cit**, p. xiii.

17. Watson, K (1983): **Some Contemporary Problems and Issues Resulting from Educational Expansion in South East Asia**, (mimeo) Paper presented at the 1983 Conference of the Association of South East Asian Studies in the United Kingdom. Forthcoming in **Modern Asian Studies.**

18. Postlethwaite, T.N. and Thomas, R.M. **Schooling in the ASEAN Region**, (Pergamon Oxford Press 1980), p.18.

19. Kunstadter, P. (ed.): **Southeast Asian Tribes, Minorities and Nations**, (Princeton Univ. Press, 1967); **Contributions**

to South East Asian Ethnology (1982). Vol.1, National University of Singapore.

20. Reid, A. "Indonesia: Revolution without Socialism" in Jeffrey, R (ed.) Asia: the Winning of Independence, London, Macmillan,(1981) pp.113-162.

21. Shahani, L.R. (1970), The Philippines, The Land and People, Manila, National Bookstore Press.

22. Fishman, J.A.National Languages and Languages of Wider Communication in Developing Nations. (Stanford Univ. Press 1972), pp.191-223.

23. Rustow, D.A. : "Language, Modernization and Nationhood - An Attempt at Typology" in Fishman, J.A. et al (ed.): Language Problems of Developing Nations, (Wiley, New York, 1968), p.102.

24. McCoy, A.W. "The Philippines; Independence without decolonisation", in Jeffrey, op.cit pp.23-70.

25. Platt, J.T. The Chinese Community in Malaysia: language policies and relationships, in McGarry J, et al (ed.), op.cit. pp.164-176.

26. Coughlin, R.J. Double Identity: the Chinese in Modern Thailand (Hong Kong University Press, 1960); Skinner G.W: Chinese Society in Thailand: An Analytical History (Iathaca, NY, Cornell Univ. Press 1957).

27. See Kuo E.C.Y: "A Sociolinguistic Profile" in Hassan R. (ed.): Singapore: society in transition. (East Asian Social Science Monographs, OUP 1977), pp.134-148.; Harrison, G. "Mandarin and the Mandarins: language policy and the media in Singapore", Journal of Multilingual and Multicultural Development, Vol.1, No.2, (1980) pp.175-180.

28. Kunstadter, op.cit.

29. Quoted in Wong, R.H.K.: Educational Innovation in Singapore (UNESCO. IBE. Paris, 1974) p.10.

30. Watson, K. Educational Development in Thailand, (Hong Kong, Heinemann Educational Books (Asia) Ltd.' 1980)

31. Reply of the Prime Minister at the Dewan Rakyat, 7th April 1976.

32. Rukun means "fundamental principles" and negara means "nation or country". For a discussion of the Rukunegara see Milne, R.S. "National Ideology and National Building" in Malaysia, Asian Survey, July 1970, pp.563-573 and Syed Hussein Alatas, "The Rukunegara and the Return to Democracy in Malaysia" in the Pacific Community, Vol.2, No.4, 1971.

33. Report of the Education Committee (Govt. Printers, Kuala Lumpur, 1956), p.18.

34. Education Ordinance, 1957, p.1.

35. McGee, T.G. Population: a Preliminary Analysis in Malaysia, (ed, Wang Gunguwu Pall Mall 1964) p.81.

36. Wong, F.H.K. Comparative Studies in South East Asian Education (Heinemann 1973), p.114.

37. Adam, R. "The Education of Minorities" in **Australian Journal of Higher Education**, Vol.3, No.2, 1968, p.105.

38. See Watson, J.K.P. "The Education of Racial Minorities in South East Asia with special reference to the Chinese,in **Compare** 6, 2 Sept 1976 and "A conflict of Nationalism: the Chinese and Education in Thailand, 1900-1960", in **Paedagogica Historica** XVI/2, 1976.

39. Quoted in Noss,R. **Language Policy and Higher Education and Development in South East Asia.** Vol.3, Part 2, UNESCO and IAU, 1967, p.12.

40. Chai Hon-Chan, **op.cit** p.38.

41. Inglis, C. "Chinese Education in South East Asia" in Orr, K. (ed.), **The Appetite for Education in Asia,** Development Studies Monograph No.10, Australian National University, p.126.

42. This is discussed in Watson, K. (1980) **Educational Development in Thailand.** op.cit.

43. Watson, J.K.P, **A Conflict of Nationalism: the Chinese and Education in Thailand, op.cit**

44. Franke, W. Some remarks on Chinese Schools and Chinese Education in Thailand and Laos. **Malaysian J. of Ed,** Vol. 11 No, 1/2 Dec. 1974) p.14.

45. Inglis, **op.cit.** p.123.

46. Maxwell W.E. "The Ethnic Identity of Male Chinese Students in Thai Universities". **Comp. Ed. Review,** Vol.18, No.1, Feb. 1974, p.66.

47. Fraser R.M. **Fisherman of South Tahiland - the Malay Villagers.** (Holt, Rinehart and Winston, N.Y. 1966) p.52.

48. Suhrke, A. "The Thai Muslims - Some Aspects of Minority Integration" in **Pacific Affairs,** Vol.43, No.4, 1970/71; Suhrke, A,"Loyalists and Separatists: The Muslims in Southern Thailand" in **Asian Survey,** March 1977, Vol. XVII No.3.

49. Kuo, **op.cit** p.140.

50. Harrison, **op.cit.**

51. Chai Hon-Chan, **op.cit.** p.61.

52. Chee, T.S. "Issues in Malaysian Education: Past, Present and Future' paper presented at the Second National Conference of the Asian Studies Association of Australia, University of New South Wales, 14-19 May, 1978.

53. Watson, J.K.P, "Cultural Pluralism, Nation Building and Educational Policies in Peninsular Malaysia", in **Journal of Multilingual and Multicultural Development,** Vol 1., No.2, 1980, pp.155-174.

54. Chai Hon-Chan, **op.cit** p.24.

55. Loh Fook Seng,P. **Seeds of Separatism - Educational Policy in Malaya 1874-1940.** (OUP Kuala Lumpur 1975).

56. Watson, K. "Education and Colonialism in Peninsular Malaysia" in Watson, K. (ed.) **Education in the Third World** op.cit. pp.88-107.

57. See Watson, J.K.P. " The Problem of Chinese Education in Malaysia and Singapore in **Journal of Asian and African Studies** - Vol. VIII 1-2, 1973 and "The Education of racial minorities in South East Asia, with special reference to the Chinese", **Compare,** Vol, 6, No.2, 1976.
58. Hirschman, C. "Educational Patterns in Colonial Malaya" **Comparative Education Review,** Vol.16, No.3, 1972.
59. See Le Page, R. **The National Language Question,** (OUP, 1964); Roff, M."The Politics of Language in Malaya" in **Asian Survey,** May 1967.
60. From the National Language Act.
61. Watson, (1973) and (1982) **op.cit.**
62. Chai Hon-Chan **op.cit** p.37.
63. Chee, T.S. **op.cit.,** p.25; National Operations Council, **The May 13 Tragedy - A Report,** Kuala Lumpur, (1969). An account of the events leading up to these disturbances is also given in Bloodworth, **op.cit,** Chapter 32.
64. Pillai M.G.G., "The MCE Drama" in **Far Eastern Economic Review,** 80, 17, 1973.
65. Rudner, M. "Education, Development and Change in Malaysia" in **South East Asian Studies,** Vol.15, 1, pp.23-62; 1977; Selvaratnam, V. **Decolonization, the Ruling Elite and Ethnic Relations in Peninsular Malaysia,** Sussex, IDS Discussion Paper No.44. (1974).
66. Selvaratnam, V. Rabushka **Race and Politics in Urban Malaysia,** Stanford, (Hoover Institution Press, 1973)
67. Report of the committee appointed by the NOC to study campus life of students of the University of Malaya. The Majid Report. (Govt. Printing Office, Kuala Lumpur, 1971).
68. Chee, **op.cit,** p.38.
69. Chai Hon-Chan, **op.cit.**

10 EDUCATION, NATIONAL UNITY AND CULTURAL DIVERSITY IN NIGERIA

MARK BRAY

With a population of approximately 100 million, which represents about one fifth of the entire population of Africa, Nigeria is appropriately described as the giant of the continent. Because of its petroleum resources, Nigeria is relatively prosperous. However, it is also a very diverse country, which suffers from threatened political instability. Memories of the tragic Biafran war remain strong, and Nigeria's leaders since the war ended in 1970 have emphasised the need to ensure that such a crisis will not recur. However, the task of forging a national identity is not easy, and divisive tensions in Nigerian political life are still clearly evident.

Education is considered to play a key role in developing a sense of unity, and the 1970's and early 1980's witnessed considerable investment at all levels of the formal system. Within the education system, the needs of the country have usually demanded that, where national and local interests conflict, the former should receive priority. However, the experiences of the last decade have shown that national unity is not as easy to foster through the education system as has sometimes been supposed.

CULTURAL PLURALISM AND POLITICAL DEVELOPMENT IN NIGERIA

The rivalry of three main ethnic groups plays a strong role in Nigerian politics. The groups are the Hausa-Fulani, who live mainly in the north and who number about 14 million; the Yoruba, predominantly in the south west, and who number about 10 million; and the Ibo, for the most part in the south east, and who also number about 10 million. In addition to these three groups, there are many smaller ones. One survey has counted 395 indigenous Nigerian languages, and has emphasised that its data are still incomplete.[1]

The boundaries of Nigeria, like those of most African countries, were arbitrarily determined by European colonial powers at the end of the last century. Many ethnic groups gain for their own areas separate portions of federal funds. More recently, the increasing pressure on resources and the decline in world oil prices has made the Nigerian economy, strong in African terms, much more vulnerable. The recent

were divided by these borders, and now find themselves in different countries, expected to adopt different national identities. At the same time, the groups which found themselves encompassed by Nigeria's boundaries had no common identity in the pre-colonial era. Indeed, some had traditions of warfare with each other and of oppression. In one sense, therefore, the unity which Nigeria's leaders are attempting to build is somewhat artificial.

During the colonial period, the lack of unity in Nigeria was less of a problem than it later became. The North was administered separately from the South, and partly because the government was largely imposed by decree, consensus on development strategies was less important. In the post-colonial era, however, the lack of unity has been more problematic. Moreover, disunity has partly been exacerbated by educational development, for on the one hand unequal educational provision has increased development imbalances, and on the other hand extension of education has made peoples aware of the opportunities which are either denied or open to them.

The 1960's opened with optimism for Nigeria, for at the beginning of the decade a newly elected democratic government proclaimed the nation's political independence from the United Kingdom. In 1966, however, this government was overthrown in a military coup, and the following year the country was plunged into civil war. After the termination of the war in 1970, military rule continued until 1979. Finally, in that year a popularly elected civilian government once again resumed power.

Many of Nigeria's problems have been caused less by its extreme diversity than by the dominance and rivalry of the three large groups. In 1967, chiefly in order to reduce this rivalry, the four main regions of the country were divided into 12 states. By the early 1970's, it was evident that this 'divide and rule' strategy had not gone far enough. Allegations of discrimination with states, most of which were based on ethnic group allegiance, recurred, and in 1976 it was decided again to reorganise the country, this time into 19 states.

During the 1970's, however, a new factor came strongly to the fore, namely the existence of unprecedented revenues from petroleum. Revenues were collected by the federal government, and since large portions were distributed individually to state governments, demands for more states increased. Since 1976, there have been many such demands. Ostensibly, they have often been based on cultural factors such as that particular groups have no tradition of co-existence and should be accorded greater autonomy. In practice, this argument has been heavily underscored by an economic motive, and most of those have pressed for new states have been more concerned to

expulsion of the Nigerian "Gastarbeiter", the Ghanians, is one potential consequence.

Demands for new states have continued, and it is widely anticipated that several will be created in the near future. Even after they have been created, it is unlikely that demands will die down, and cultural arguments will continue to be mixed with economic motives. Especially because of its colonial connotations, and because of its negative and divisive implications, the word 'tribe' is rarely used in modern Nigeria. But since states are quite acceptable reference points, to a large extent, 'statism' has replaced tribalism. Observers therefore make their own deductions about implied allegiances with a different vocabulary.

THE ROLE OF EDUCATION IN PROMOTING UNITY

Considerable faith has been placed in the ability of the education system to promote national unity. The 1977 National Policy on Education described it as the greatest instrument available for promoting unity,[2] and major investments have been initiated with unification specifically in mind. The primary, secondary and tertiary sectors will here be considered in turn.

(a) Primary Education

Nigeria has become well known in the developing world for its massive Universal Primary Education (UPE) campaign, which was launched in 1976. Among the campaign's principal objective was the reduction of regional imbalances, and thus the reduction of regional and ethnic tensions. It was hoped that the primary school curriculum would also promote unity. Experiences of the campaign showed that its initiators had been over-optimistic, however, and by the early 1980's most observers and participants felt somewhat disillusioned.

As originally conceived, the UPE scheme was formidable in scale. The 1971 primary school enrolment was 3,895,000, and by 1973 had expanded to 4,747,000. The Third National Development Plan envisaged an intake of 2.3 million in 1976, to bring the total to 7,400,000.[3] Enrolments were then expected to reach 11,521,000 in 1979/80 and 14,100,000 in 1981/2. In other words, the primary sector was to expand nearly fourfold within ten years. In the early stages, schooling was to be voluntary. But from 1979, it was planned that primary education for all would become compulsory. The quantitative achievements of the early stages of the campaign were remarkable. The enrolment of the first year was over 8.2 rather than 7.4 million, and reached 9.5 million the following year. Expansion in some areas was particularly notable. Kano State, for example, was the most populous but the least educationally developed. Enrolments in Kano jumped from 160,000 in 1975/6 to 342,000 in 1976/7. And in Dutse Local Government Area of the same state, the number of schools increased from 17 in 1975/6 to 162 the following year.[4]

As time progressed, however, the campaign encountered

increasing qualitative, financial and logistic difficulties. Expansion on this scale required a very large number of teachers, and, despite the creation of crash training courses, available qualified staff were inadequate in number. The most serious shortages were encountered in the Northern States, in which both expansion and needs were greatest. Even before UPE was launched, only 13 per cent of the Kano State primary school teaching force was qualified, and in the launching year the proportion fell to 9 per cent.

The national planners also underestimated the costs of UPE. In 1974, Chief A.Y Eke, then Federal Commissioner for Education, calculated that UPE would require an annual recurrent expenditure of only N 200 million.[5] The actual recurrent allocation just for the first year was N515 million. This was part of a record vote of N738 million for the Federal Ministry of Education, which the previous year had been only N101 million.

With expenditures of this magnitude, the federal authorities soon found themselves overcommitted. Shortly after the scheme wa launched, therefore, the national government announced that it would no longer bear sole responsibility for UPE, and that state and local governments would have to bear part of the burden. In several provinces, this resulted in both substantial scaling down of targets and the reintroduction of fees.[6] The element of compulsion, which had been scheduled for 1979, was also abandoned.

In 1980, implementation difficulties caused the Commissioners of Education of the ten Northern States to declare the UPE scheme a disaster.[7] Especially in view of the euphoria with which the campaign had been launched just four years ealier, this was a disappointing outcome. By that stage, moreover, it was clear that those who favoured the campaign should have taken more account of quality as well as quantity. In quantitative terms, some gaps between the developed and less developed states were reduced. But qualitative gaps seemed as wide as ever, and may have increased. Even before UPE was launched, many children in the far north left school without being able to read or write in any language, and quality declined even further with the massive expansion which the campaign involved.

In matters of curriculum also, the initiators of the campaign had been over-optimistic. Their hopes had been based on the premises that children would all learn English, the official language, and would thus be able to communicate with each other. They also hoped that, by learning about the topography and customs of other parts of the country, children would acquire mutual understanding and respect.

Even the language issue proved less than simple, however. During the colonial era, when the task of nation building was less important, primary pupils usually learned in their vernacular for the first few years before later changing to English. In the years following Independence, English was assigned a more prominent role in promoting unity, and since the authorities wanted children to learn as much of the language as possible, they argued that it would be best for them to go "straight for English" from Class I.

In the mid-1970's, this policy was changed again and vernaculars were made the official teaching medium for the first three years. This policy was introduced partly because the mass expansion necessitated recruitment of teachers who could themselves only speak poor English, and partly because the "straight for English" approach was considered to obstruct children's education progress. English should now be taught as a subject from Class I, but should only become the medium of instruction in Class IV.[8] In this instance, the objective of national unity would seem to have taken second place the needs of the individual.

Many practical problems still remain, however, for it is impossible to provide tuition in every one of Nigeria's 395 languages. Particularly in multilingual areas, it is difficult to decide which vernacular should be used at school. For example, although the government of Gongola State has decided to make Hausa the medium of instruction for the early years, it is still not the mother tongue of a large number of children. They are therefore faced with learning one 'foreign' language in the early years and another later on. In addition, the fact remains that progress up the educational ladder is still highly dependent on a good command of English. Thus children in those schools and states in which English is still the medium from the beginning are still likely to have an advantage over the others, and inequalities will be perpetuated.

A further aspect of the language issue is related to religion. For many years tensions have existed between the Muslim communities of the north and the Christians in the middle belt and south.[9] This has been one reason for the present economic and educational imbalance, since schools of the Western type were first introduced by Christian missionaries in the south. Northern Muslims thus came to associate the schools with Christianity and in consequence rejected the former with the latter. This association continues and is a further reason for northern resistance to education. The Muslim communities have their own long-established system of education, but the training it provides, which is mainly confined to learning the Koran, has limited use in the modern economy and little real attempt has been made to use it as a base to develop a modern system of education.

One reason for the lack of official interest in Islamic education has again been the need for national unity, for the country at present cannot contemplate a duality of education systems. In consequence cultural differences again have to sacrificed for the goal of unity. As one way to allay Muslims' suspicions, the authorities have decided that Arabic should be taught in northern schools. Yet this again has the strong drawback of overloading the curriculum and making it almost impossible for the northern child to advance as rapidly as his southern counterpart. Not only is a child faced, in some northern states, with learning Hausa, English and Arabic in Class I (none of which may be his mother tongue), but he also has to cope with two completely different alphabets which operate in opposite directions. The disadvantages of this are obvious. However it is difficult to see how it can be avoided in the short run, because without Arabic in the curriculum, many children would not be permitted to attend school at all.

The need for a national focus produces other anomalies also. For a Christian child it is logical to attend school from Monday to Friday and relax on Saturdays and Sundays; but for a Muslim child, with Friday as the holy day, the pattern of the week should be (but officially is not) quite different. Similarly, it is frequently suggested that holidays should be arranged to coincide with the planting and harvesting seasons when the children are needed at home; but in a country as large as Nigeria with completely different climates in the north, the middle belt and the south, no single calendar can operate. Likewise, geography, social studies and science textbooks should emphasise the local surroundings as well as have a wider focus; but the costs of production, particularly if those books must be written in a local language, may be prohibitive. Examinations should be geared to what a child has learnt, which should itself be geared to his environment; but a multiplicity of different examinations raises problems of standardisation and comparability which inhibit national mobility and integration. History teaching should of course be accurate; but the truth may be that in the past different ethnic groups have lived in disharmony rather than the opposite.

b) Secondary Education

At the secondary level also, governments are succeeding in overlaying inter-tribal rivalries with inter-state ones. However, the former are still evident, and the problems experienced at the secondary level are not much less than those at the primary level.

The National Policy on Education requires that "Every secondary school should become a unity school by enrolling students belonging to other areas or states."[10] In practice, however, state governments are not anxious to pay for the education of children from other areas, and it is difficult for non-indigenes to gain admission to post-primary institutions. Moreover, the same regional quantitative and qualitative imbalances exist at the secondary as at the primary level.

In connection with the shaping of values, Harber's work in Kano State is of major significance. Having investigated the national awareness of pupils of four secondary schools, he found that most pupils had a good knowledge of such national symbols as the flag and the pledge, and that the schools had played a major role in imparting this knowledge. However, when pupils were asked who they considered to be the most important men in Nigerian history, their views of the world appeared to be through very ethnically tinted glasses. Hausa/Fulani children opted for northern leaders such a Murtala Mohammed, Abubakar Tafawa Balewa and Ahmadu Bello, while southern pupils opted for southern leaders such as Obasanjo, Azikiwe and Awolowo. Thus although the pupils had a good knowledge of national symbols, at least some parts of their outlook remained ethnically oriented.[11]

Harber also asked pupils where they would and would not like to live. The most interesting information, he suggests, was contained in the answers to the second question. A sense of community cannot develop unless there is widespread trust. Yet

"one fifth of the Hausa/Fulani pupils stated that the reason they did no want to live in a particular area of Nigeria was one of outright hostility or tribalism. This is a disturbingly high proportion and a more overtly worded question, which it was felt impossible to ask, might well have solicited even more hostile responses. Another 23 per cent of Hausa/Fulani pupils gave the reason that the people in the area in which they did not want to live were 'different' in some way and that they did not share a similar identity. The other 57 per cent explained their preferences in terms of weather, unpleasant environment, lack of educational opportunity or lack of utilities."[12]

Among the southerners, perhaps because of their greater familiarity with different ethnic cultures, fewer respondents referred to other peoples being different. However, 25 per cent gave a reason displaying hostility or tribalism, 13 per cent gave the reason that the people were different, and 62 per cent gave other reasons.

When Harber examined the hypothesis that pupils who have been at school for a greater period of time might have a greater tolerance of racial and cultural differences, he was unable to find a correlation. He also found no evidence of a relationship between a high knowledge of national symbols and a lower level of inter-ethnic hostility. His conclusions therefore suggest that the rationale for the educational investment may have been misconceived.

The experiences of Nigeria's Federal Government Colleges also demonstrate the difficulties of forging unity out of diversity. There are currently 39 colleges in the country - one mixed and one solely for girls in each state, plus an additional one for boys in Lagos. The colleges operate under the direction of the Federal Ministry of Education and are intended to have a specific unifying function. Students are selected from every state according to an equal quota, and the colleges are based on the idea that children of all ethnic groups, by growing up together, will become acquainted with each other, and that much of the strife caused by ignorance will therefore be avoided.

The extent to which the colleges actually reduce ethnic divisions must again be queried, however. There is no doubt that because pupils cannot communicate with each other in their own languages, the standard of written and spoken English is high. But Harber's work in the Kano Federal Government College indicated that, at least in the short run, the policy was having the opposite effect to that intended. Experience of pupils from other ethnic groups did seem to reduce the negative mystique about the other groups, but day-to-day rivalries in the competetive school atmosphere brought into sharper focus latent inter-ethnic tension. There is little reason to supose that the characteristics of the Kano Federal Government College are substantially different from the others.

c) The Tertiary Level

The impact of regional tensions has also been clear at the tertiary level. Until 1973, there were six universities in Nigeria. In the mid-1970's, the number was increased to 13, and at the end of the decade the federal government decided to establish a university in every state. This decision was not based on careful assessment of man-power needs and resources, but rather was motivated by a desire to allocate resources equally and to be considered to be even handed.

Even this move has not solved the problems of imbalance, however. First, it took no account of the fact that some states have much larger populations than others. Second, it failed to equalise the quality of the institutions. Third, although admissions are supposed to reflect Nigeria's federal character and embrace students from all states, some universities have difficulty in managing this - there are very few Northern students in the South, whereas there are many Southerners in the North. And finally, the moved failed even to equalise the number of institutions. Oyo State already had two universities, and since state governments were permitted to open their own institutions, the objective of equality was further upset. Anambra State opened its own university in

1980, and Bendel and Ondo States embarked on plans to do likewise.

Ethnic politics at the university level were also illustrated in 1979 by a controversy surrounding the operation of the Joint Admissions and Matriculation Board (JAMB). The Board had been established the previous year to coordinate admissions into Nigerian universities. The two criteria on which it was to admit students were academic merit and encouragement of educationally disadvantaged areas. These criteria conflicted, however, and led to major argument in which the opposing parties were divided along ethnic lines. The 1979 allocation of places apparently favoured the disadvantaged Northern states. For example, while only 12 per cent of Bendel applicants were offered places, the proportion rose to 43 er cent of Sokoto State applicants. Translated into absolute terms, however, Bendel's alloation meant 2,160 students, whereas Sokoto's was only 198. Both groups felt that their allocations were too small, and major student protests in 1979 led to the temporary closure of five universities and the abandonment of the Board's role as the sole decision-maker on admissions.[13]

The experience of a different body has been more encouraging, however, and is worth mention. It is the National Youth Service Corps (NYSC), which was initiated in 1973 and through which all university and Advanced Teachers' College graduates must perform a year's national service. The majority of graduates who do not have another specific skill will become teachers, and all have to perform some kind of community service such as road construction. Corpers are required to serve in a state other than that of their origin, and there is evidence that the majority of participants acquire more positive attitudes towards fellow Nigerians.[14] The NYSC has also ameliorated educational imbalances by permitting the less developed Northern states to benefit from the greater number of Southern graduates. The NYSC is not without its problems, but it is encouraging to observe that there is one project which seems to be achieving at least some unification.

CONCLUSIONS

Although there is evidence from other countries that the education system can facilitate national unification, [15] many complimentary factors are required to achieve this result. The existence of a common language, for example, should be considered a necessary but insufficient factor in unification. The education system reflects society at least as much as it shapes it, and teachers play a particularly important role. There is no evidence that teachers in Nigeria have attitudes that are more nationally oriented than are those of most other members of society. Expansion of both primary and secondary education has been based more on faith in its unifying ability than on careful appraisal of the evidence. And the decision to establish a university in each state was based on even less positive motives. The decision was chiefly a response to the need for the federal government to be seen to distribute resources evenly, regardless of the manpower needs and resources of the nation.

Hoy has suggested that as comparativists, we should ask whether specific examples are unique case-studies or continuum-located examples from which others may gain insights.[16] Many aspects of the Nigerian situation, such as its particularly wide cultural diversity and the impact of the oil boom, are perhaps unique. But in other respects, Nigeria might be considered a continuum-located example. For instance, the education system currently emphasises national unity at the expense of individual and local diversity. With time, this will probably cease to be so pressing, and a balance may be restored. Similarly, both general development on the Western economic model and Universal Primary Education are goals towards which other developing nations aspire. The sudden arrival of wealth has permitted Nigeria to become a leader in Africa, and to tread a path which others may follow. Unfortunately, the difficulties in using the education system to promote unity in other countries are likely to be as great as they are in Nigeria.

NOTES AND REFERENCES

1. Keir Hansford et al., 'A Provisional Language Map of Nigeria', **Savanna**, Vol.5, No.2, 1976.
2. Federal Republic of Nigeria, **National Policy on Education,** Federal Ministry of Information, Lagos, 1977, p.5.
3. Federal Republic of Nigeria, **Third National Development Plan 1975-80,** Government Printer, Lagos, 1975, Vol.I, p.251.
4. Mark Bray, **Universal Primary Education in Nigeria: A Study of Kano State,** Routledge and Kegan Paul, London, 1981, pp.67-70.
5. **New Nigerian,** 17th August 1974. One naira (N1) is approximately equivalent to Stg 0.80 pence.
6. Bray,**op.cit.,** p.99.
7. **ibid,** p.159.
8. The Federal instruction (as contained in the **National Policy on Education,** op.cit., p.8) only states that the medium of instruction will "initially" be the mother tongue, and English "at a later stage". Most states interpreted this to mean the vernacular for the first three years and English thereafter.

9.   There are many Muslims in Lagos and the south west as well. However, tensions between them and Christian communities have not been so marked.
10. Nigeria, **National Policy on Education,** op.cit., p.12.
11. Clive Harber, 'Schoolchildren and Political Socialisation in Kano State, Northern Nigeria', **Development Research Digest,** No.4, 1980, p.63.
12. **Ibid.**
13. 'JAMB Today, None Tomorrow?', **West Africa,** 9th March 1979, pp. 625-6.
14. Otwin Marenin, 'National Service and National Consciousness in Nigeria', **Journal of Modern African Studies,** Vol. 17, No.4, 1979, p.653 and passim.
15. See for example David Koff and George Von der Muhl, 'Political Socialization in Kenya and Tanzania - A Comparative Analysis', **Journal of Modern African Studies,** Vol.5, No.1, 1976.
16. Charles Hoy, 'Comparative Methodology and its Application to Multicultural Societies', in this volume.

11 COMPARATIVE METHODOLOGY AND ITS APPLICATION TO MULTI-CULTURAL SOCIETIES
CHARLES H. HOY

The articles in this book have all been written by Comparative Educationists - that is academics or professional educators whose experience and expertise has been acquired over a lengthy period of time, studying and working in the field of education in a number of different countries. That is not all they have in common. All contributors have chosen to present their information in a way which makes possible the clearest interpretation. Each has written strictly independently of the others. The common title and theme of the articles allowed them to do this under an umbrella which paid scant regard to the methodology of presentation or of patterns of investigation into the themes themselves. True there could be the assumption that readers of a text entitled 'Education in Multicultural Societies' would all be familiar with educational policies and practices in countries where there are examples of multicultural groups. However, it is more than probable that some explanation of the concern of comparative education is necessary before the reader is able to appreciate fully the claims of the other contributors in this field. This then becomes the first task of this particular chapter. After that a summary of the current debate over methods of study within comparative education will be exemplified through research undertaken by the writer. Finally, an analysis of the expected findings from the comparative study of education in multicultural societies is presented in the light of contemporary research in this area.

Before expecting readers to grasp fully the implications of the other chapters in this book, and the effect these ideas and postulations might have on their own sector of education in their own country, it is important to consider the field of comparative education in some detail. The very title implies a reflexive property which offers a distinct means of viewing ourselves and our policies and practices in a different light, hopefully more clearly, as a result of seeing our educational practices mirrored in the examples shown by other countries.

This feature is implicit, in my opinion, in each of the contributions in this book. Let us attempt to make these underlying assumptions explicit by considering briefly the main developments and purposes of comparative education.
All things are defined and thereafter understood, by comparison. It is therefore to comparison that we must look if we are to gain insight into the subtle differences in practices, philosophy and objectives contained within an educational system. In this chapter an attempt is made to operationalize 'comparison' in educational terms, and to seek answers to common problems in multicultural education primarily by posing questions and offering suggestions. Through this arrangement the reader is inducted into the discussion of the problem/dilemma that is ever present within comparative education: namely, is it exclusively an area-study based subject, or does it contain an essential methodological basis from which 'comparison' between, amongst, within and through educational systems can be made?

First then, what does educational comparison entail? Over the generations of contributors to the field of comparative education, starting with Jullien de Paris in 1817, through Sir Michael Sadler to Isaac Kandel and Joseph Lauwerys, there has been an attempt to formulate this activity of 'comparing' into a composite phenomenon readily identifiable and universally recognised for what it was. The fact that so many attempts have been made leads one to assume failure in the past, but what of the present generation? My own brief definition may be helpful here: Comparative Education consists of a body of knowledge of foreign educational systems held together through an understanding of the methods of studying and applying such knowledge. Other educators have offered different definitions. For example, Brian Holmes writing in the introduction to Philip E. Jones "Comparative Education: Purpose and Method" in 1971 defines comparative education as "a theoretical generalizing social science consisting of those theories, hypotheses, models and laws which facilitate our understanding of the processes of education".[1] In that same text, Holmes identified the aims and purpose of the subject as both theoretical - to improve our understanding of education as such, and in particular, our own national problems in education - and practical - it should help administrators to reform their schools more effectively and efficiently. Edmund King in "Other Schools and Ours" sees comparative education "as achieving a fair relative assessment of two educational systems".[2]

In essence, comparative education provides particular evidence to illuminate and apply social science techniques within an educational framework - for example the use of comparative methodologies as acceptable alternatives to experimentation, arguing in favour of time-saving comparisons in place of lengthy pilot schemes. Through its concentration upon problems, themes and topics common to a number of societies, comparative education offers an alternative focus for analysis and interpretation of difficulties within the educational context in one country, wherever that might be. Through the study of comparative eduation we arrive at some check to our own uncritical ethnocentric bias. The realization that there are other teaching styles, other ways of organizing the classroom, the curriculum, the schools, which have already been tried and adopted in other countries, provides a powerful model for reform strategies to be argued in our own schools. Given the political realities of the new Europe, for example, comparative education can provide knowledge about our common educative society by focussing on the development of shared objectives for a European Education Policy - if such were ever to be postulated in the future - and offers an appreciation for the harmonization and equalization/reciprocation criteria of the European Economic Community. In the education of teachers and through them the children, it anticipates the requirments of future European and World Citizens in awareness and acceptance of differences between member States through the distinctive cultural imperatives of their educational systems.

Comparative education points to our responsibilities to developing countries too, through the service provided in high income countries for training and advising in educational developments in other countries. With the realization that the structure of a nation's educational system is characteristic of its culture, comes a greater respect for indigenous alternatives to the educational industry of high income countries. As one aspect of this concern, comparative education provides the forum for discussion of the role of the international agencies for educational research, and for an assessment of their published findings and programmes of current research; e.g. the activities and influence of U.N.E.S.C.O., the International Bureau of Education in Geneva, and the Council of Europe Commission for Cultural Cooperation to name but three.

As the concerns of the subject became more clear, so did the need for specific methods of handling the concepts, relationships and findings from such studies. Individual descriptions of case studies or area studies declined in importance while an increasing need to explain and analyse cross national variables, in such a way that their applicability to other scenes was immediately recognisable, became evident. From such beginnings there developed the host of sophisticated methodologies and techniques we have at our disposal today to study comparative education. In chronological terms the methodology has progressed from 'traveller's tales', Horace Mann and Michael Sadler are two good examples, through descriptive studies, Isaac Kandel and Nicholas Hans illustrate that mode, to the scientific and analytical studies of the present day. Advocates of different emphases within this current phase include Edmund King - from an ecological and historicist approach - and Brian Holmes, with his problem-solving approach. Other contributions have been systematized by George Bereday, who centres his work on area studies first, with comparison as a later stage, and Harold Noah and Max Eckstein, who supported an inductive correlational approach made possible in a world of infinite data banks and main frame computer systems. With one or two notable exceptions however, few studies have been made of multiculturalism from a comparative education viewpoint.

Having briefly surveyed the development and range of the subject, our next concern is to consider the extent to which comparative education can be thought analogous to other comparative disciplines of politics, physiology, philology, religion etc. as applied to educational matters.[3] If it can, then the methods of approach and the patterns of study developed in these disciplines could well be used in comparative education, to advance the analysis of comparison and its application to multicultural societies in particular. Additionally, if comparative education can be considered analogous to the other comparative subjects, then could not educational comparison be defined universally as an example of comparative methodology whose application lies in the field of education?

What then characterizes comparative studies in education? What aspects of different educational experience can be brought together to produce the anticipated outcomes, which will show that comparison has taken place? Indeed what evidence is there that in comparing things, people are consciously undertaking one definable activity? Have we not rather methods of comparing things which depend for their usefulness upon the purpose for which the comparisons are being made? All too often is not this part of the comparative process left to the reader or the listener to interpret as they think fit? When are the methodological assumptions made explicit, if at all? If not, can we say that a process of comparison is being pursued equally for all followers of the arguments over multiculturalism being presented in this text? Philip E. Jones in his "Comparative Education: Purpose and Method"[4] discusses the contribution of a number of methodologies, including the International Evaluation of Achievement study of mathematical achievement, which he decides "compares, and compares well".[5] In that same concluding chapter he reminds us that "some comparative educationists do not, in the final analysis, compare at all".[6] Do others, such as newpaper writers or the media generally, ever leave the impact of their information and opinion to chance? Jones goes on to state that in his opinion, "proper comparisons can only be made when there is a considerable degree of cultural similarity between nations, that is when cultural conditions are **judged** very similar".[7] W.D. Halls in Comparative Education Vol.13 No.2 pointed to the same phenomena, and took the argument a stage further:

"What is <u>not</u> meant (by comparative studies in education) is the mere study of education in foreign countries, whether this is subsumed or not under the term 'area studies'. Yet one has only to count the number of articles appearing in the three main journals devoted to the field or scan the bibliographical lists to realize that this kind of study, from which the comparative element is singularly often lacking, is the principal occupation of 'comparative educationists'".[8]

Both Halls and Jones end by expressing comparable aspirations which underline the need for some agreed methodological foundations simply in order to gain more from 'comparative' information.

We need not only scientific method, but also an adequate basis for comparing, and it is here that typologies, classifications, models, and/or theories are of value because singly or in some combination they may provide the means of understanding and ordering the data",[9]

is the way Jones sums up the problems; while for Halls:

"the way ahead lies in greater academic independence, in less dogmatism regarding methodology, and in deliberately placing limitations on our own competence."[10]

Such sentiments would appear to be equally supported by Holmes judging from his recent very important work on the subject, "Comparative Education: some Considerations of Method", which he offered in the hope that it would "stimulate discussion and promote co-operation", adding that "Much still needs to be done to improve techniques and models of analysis if the social functions of comparative education are to be performed adequately.[11]

Let us look for a moment at the modes of comparison which have been used by the authors of the other chapters in this text. Have they left comparison to the reader? Have they stated their assumptions and prejudices, and their plans before striking out into their specialist area of knowledge and concern? Have they made explicit their classificatory system? What aims of objectives have they advanced for expecting their contributions to be published in this collection? What approaches, what type of data and what analytical patterns have been offered; and more importantly, what type of findings have been offered, either as unique case studies or as continuum-located examples for others to gain insight from? While it may be presumptuous of this writer to offer "an adequate basis for comparing"[12] education in multicultural societies, nevertheless an attempt will be made to provide reasons for the assumption that without such a system, any comparisons made are likely to lack either legitimation or reliability, or both. A systematization of arrangement or format is not being advocated, but it might have been advantageous from a comparative point of view if contributors to this text had agreed on a summary outline, which at its most simple could have accommodated a patterning of aim, approach, type of data, and findings.

The topic, however, is too wide and the interpretations too far reaching for anything other than the most cursory of comments here. What can be done is to offer an interpretation of the methodological debate and mention the writer's contribution to the discussion - a contribution which attempts reconciliation and commonality, almost integration, rather than differentiation and a uniqueness of approach. Such method draws on parts of the seemingly opposed stands of Bereday[13] and Noah-Eckstein[14] with not a little help from the problem-centred approach of Holmes[15], to produce an eclectic methodology. While other workers in the field have considered ways of organising comparisons, it has been these three independently produced and advocated arguments which have caught the imagination and the questioning of comparative educators over the past twenty years. Philip E. Jones provides a first rate account of the methods of the first and third of these contributors to the analysis, while the explanation given by Noah and Eckstein in their own book is emminently readable and portrays their position clearly.

Bereday strongly believes in the collection of data about foreign systems in order to gain a breadth of perception about education, and in his first stage he emphasises the purely descriptive aspects of educational data from different countries. The second stage of his methodology encompasses interpretation and evalution of the previously described systems in terms of other related information such as historical, geographial, economic and social data. These two stages taken together constitute the 'area studies' section of comparative education for Bereday. The amount of detail required will be determined by the nature of the investigation, but generally speaking Bereday advocates the collection of as much information as possible so that some selection can be made during the interpretive stage. The actual process of comparison is performed by Bereday in two stages. Juxtaposition, stage 3, entails looking closely at similarities and differences in the data analysed in stage 2 for two or more countries, and formulating a hypothetical relationship between aspects of the data which command attention. By means of simultaneous comparison using the hypothesis between the countries, Bereday is able to produce a conclusion. Applying the hypothesis to each country after this preliminary matching produces the final, objective and consistent conclusion in stage 4. Here the hypothesis will be verified in whole or in part, or refuted, or shown to have produced some useful though inconsistent results.

The approach is logical and it demands little preparation before the actual collecting stage is begun. This purely inductive method of approach is also advocated by Harold Noah and Max Eckstein. Their method starts with the formulation of some relevant hypothesis relating educational practices in a number of countries. However, the origin of the hypothesis is of less concern in this method. Instead, the main procedure centres on the collation of information, focussed upon by the hypothesis. Every possible item is assessed, measured and graded in terms of its relevance to the hypothesis, and through this to every other educational item considered. Correlations are looked for, investigated further as appropriate, and the final outcomes noted. The search produces a residual factor or factors which explain the comparison between eduational practices in the countries studied. The process can be repeated using similarly related hypotheses, and by this means a fuller understanding of the reasons for particular educational practices is achieved.

Of the two methods of arguing, that of induction means arguing from the particular to the general, and deduction arguing from the general to the particular. Bereday and Noah-Eckstein employ the former, while Holmes in his problem-solving approach applies the latter method of working, preferring to describe his approach as a hypothetico-deductive one. Essentially the method is to focus our attention on an issue in education - such as education in multicultural societies - which has relevance to more than one country, to refine our perception of the problem and offer some solution to it. Problems according to Holmes often result from asynchronous changes in society or parts of society, as for instance between different cultural groupings within one country. Educational problems in particular have been initiated by the over-riding 'explosions' in expectations and aspirations, knowledge and population, this latter both absolutely and in terms of relative changes, fluctuations and oscillations over time. Society in terms of both institutional provision and normative or attitudinal aspects, has not kept pace with these changes, and so policies which are directed to the solution of these problems must be formulated in such a way as to enable rational decisions to be made on the basis of predicted outcomes. The problem on hand will determine the degree of importance to be attached to each of a number of identified contextual factors. In the problem-solving approach, the factors identified are classified according to their character. Ideological factors (norms, attitudes and values), institutional forces, and natural resources make up the basic patterns. These are cut across at many points by economic, religious, political, racial, educational and linguistic factors for example. However, despite the amount of care involved in the construction of this logical framework, it is still true that the judgements involved are no less intuitive than those in the other comparative approaches.

The essential differences between these three approaches is that Bereday starts immediately with the collection of data on education and related issues, the Noah-Eckstein approach starts with the formulation of a hypothetical relationship between the two, while the problem-solving approach of Holmes initially concentrates on the appreciation of a 'problem' by the investigator. The directions of study imposed by the three methods are therefore divergent from the start. The question of which method to choose, would then appear quite simple, as long as researchers know where they want to go in their comparison. The only real difficulty is that the methods are necessarily complicated and involved. What is offered by the eclectic method is a simplification of these procedures for those who are involved in studies of multicultural comparisons for the first time, without necessarily limiting their more experienced counterparts in pursuing more complex comparisons.

Returning to my earlier definition of comparative education, an understanding of the methods of studying and applying knowledge of foreign educational systems, presupposes an appreciation of the ways of comparing things. We have written elsewhere[16] that there are many ways of comparing things, and since not all enquiries aim at the same kind of result, it follows that there is unlikely to be one single most appropriate method of approach. While specific 'standard' methodologies exist, for example those of Bereday, Noah-Eckstein, and Holmes, there has been no comparative studies of the effect of using these approaches to investigate the same study, as far as is known to the writer.[17] Nor has there been an attempt to combine facets of these three methodologies into an eclectic approach, other than that offered by the present writer.[18]

The constraints placed upon the researcher in the Bereday approach are minimal - he or she can go ahead and collect, interpret and evaluate data. This I judge to have been the method adopted by James Banks, Dudley Hick, James Lynch, Colin Brock and Mark Bray. However, no classification is as simplistic as that. James Banks for example, introduces the concept of 'new pluralism' which offers researchers a multitude of applications in a comparative context now that almost every nation contains sizeable ethnic goups. Many would see in his assertion "We treat them all the same" a common teacher response to ethnically probing questions the world over. James Banks advocates that teachers should recognise differences, not in any forceful manner but as a matter of fact, and the typologies he offers from American experience of curriculum reform provide food for thought in other contexts too.

On the other hand Keith Watson has approached the theme of cultural diversity first and then provided examples from South East Asia to illustrate his chosen hypotheses; in essence a very different route from that of an area study. Dan Dorotich and Werner Stephan provide a frank comparative assessment within their chapter from the political, social, economic, cultural and psychological dimensions of the two societies they analyse. Or again, Alan Davies has started from a priori statements and interwoven a comparative argument. These are more in the Noah and Eckstein or Holmesian modes of comparative study, and yet any or all of them could be used fruitfully as a basis for extension along the lines of the eclectic comparative methodology suggested later in this chapter.

Returning to the area studies, the essential feature present in them all is the factual information whether presented chronologically or by following another typological rationale. The task for the researcher is to extract the information relevant to their own study. From Dudley Hick comes the question of whether nationalism ought to be achieved through the single pillar of assimilation, or by some form of accommodation. The issue is debated against the gathering climate of integration in Australia, and thereby offers useful comparative research destinations. Equally his acknowledgment of the need for the reciprocal recongition of differences, on the part of the majority as well as minority groups, as precursor to cultural and structural pluralism within a multi-cultural society, provides a powerful platform for further analysis of other communities. Similarly James Lynch prescribes multicultural education for everyone as the way to achieve shared values in Australian society - a thought not a million miles from James Banks advocacy. Both see the importance of emphasising the common multicultural heritage in each country.

Colin Brock makes the point that not only are people from the Caribbean a multicultural group themselves, but because elements of those groups have settled in North America, Europe and the British Isles they offer a bountiful comparative example of acculturation patterns in these three distinctive areas. Mark Bray offers a Nigerian case study emphasising language, religious diversity and the political dimension; each categorization offering a comparative extrapolation, with Bray acutely conscious of the difference between the useful-ness of unique case studies and continuum-located examples. Finally, of course, the separation of contexts between Developed and Developing Countries in Sections II and III provides the enterprising researcher with a further contexutal comparison.

Overall it is not a question of whether models or unique case studies provide the most useful comparative analysis, but rather that each complements the other at different stages of the researcher's work. There are indeed different paths to the same comparative objective. Following Noah and Eckstein, the task is not so much focussed upon data collection as upon manipulation and handling of the consequential hypothetical outcomes from the analysis, while searching for a residual factor. Keith Watson's contribution gives this impression, and my own is in similar vein. By contrast the attention of the researcher using the problem-solving approach is focussed more and more acutely at the specific data made relevant by the rigorous intellectualization of the problem.

Where there is an abundance of data, the Bereday approach is useful; where there is a store of inter-related variables and the researcher is at ease in the manipulation of these sources, the Noah-Eckstein approach is useful. Equally the problem-solving approach is apropriate where there is a definite characterization of normative and/or institutional inconsistencies in the situation being studied.

The destinations of these three directions of study are then likely to be the following. Bereday's approach will produce an interesting increase in general understanding of the situations compared. Noah-Eckstein will if pursued rigorously, continue to uncover unsuspected relationships between the situations compared, while Holmes will produce predicted policy solutions identified from part of the context of the situations. The suggested benefit of the eclectic approach is the possibility it allows of limiting the hypothetical findings, while at the same time permitting a rigorous investigation. The major concern of this approach, in an attempt at justification of the hypothesis chosen - on the basis of what is termed the Initial Survey, is the necessity to state the criteria for such an hypothesis. In addition it allows for replication of the inductively formulated hypothesis by others evaluating the Initial Survey. Thus a method of approach not too dogmatic or limiting, yet one which could be used as a pedagogic tool by students and others interested in education at all levels of comparative analysis, is suggested.

The eclectic approach comprises four stages, which combine facets of all three of the approaches described above without stipulating that researchers must make a definite choice right at the commencement of their investigations. As a comparative methodology the approach can be used at different levels of expertise by a wide range of students wishing to explore multiculturism from an established comparative perspective. Stated briefly it comprises:

1.   The identification of a **Primitive Hypothesis** that there is something comparable between the situations 'A' and

'B'. This is defined as precisely and succinctly as possible, in order to determine the field of concern in the study.

2. The **Initial Survey** consists of a preliminary description of the situations as defined above in educational and other terms. This is followed by a preliminary evaluation using economic, political, sociological, cultural/anthropological, religious and educational components, aimed at a presentation of the educational characterization of the two situations.

3. From these two stages will develop an appreciation of the complex relationships displayed in the two situations 'A' and 'B'. This can then be formulated as a **Hypothesis** depending upon the particular outcome of stages 1 and 2, and the interests of the individual researcher.

4. The **Investigation** proceeds with the deduction of **Logical Effects** which follow from the hypothesis. This can include rigorous measurement and correlation coefficients; descriptive or ethnographic evaluations and the drawing of conclusions or some combination of the two. The fundamental principle involved in this stage is that the researcher selects rigorously the variables and measures with which to test the hypothesis by using data which is different from that previously considered in the Initial Survey. The outcome is then a comparative statement or statements relating the variables first encountered in the Primitive Hypothesis. See table 1.

The diagramatic representation of the method, shown overleaf, shows the four separately identified stages of Primitive Hypothesis, Initial Survey, Hypothesis Formulation, and the Investigation of Logical Effects in Situations 'A' and 'B'. Naturally the method can be extended to other situations in which comparability is suspected, while the outcomes from the hypothesis can be investigated in other countries, for other societies, or in other Situations in addition to those originally considered.

That summarises the argument and the writer's position in relation to it. What remains to be done is to give application to the different methods, and to analyse the findings from the writer's research and from other contemporary research into multiculturalism in a number of societies.

A comparative analysis of education in multicultural societies using four case studies now follows. The four cases are the result of the application of the eclectic approach and the problem-solving approach to two investigations, and are therefore in two pairs. The first set are concerned with the indigenous minorities in North America and Australasia,[19] the second with the Welsh, Scots and Northern Irish minorities within the United Kingdom.[20] The first set, Case Studies A

TABLE I

The Eclectic Approach

Primitive Hypothesis	Initial Survey	Hypothesis	Investigate Logical effects
Comparability suspected	Describe and evaluate	Formulated	Outcomes investigated together with effects in other situations

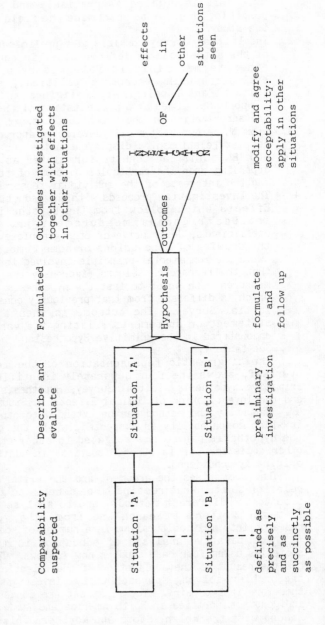

| defined as precisely and as succinctly as possible | preliminary investigation | formulate and follow up | modify and agree acceptability: apply in other situations |

and B, utilized the problem-solving approach and the eclectic approach respectively for the study of indigenous minorities; the second set, Case Studies C and D, the problem-solving and eclectic approaches respectively for the study of the 'national' minorities within the U.K., as shown:

CASE STUDY	TYPE OF MINORITY	METHODOLOGY ADOPTED
A	Indigenous	Problem-solving
B	Indigenous	Eclectic
C	National	Problem-solving
D	National	Eclectic

Case Study A: Indigenous minorities using the problem-solving approach.

The aim of this study was to investigate the possibility of achieving native self-sufficiency, i.e. to solve the problems resulting from asynchronous changes caused by technological, population and other factors, in the minority areas. The study using the problem-solving approach presented an historical perspective through economic, legal and social behaviour patterns of the natives both before and during initial settlement by the whites. An attempt was then made to find a rationale in the different policies determining the treatment of natives, and the study concluded with a discussion of the possibility of establishing a general pattern of development for the indigenous minority groups in these four areas.

It was relatively easy to document the degree of social lag or asynchronous rates of change between native self-sufficiency before settlement and the situation today. Hence the search for policy solutions to reduce and eliminate this 'lag problem' was undertaken. Comparison of the outcomes from each area formed the basis for the prediction that with the education of both minority and majority societies, the Maoris and then the Aborigines followed at a distance by the Canadian and then the American Indians could be self-sufficient again. A straight forward problem-solving study had thus been undertaken, with the directing policy solutions being tested in turn in each of the minority areas.

Case Study B: Indigenous minorities using the eclectic approach.

Analysing this case using the eclectic approach the primitive hypothesis considered the relations between English settlers and indigenous minorities as likely to produce similar conflicts and similar policies. The same initial conditions applied with differences in length of contact time, but outcomes were related. Comparison allowed an assessment of the different stages reached in different areas. The data referenced in the brief Initial Survey to formulate the hypothesis included: date first contact, number of white settlers at different dates, and the number of the indigenous

FIGURE I. CASE STUDY APPROACHES

Case	A	B	C	D
Aim	Investigate possibility of achieving native self-sufficiency	Investigate similarities between conflicts, & find whether these have sponsored similar policies	Investigate possibility of self determination for national minorities	Investigate whether minorities participate more if supported more
Approach	Problem approach, with generalized normative statement pointing to inconsistencies in cultural and in educational areas	Eclectic with hypothesis communication with 'home society' vs. accommodation of minority group	Problem, with generalized normative statement pointing to inconsistencies in economic and political areas	Eclectic with hypothesis support from general society vs. participation by minority in general society
Type of data	Government and academic studies of each minority group's status, attitudes and demands	Measurement of degrees of contact, & acceptance. Marital contact, social groupings, status of offspring, legal barriers	Government and academic studies of each minority group's status, attitudes, demands	Measurement of legislative support and personal participation in all areas
Findings	Achievement possible if majority adopt accepting educational patterns, e.g. from Maoris case	Similar policies in similar density contacts. Rural and urban dichotomy	Achievement not possible in economic and political areas. Cultural, social, religious and educational possible; e.g. Northern Ireland pattern	Educational area important for use made by minority groups in maintaining cultural and leadership tradition

population, and the initial policy vis-a-vis indigenous groups. Also included was data on mixed marriages and status of offspring in the different areas - to afford some assessment of the degree of acceptance shown by the settlers; distance from home society and the extent of the communication maintained with home. Other data included the extent of attempts at education and the expectations through education.

All of these offered possible hypothetical relationships. using this approach the hypothesis formulated was that the smaller the extent of communication with the home society, then the greater would be the accommodation with the indigenous peoples. The hypothesis was particularly concerned with educational and social provision for indigenous groups. Stage four, the deduction of logical effects from this statement considered the creation of measurement indices and the systematic testing of these deductions, and assessment of the outcomes of the hypothesis. The definition of home society here referred to the dominant cultural group. Communication can be measured by travellers, letters, ships in the past; composition of social groupings, clubs, pressure groups for discussion etc. in the present. Accommodation can be determined by the status of mixed marriages and offspring, the presence of any legal opposition to indigenous groups, and the establishment of educational provision, and its nature.

Difficulties may arise due to the kinds of data available for this type of study, both in historically available sources and in the reliability of case studies of group composition in mixed areas. The investigation can, however, be handled easily, with measurement indices and testing quite feasible. It was anticipated that the hypothesis would e confirmed in the past, or in places having a small degree of communication with the home society, and refuted or not confirmed in urbanized areas. That is, the hypothesis applied where whites immigrated into minority areas, but not when minority group members later emerged in white areas possessing a strong coherent cultural grouping. Minorities in that case being more accommodated on the periphery of the dominant cultural areas, for example under shanty town urbanization patterns.

Case Study C: National minorities using the problem-solving approach.

Adopting a similar pattern of analysis to that used in Case A, a generalized normative statement of the ideal type would be that the U.K. national minorities ought to have self-determination. Specific hypotheses can then be determined: for example, if these minority groups are given self-determination then the outcomes or policies in the political, economic, cultural, eduational areas, and on religious matters, will be predicted. Where such outcomes are not realizable, there will be inconsistencies; so that by a process of intellectualizat-ion the problem-solving approach will focus attention on normative inconsistencies, or inconsistencies within the institutional field, and between the normative and institutional areas. In other words, it will attack inconsistencies between what devolutionists in the United Kingdom say they want, and what in the end they are prepared to sacrifice under such a policy.

For example, attitudes towards self-determination on religious matters may conflict with attitudes towards self-determination in the political realm. It is alright for Wales to control its own independent Church, but not its own independent parliament; its own schools, but not its own universities; its own Eisteddford and Museums, but not its own social security arrangements. Pre-requisites for the realization of self-determination were postulated as a retention of, or a transference to, minority control over cultural, educational social and religious areas, while the economic and political areas would be fought over before a modus vivendi were achieved. These directing policy solutions can then be applied in turn to each minority, and predictions made as to the degree of acceptability of the proposals. Using this approach, the acquisition of data is unlikely to cause any difficulty, and the approach can therefore be easily applied.

Case Study D: National minorities using the eclectic approach.

The approach followed in this case was the eclectic method with subsequent analysis following the Noah-Eckstein model. However, in place of the regression to find a residual cause, the interpretation of deviant findings was undertaken using the Hopper typology.[21] The hypothesis was formulated in terms of general society support for the minorities and their participation in the national culture of their respective countries. The data from which the hypothesis was considered came from legislative enactments, thereby being independent of the Initial Survey sources, while participation by the minorities was determined in economic, political, social, fine cultural, religious and educational terms.

The findings showed that the educational area confirmed the hypothesis, with the other areas either completely or partially refuting it. This resulted in the deviant educational relationship being investigated further; and the study concluded that a successful resolution of the dilemma facing minority group members who desired acceptance within the general society without abandonment of their cultural heritage was possible, given certain policies in the educational field. The acquisition of data was not a methodological difficulty, and the approach was readily applicable to the investigation.

A chart showing the aim, approach, type of data and findings for each of the four studies is given (see figure 1).

Case study A proved concise, a real problem-solving study, with attention directed towards the achievement for all groups of a policy similar to that enjoyed by the Maoris already. In Case study B, while a realistic hypothesis was produced, the method is not as useful as it might be due to difficulty in gaining access to the right kind of reliable data; the validity of the findings is therefore questionable. For Case study C, when the objective is to produce a resolution of the dilemma over self-determination, this approach is most appropriate. Relative degrees of inconsistency can be determined and attention directed to the application for the others, of what in the economic and political areas for one group was a sucessful model at one time, namely the Northern Ireland Stormont Parliament model of devolution. However, there would have to be a number of changes to that particular constitution before it could be tried elsewhere in anything like a workable form. In Case study D, the eclectic approach was able to produce a realistic hypothesis which subsequently enabled the study to pick out the importance of the educational component from the correlational analysis. The further investigation carried out on this deviant case, usefully highlighted the different usage made of the educational system by different minority groups.

Although there is inevitably a gap between the hypothesis as formulated by the eclectic method and the initial surveyed data, the approach minimizes this inductive gap, and produces overt rationalizations for the choice based upon analysis of the data according to the specified primitive hypothesis. Consistency, and a lack of internalized normative judgements associated with the production of the hypothesis, should result from this eclectic approach. Reproduceability of analysis and findings is then more likely, and our overall knowledge of comparative studies thereby increased. Where there are inconsistencies within normative statements, or between normative statements and the institutional patterns related to these, then the problem-solving approach is likely to focus attention quickly but exclusively, on policy solutions which will minimize those particular inconsistencies.

In summary, the problem-solving approach allows for intuition only at the start when the 'problem' is first tentatively identified, and before a process that Holmes calls "intellectualization" is begun. In contrast, Noah and Eckstein systematically allow for intuition, almost in an uncontrolled way, in their approach; while Bereday has it at the end, in directing the attack on the hypothesis. The eclectic approach puts it firmly in the middle where it can offer an rationalization for the hypothesis, yet not interfere with the necessary deductive testing based upon the hypothesis. It might be argued that some people who know what comparison means, and who are sure of where they are going, ought to start straight in. For the rest however, the initial survey is a necessary pre-requisite in their education as comparative methodologists, whether they be investigating multiculturalism or some other topic.

The eclectic method clarifies the ambiguity over where and when the data is collected and analysed. It also explains clearly the function of the hypothesis. However, what is more important than subscription to any one method, is an appreciation for comparative studies themselves. Comparative education is much more sophisticated in its analytical patterns and methodological frameworks than other comparative disciplines, but it remains necessary for comparative educationists to appreciate these positions, and to see that they are more prominently referred to and used in the future.

Notes and References

1. Jones, P.E. **Comparative education: purpose and method,** University of Queensland Press. 1971, p.10.
2. King, E.J. **Other Schools and Ours,** Holt, Rinehart and Winston, 1963. p.27.
3. See Simsova, S. "Resources for comparative education" in **Communication in Education** British Comparative Education Society Conference proceedings, 1979.
4. Jones, **op.cit.** p.173.
5. **Ibid.** p.162.
6. **Ibid.** p.162
7. **Ibid.** p.163 (emphasis in original.)
8. Halls, W.D. "Comparative Studies in Education 1964-1977: a Personal View". **Comparative Education** (Oxford) Vol.13, No.2, 1977, p.81.
9. Jones, **op.cit.,** p.165.
10. Halls, **op.cit.,** p.86.
11. Holmes, B. **Comparative Education: Some Considerations of Method.** Allen and Unwin, 1981, p.15.
12. Jones, **op.cit.,** p.165.
13. Bereday, G.Z.F. **Comparative Method in Education.** Holt, Rinehart and Winston. 1964.
14. Noah,H.J. and Eckstein, M.A. **Towards a Science of Comparative Education.** Macmillan, 1969.
15. Holmes, **op.cit.**
16. Hoy, C.H. "The interaction of minority groups with the majority: methods of approach for comparative studies". Paper submitted to 3rd World Congress of Comparative Education Societies: 1977. See **Diversity and Unity in Education,** Holmes, B. (ed.) Allen and Unwin. 1980.
17. Use of similar methods of study can be identified e.g. Coupland, R. in **Scottish and Welsh Nationalism: a Study** followed a Bereday approach; Lijphart, L.A. in **The**

Politics of Accommodation: Pluralism and Democracy in the Netherlands who followed a Noah-Eckstein approach; and Gordon, M.M. in **Assimilation in American life: the role of race, religion and national origins** following a Holmes approach. However, in no case was there an attempt to study the same situation using more than one approach.

18. See Hoy,C.H. **Education and Minority Groups in the U.K. and Canada: a comparative study of policies and objectives.** Ph.D. (unpub.) London, 1975.

19. See Hoy, C.H. **The minority indigenous populations of North America and Australasia: a comparative study of recent administrative policies and educational objectives** M.A. (unpub) London, 1969; and see note 16 above.

20. Hoy, C.H. 'Education and Minority Groups in the U.K.: the case of the Scots, Welsh and Northern Irish'. **Compare** (Oxford) Vol.6., No.1. 1976. p.14.

21. Hopper, E. "A typology for the Classification of Educational Systems' **Sociology** Vol.2 No.1. January 1968. pp.29-46.

12 FURTHER READING: AN INTERNATIONAL BIBLIOGRAPHY

TREVOR CORNER

This bibliography has been compiled from further reading suggested by the contributors. It is intended to develop the interest of the reader beyond the text itself, but is only a limited and personal view of the vast range of publications on the relationship between education and cultures. Internationally, books that review the strictly academic interpretations of multicultural education are included with historical or comparative readings, as well as some which are intended as background readers to introduce individual countries. Theories, if such exist at all in multicultural education, are in a constant flux of change and it would be inappropriate to conclude that the vastness of the potential reading available is any guide to the certainty of knowing what can and should be done. Briefly then, an introduction to a few current publications in Britain is followed by some suggested further references and sources of information for chapters three through to eleven.

A substantial proportion of books published on British multicultural education contain useful reviews of reading; to take just three examples covering different approaches:-

Barton, L. and Walker S., (Eds.) **Race, Class and Education** Croom Helm, London 1983.

Edwards. V, **Language in Multicultural Classrooms** Batsford, London 1983.

Lewis, E.G. **Bilingualism and Bilingual Education** Pergamon, London 1981.

The range of references that follow from the first chapter could be substantial if all the countries mentioned were included. There are however very few texts that use a comparative analysis; four books that, whilst not being comparative, allow for comparisons to be drawn are:-

Further Reading

Megarry J, Nisbet. S, & Hoyle. E, **Education of Minorities**, World Yearbook of Education 1981. Kogan Page, London.

Seton-Watson. H, **Nations and States**, Methuen, London 1977.

Ashworth, G.(Ed) **World Minorities in the Eighties** (3 vols) Quartermaine, Sunbury 1977-1980.

Haugen. E, McClure, J, Thomson, D. **Minority Languages Today**, Edinburgh U.P. 1981.

A very limited selection of readings which elaborate on chapters one and two which the reader may care to follow up are:-

Durkacz. V. **The Decline of the Celtic Languages**, (John Donald, Edinburgh, 1983).

Miller, J. **Many Voices: Bilingualism, Culture and Education**, (R.K.P. London 1983).

Institute of Education, London. **Linguistic Minorities in England**, (Tinga Tinga, London 1983).

Stubbs, M. & Hillier, H. **Readings on Language, Schools and Classrooms**, (Methuen London, 1983).

Lynch, J. **The Multicultural Curriculum** (Batsford, London 1983).

Stenhouse, L. Verma, G, Wild. R, Nixon. J, **Teaching about Race Relations** (R.K.P. London 1982).

Verma, G. & Bagley, C. **Self-concept, Achievement and Multicultural Education** (Macmillan, London 1982).

Runnymede Trust. **Britain's Black Population** (Heinemann London 1980).

Aitken, A.J. & McArthur, T. **Languages of Scotland**, (Chambers Edinburgh, 1979).

O'Connor, K. **The Irish in Britain** (Gill and Macmillan, Dublin, 1974).

All the above references tend to seek ways for positive action in the development of multicultural education; they have been affected considerably by research and publications from North America, and notably the detailed Canadian surveys of ethnicity and language in the late 1960s. There is currently a second wave of research going on across Britain though perhaps the largest and most detailed surveys e.g.

Rosen and Burgess, **Languages and Dialects of London School Children** (1980) and the reports of the Linguistic Minorities Project have been in the Greater London area.

There are a growing number of centres in Birmingham, Coventry, Leicester, Bradford, Sunderland, Aberystwyth, Dublin, Glasgow and elsewhere which have started to produce detailed work on the ethnic composition of their immediate regions. Taken in conjunction with more national reports, such as Rampton and Swann, there should be a considerable increase in the amount of information and opinion available during the mid-1980s.

Chapter 3 **(The Interaction of Language and Culture)**

As indicated by this chapter the relationship between language and culture (and thus eduation) is intimate and complex. This is itself indicated by the massive and wide-ranging literature on the study of languages, socio- and psycholinguistics, and role of language in learning. Such studies have traditional roots which continue to be called upon: for example Sweet's book **The Practical Study of Languages** published in 1899 is still used in many language courses, as is Wilhelm Von Humbolt's classic of its time **Linguistic Variability and Intellectual Development.** Some early publications generally regarded as important in the study of language and culture up to the 1960's are:-

Benedict, Ruth. **Patterns of Culture** (Houghton Mifflin, Boston, 1934).

Weinreich, Uriel. **Languages in Contact: Findings and Problems** (Mouton, The Hague, 1955).

Allport, Gordon. **The Nature of Prejudice** (Cambridge, Mass, Addison-Wesley, 1954).

Hymes, Dell (Ed.) **Language in Culture and Society** (Harper and Row, New York, 1964).

Landar, Herbert. **Language and Culture** (Oxford University Press, New York, 1966).

de Saussure, Ferdinand. **Course in General Linguistics** (McGraw Hill, New York, 1966).

Ideas from socio - and psycholinguistic studies have had an important impact on teachers' education and subsequent attitudes towards the acquisition of language, standard and dialect forms, as well as the benefit or otherwise of bi - or multi-lingualism. Some readings which indicate the general trend in thinking over the past 15 years at varying levels of sophistication are:-

Further Reading

Barth, Fredrik. **Ethnic Groups and Boundaries** (Universitets Forleget, Bergen and George Allen and Unwin, London, 1969).

Gumperz, J.J. & Hymes, D. (Eds.) **Directions in Sociolinguistics: the Ethnography of Communication** (Holt Rhinehart and Winston, New York, 1972).

Douglas, Mary (Ed) **Rules and Meanings** (Penguin, Harmondsworth, 1973).

Banman, Richard & Sherzer, Joel (Eds.) **Explorations in the Ethnography of Speaking** (Cambridge University Press, London, 1974).

Glazer, N. & Moynihan, (Eds.) **Ethnicity, Theory and Experience** (Harvard University Press, 1975).

Giles, Howard. (Ed) **Language, Ethnicity and Intergroup Relations** (Academic press, London, 1977)

Scherer, M.R. & Giles, H. (Eds). **Socialmarkers in Speech** (Cambridge University press, London, 1979).

Hudson, Richard, A. **Sociolinguistics** (Cambridge University Press, London 1980).

Milroy, Leslie. **Language and Social Networks** (Basil Blackwell, Oxford, 1980).

Aitchison, Jean. **Language Change: Progess or Decay?** (Fontana, 1981).

Davies, Alan. 'Language and Ethnicity'. Special Issue of the **Journal of Multilingual and Multicultural Development** 3/3 (Clevedon Avon, 1982).

Saville-Troike, M. **The Ethnography of Communication: An Introduction** (Basil Blackwell, Oxford, 1982).

Gumperz, John J. (Ed) **Discussion Strategies: Language and Social Identity** (Cambridge University Press, London, 1983).

Some books looking more specifically at bilingualism:-

Sharp, Derrick. **Language in Bilingual Communities** (Edward Arnold, London, 1973).

Fishman, Joshua. **Bilingual Education** (Newberry House, Mass, 1976).

Hornby, Peter, (Ed.)**Bilingualism Psychological, Social and Educational Implications** (Academic Press, New York, 1977).

Further Reading

Miller, Jane. **Many Voices: Bilingualism, Culture and Education** (Routledge and Kegan Paul, London 1983).

Language development in children and the impact of schooling:-

Opie, Peter & Opie, Iona **The Lore and Language of School Children** (Clarendon Press, Oxford, 1959).

Christophensen, P. **Second Language Learning: Myth and Reality** (Penguin, Harmondsworth, 1973).

Rosen,H & Rosen, C. **The Language of Primary School Children** (Penguin, Harmondsworth, 1973).

Trudgill, Peter. **Accent, Dialect and the School** (Edward Arnold, London, 1975).

International Review of Education. Special Number. 'Language in a Multicultural Setting', XXIV/1978/3 (Nijholt, The Hague).

Cattenden, Alan **Language in Infancy and Childhood** (Manchester University Press, 1979).

Rosen, Harold & Burgess, Tony **Language in Infancy and Childhood** (Manchester University Press, 1979).

And finally, a selection of area studies:-

Dakin, J, Tiffen B, & Widdowson, H.G. **Language in Education: The Problem in Commonwealth Africa and the Indo-Pakistan Subcontinent.** (Oxford University Press, London 1968)

Laird, Charlton. **Language in America**, (Prentice-Hall, New Jersey, 1970).

Busso, Keith. **To give up on words: silence in the Western Apache Culture** (South Western Journal of Anthropology Vol.26, 1970, pp.213-230.)

Gorman, T.P. (ed) **Language and Education in Eastern Africa**, (Oxford University Press, Nairobi, 1970).

Fishman, Joshua, Cooper,R.L. & Roxana, M.A. **Bilingualism in the Barrio**, (Bloomington Indiana University Publications, 1971.)

Brass, P.R. **Language, Religion and Politics in North India**, (Cambridge University Press, London 1974).

Lewis, Glyn. **Bilingualism and Bilingual Education**, (Pergamon Press, Oxford, 1981.)

Chapter 4 **(Multiethnic Education in the U.S.A.: Practices and Promises).**

This chapter, which particularly emphasises the changes in the curriculum and educational practice necessary for multicultural awareness, is dealing with a country which had a strong educational ideology based on the 'melting pot' of races, along with a weaker strand of thinking which has acknowledged the diversity of races that make up its population. The following readings indicate some very recent publications relevant to multicultural education for teachers.

Sowell, Thomas **Ethnic America: A History,** (Basic Books, New York, 1981).

A thoughtful and provocative history of ethnic groups in the United States which has evoked considerable discussion and debate. Sowell blends historical analysis with reasoned opinion.

Gordon, Milton M. **Assimilation in American Life: The Role of Race, Religion, and National Origins,** (Oxford University Press, New York, 1964).

This seminar and classic work has deeply influenced ethnic studies teaching and research in the United States.

Banks, James A (Ed) "Multiethnic Education at the Crossroads," **Phi Delta Kappan,** Vol. 64 (April, 1983), pp.559-585.

A collection of articles covering a wide range of topics, including the historical developments of multiethnic education in the United States, bilingual/bicultural education, multiethnic and global education, and multiethnic education in Europe.

Gollmick, Donna M & Chinn, Philip C **Multicultural Education in a Pluralist Society,** (The C.V. Mosley Company, St. Louis, 1983).

Multicultural education is conceptualized broadly in this book, which discusses ethnicity, religion, language diversity, socioeconomic status, sex and gender, age, and exceptionality.

Glazer, Nathan & Moynihan, Daniel (Eds) **Ethnicity: Theory and Experience,** (Harvard University Press, Cambridge Ma.,1975).

An outstanding and seminal collection of essays which focus on ethnicity in the United States and in other nations. Martin Kilson, Milton Gordon, Talcott Parsons, and Andrew Greeley are among the contributors.

Banks, James A. **Multiethnic Education: Theory and Practice** (Allyn and Bacon, Boston, 1981).

This book discusses the historical, conceptual, and philosophical issues in the fields of multiethnic and mutlicultural education. It also includes a chapter on teaching strategies for multiethnic education.

Appleton, Nicolas. **Cultural Pluralism in Education; Theoretical Foundations,** (Longman, New York, 1983).

This book includes a thoughtful theoretical analysis of the concept of cultural pluralism and its implications for schooling.

Baker, Gwendlyn C. **Planning and Organizing for Multicultural Instruction.** (Addison-Wesley, Reading, M.A; 1983).

This introductory book is designed to introduce educators to multicultural eduation. Topics include planning for instruction, organizing for instruction, and instruction.

Banks, James. A. **Teaching Strategies for Ethnic Studies,** (Third Edition, Boston, Allyn & Bacon, 1983).

Teaching strategies, with grade levels designated, and bibliographies for teachers and students are key features of this book. An historical overview and a chronology of key events for all major ethnic groups in the United States are also included.

Garcia, Ricardo L. **Teaching in a Pluralistic Society: Concepts, Models, Strategies.** (New York, Harper and Row, 1982).

This introductory book on ethnic divesity and American education discusses a range of topics, including schools and their communities, and various models and strategies related to teaching cultural diversity.

Longsteer, Wilma. **Aspects of Ethnicity: Understanding Differences in Pluralistic Classrooms.** (Teachers College press, New York, 1978).

The author presents an interesting definition of ethnicity and describes a process that teachers can use to study ethnic behaviour in their own classrooms.

Schniedewind,N. & Davidson, E **Open Mind to Equality: A Sourcebook of Learning Activities to Promote Race, Sex, Class and Age Equity.** (Prentice-Hall, Englewood Cliffs, N.J., 1983).

This book conceptualizes multicultural education broadly and includes specific activities and lessons for use by teachers.

Chapter 5 (Multicultural Education and Society in Canada and Yugoslavia)

There is a considerable amount of information on ethnic nature of the Canadian population. Many articles draw from the **Report of the Royal Commission on Bilingualism and Biculturalism** (Queen's Printer, Ottawa, 1974) and the **1971 Census of Canada,** and its supplementary bulletins - **Population Ethnic Groups, Immigration and Population Statistics,** etc. Compared to many other countries, Canadian information is exceptionally detailed.

During the 1950's and 1960's there was much debate on the 'French versus English language' question. Two standard works on this are:-

Wade, M. (Ed)   **Canadian Dualism: Studies of French-English Relations** (Toronto and Quebec City, University of Toronto Press and Laval University Press, 1960).

Cook, R.   **Canada and the French Canadian Question** (Macmillan, Toronto, 1966).

During the 1970's it was felt that the French/English cultural debate overshadowed the interests of other minorities, and the whole question of multiculturalism began to receive wider attention. Some general texts, and others dealing with the interests of specific minorities are:-

Porter, J. **The Vertical Mosaic** (University of Toronto Press, 1965).

Davis, M & Kranter, J.R. **The Other Canadians; Profiles of Six Minorities** (Methuen, Toronto, 1971).

Sheefe, N.(Ed) **Many Cultures, Many Heritages** (McGraw-Hill Ryerson, Toronto, 1975)

Migus, P.H.(Ed)**Sounds Canadian; Language and Cultures in a Multi-Ethnic Society** (Peter Martin Associates, Toronto, 1975).

Palmer,H.(Ed) **Immigration and the Rise of Multiculturalism** (Copp Clark, Toronto, 1975).

Burnet,J & Palmer, H. (Eds.) **Generations: A History of Canada's Peoples** (McLelland and Stewart, Toronto, 1976).

Further Reading

Radecki,H & Heydenthorn, B **A Member of a Distinguished Family; The Polish Group in Canada** (McClelland and Stewart, Toronto, 1976).

Anderson,G.M. & Higgs, D **A Future to Inherit; The Portuguese Communities in Canada** (McClelland and Stewart, Toronto, 1976).

Reid, S. (Ed) **The Scottish Tradition in Canada** (McClelland and Stewart, Toronto, 1976).

Doughty, H.A. et. al., **Canadian Studies; Culture and Country** (Wiley, Toronto, 1976).

Chinton,A. & McDonald, N. (Eds) **Canadian Schools and Canadian Identity** (Gage Educational, Toronto, 1977).

Mallea,J. **Multiculturalism and Canadian Education** (McClelland and Stewart, 1977).

Avery, D. **Dangerous Foreigners** (McClelland and Stewart, Toronto, 1979).

Reitz, Jeffrey. **The Survival of Ethnic Groups** (McGraw-Hill Ryeson, Toronto, 1980).

Anderson, Alan & Frideres, J. **Ethnicity in Canada** (Butterworth, Toronto, 1981).

Despite these, and a host of other publications, there is considerable questioning of the progress of minority rights and the impact multiculturalism has made in educational practice:-

Wilson,J. **Canada's Indians** (Minority Rights Group, London, 1977).

Linguistic Minorities and National Unity Special Number 1. **Compare** (Vol.8, No.1, 1978) Articles by Lipton and Lawson, Lupol, Macleod, Gulatson.

Young, J. C. 'Education in a Multicultural Society: What Sort of Education?' **Canadian Journal of Education** (Vol.4, No.3, 1979).

Dorotich, D.(ed) **Education and Canadian Multiculturalism: Some Problems and Solutions** (Canadian Society for the Study of Education, Yearbook 8, University of Saskatchewan, 1981).

Legendre,C. **French Canada in Crisis** (Minority Rights Group, London, 1982).

Detailed statistics on the peoples and nationalities in Yugoslavia are published in the national census data (**Federal Statistics Office Beograd, 1971 Census** and in subsequent bulletins.)

Discussion on the general background in social and political developments can be gained from:-

Harvart, Brank,**An Essay on Yugoslav Society** (International Arts and Science Press, New York, 1969.

Bicanic, Rudolph. **Economic Policy in Socialist Yugoslavia** (Cambridge University Press, 1973).

Dragic, Nada (Ed) **Nations and Nationalities of Yugoslavia** (Medjunarodna Polititca, Belgrade, 1974).

Fejto, Francois, **A History of the Peoples Democracies** (Pelican, Harmondsworth, 1974).

Ra'anan, Gabriel, D. **Yugoslavia After Tito** (Westview Press, (Boulder, Col. 1977).

Doder, Dasko. **The Yugoslavs** (Random House, New York, 1978).

Pervan, Ralph. **Tito and the Students** (University of Western Australia, 1978).

For a discussion of the Yugoslavian education system:-

Grant, Nigel **Schools, Society and Progress in Eastern Europe** (Pergamon, 1969).

O.E.C.D. **Innovation in Higher Education: Reforms in Yugoslavia** (Institute for Social Research, Paris, 1970).

Further discussion beyond the present chapter on ethnic diversity in Yugoslavia:

Dorotich, Daniel, "Ethnic Diversity and National Unity in Yugoslav Education: The Socialist Autonomous Province of Vojvodina" **Compare** (Vol8, No1, 1978)

Dorotich, Daniel, Education for Ethnic Minorities in Yugoslavia, with Some Indications for Canada **Second Banff Conference on Control and Eastern European Studies Education Presentations** (The University of Alberta, 1978) pp.16-27.

Topoloski, Ilija, "Language Rights in Yugoslavia" **Language and Society** (No.8, 1982).

Further Reading

Specialist articles on Yugoslavian education and culture occasionally appear in **The International Review of Education, Comparative Education, Harvard Educational Review**, etc.

Chapters 6 and 7 **(The Emergence of Cultural Diversity in Australia: Community Relations and Multicultural Education in Australia.)**

If Australia has only recently turned its attention to multicultural education and the need for a major rethink of policy, the growth of investigations and publications in this field in the past ten or fifteen years indicates its increasing importance. The Australian Institute of Multicultural Affairs, established since 1981, has produced a series of summaries and reports.

Examples are:-

Evaluation of Post-Arrival Programmes and Services (Globe Press) May 1982.

Review of the On-Arrival Education Program (Riall Print) April 1981.

Review of Multicultural and Migrant Education (Riall Print) September 1980.

There are a large number of councils and pressure groups acting on behalf of ethnic minorities. Some of the more important ones dealing with educational matters include:-

Australian Ethnic Affairs Council, **Australia as Multicultural Society** (Australian Government Publishing Services, (A.G.P.S.) Canberra, 1977).

Australian Ethnic Affairs Council Committee on Multicultural Education, **Perspectives on Multicultural Education** (A.G.P.S. Canberra, 1981).

Australian Population and Immigration Council and the Australian Ethnic Affaris Council, **Multiculturalism and its implications for Immigration Policy** (A.G.P.S., Canberra, 1979).

Australian Council for Education Research **New Directions in Australian Education** (Carlton, Vic., 1976).

Commonwealth Department of Education
1) **Towards a National Language Policy** (A.G.P.S. Canberra 1982).
2) **Pre-School Education** (A Review of Policy, Practice and Research (A.G.P.S., Canberra, 1981).

Commonwealth Education Portfolio, **Discussion Paper on Education in a Multicultural Australia** (A.G.P.S. Canberra, 1978).
    The media and arts have been a growing source of awareness of ethnic diversity, which the educational services have sought to use in schools and teacher training. Some resource directories are:-

Education Department of Tasmania **Resources for Multicultural Education. A Directory for Tasmanian Schools** (Tasmania, May 1979).

Stanelis, N.K. **Resources for Schools: Multicultural Education** (Schools Commission, Canberra, 1978).

Australia Council, **Ethnic Arts Directory** (Community Arts Board, North Sydney, 1980).

Special Broadcasting Service, **Ethnic Broadcasting in Australia 1979** (Sydney, 1979).

Department of Immigration and Ethnic Affairs, **Directory of Ethnic and National Group Organisations in Australia 1978-79** (A.G.P.S., Canberra, 1979).

    The historical and cultural traditions of Australia's Aboriginals has been extensively, if not always accurately documented. In addition to earlier references (in particular, K. Gilbert, **Living Black** and M. Hart, **Kulila - an Aboriginal education)** some additional historico-geographical and literary texts are given below:-

Blainey, G. **Triumph of the Nomads** (Macmillan, Sydney, 1975)

Clark, M. **A Short History of Australia** (American Library, New York, 1963).

Crowley, F.(Ed.) **A New History of Australia** (Heinemann, Melbourne, 1974).

Shaw, A.G.L. **The Story of Australia** (Faber & Faber, London, 1966).

Herbert X. **Poor Fellow My Country** (Collins, Sydney, 1975).

Herbert X. **Capricornia** (Angus & Robertson, Sydney, 1975).

Lawrence, D.H. **Kangaroo** (Heinemann, London, 1923).

Pritchard, K.A. **Coonardoo** (Halstead Press, Sydney, 1943)

Further Reading

White, P. **Voss** (Eyre & Spottiswoode, London, 1957).

Further readings on education in Australia that consider the impact of multiculturalism:-

Barcan, A.R. **A History of Australian Education** (Oxford University Press, Melbourne, 1980)

Bowen, M. (Ed.) **Australia 2000: The Ethnic Impact** (University of New England, Armidale, 1977).

de Lacey, P. & Poole, M.E. **Mosaic or Melting Pot** (Harcourt, Brace, Jovanovich, Sydney, 1979)

D'Crux, J.V. & Sheehan, P.J. **The Renewal of Australian Schools: Perspectives on Educational Planning.** (Australian Council for Educational Research, Victoria, 1978, 2nd ed.)

D'Urso, S. & Smith, R.A. (Eds.) **Changes, Issues and Prospects in Australian Education** (University of Queensland Press, St. Lucia, 1978).

Marjoribanks, K. **Ethnic Families and Children's Achievements** (George Allen & Unwin, Sydney, 1980)

Poole, M.E. et al. (eds.) **Before School Begins; Readings on the pre-school years in Australia** (Wiley, Sydney, 1975).

Chapter 8 **(Education and the Multicultural Caribbean)**

There is no single text that deals directly with the issue of multicultural education in the Caribbean. For general and historical discussion the following are useful:-

Lowenthal, D. **West Indian Societies** (Oxford Univ. Press, 1972).

Gordon, S.C. **Reports and Repercussions in West Indian Education 1835-1933** (Guia, 1968).

Gordon, S.C. **A Century of West Indian Education** (Longman, 1963).

Williams, E. **Education in the British West Indies** (University Place Bookshop, N.Y., 1951).

Books dealing with contemporary developments include:-

Murray, R.N. & Gbedemah, G.L. **Foundations of Education in the Caribbean** (Hodder & Stoughton, 1983).

Further Reading

D'Ogley,V. & Murray, T. (Eds.) **Development and Disillusionment in Third World Education; with emphasis on Jamaica** (Ontario Institute for Studies in Education, 1979).

Carrington, L. **Education and Development in the English Speaking Caribbean: A Contemporary Survey** (UNDP/UNESCO/ECLA, 1978).

Figueroa, P.M.E. & Persand G. (Eds.) **Sociology of Education: a Caribbean Reader** (Oxford Univ. Press, 1976).

Journals that include relevant articles on multicultural education in the Caribbean are, amongst others, **Social and Economic Studies, Caribbean Studies, Caribbean Journal of Education, Caribbean Educational Bulletin and Journal of Caribbean Studies.** Particular articles directly apposite to chapter 8 are:-

Parker R.S. "Small Island States", in Thompson A.R. (ed) **In-Service Education of Teachers in the Commonwealth,** (Commonwealth Secretariat, 1982), pp. 144-187.

Brock C. "The Legacy of Colonialisation in West Indian Education" in Watson J.K.P. (ed.) **Education in the Third World** (Croom Helm, 1982) pp. 119-140.

Brock C. "Problems of Education and Human Ecology in Small Tropical Island Nations" in Brock C. and Ryba R. (eds.) **A Volume of Essays of Elizabeth Halsall: Aspects of Education No.22** (University of Hull Institute of Education, 1980), pp.71-83.

Cross M. "Race, Class and Education" in Cross M. **Urbanisation and Urban Growth in the Caribbean,** (Cambridge University Press, 1979) pp. 102-128.

Cross M. "Education and Job Opportunities" in Moss R. (Ed.) **The Stability of the Caribbean,** (Institute for the Study of Conflict, 1973), pp. 57-76.

Camacho A. "Education and the Educational Opportunity" in Cross M. (Ed.) **West Indian Social Problems,** (Columbus, 1970) pp. 99-117.

Farrell J. "Education and Pluralism in Selected Caribbean Societies" in **Comparative Education Review,** Vol. 11, No. 2, 1967.

Chapter 9 **(Cultural Pluralism in the ASEAN Countries of South-East Asia)**

The chapter contains extensive references, but some additional reading on the region, and national studies are given below.

Regional Studies

Miller, T. (Ed) **Education in South-East Asia** (Ian Novale, Sydney, 1968).

Wong, Hoy Kee (Ed.) **Teacher Education in ASEAN** (Heinemann, Hong Kong, 1976).

Watson, J. **'The Education of Racial Minorities in South-East Asia, with Special Reference to the Chinese'**, (Compare Vol. 6, 2, 1976) pp. 14-21.

Chai, Hon-Chan. **Education and National Building in Plural Societies** (Australian National University, Development Centre Monograph No.6, Canberra, 1977).

Posthelthwaite, T.N. and Thomas, R.M. **Schooling in the ASEAN Region** (Pergamon Press, Oxford, 1980).

Watson, K. **Education in the Third World** (Croom Helm, London, 1980).

National Studies - Indonesia

Beeby, C.E. **Assessment of Indonesian Education: A Guide in Planning** (New Zealand Council for Educational Research and Oxford University Press, Wellington N.Z., 1979).

Malaysia

Enroe, C. **Multiethnic Politics: The Case of Malaysia** (University of California, Berkeley, 1970).

Wong, Hoy Kee, F. and Traing Hong E.E. **Education in Malaysia** (Heinemann, Hong Kong 1971).

Lok Fook Seng, P. **Seeds of Separation - Educational Policy in Malaysia 1874-1940** (Oxford University Press, Kuala Lumpur, 1975).

Watson, K. 'Cultural Pluralism, Nation Building and Educational Policies in Peninsula Malaysia', **Journal of Multilingual and Multicultural Development** (Vol.1, 2, 1980) pp. 155-174.

The Philippines

Shahani, L.R. **The Philippines: The Land and People** (National Bookstore Press, Manila, 1970).

Cheetham, J. and Hawkins, E. **The Philippines: Priorities and Prospects for Development** (IBRD and World Bank, Washington, 1976).

Singapore

Doraisaung, T.R. (ed.) **150 Years of Education in Singapore** (Teachers Training College Singapore, 1969).

Wong R.H.K. **Educational Innovation in Singapore** (UNESCO, Paris, 1974).

Skolvik, R.L. **The Nationwide Learning System of Singapore** (Institute of South-East Asian Studies, Singapore, 1976).

Thailand

Watson, K. **Educational Development in Thailand** (Heinemann, Hong Kong, 1980).

Chapter 10 (Education, National Unity and Cultural Pluralism in Nigeria).

The largest and one of the most complex of recently independent African States, Nigeria is by itself a major example of multiculturalism. It is also, by African standards, wealthy and has invested greatly in education as an agent of both unity and development. This chapter, and the suggested reading below, can only indicate briefly the massive literature, indigenous and international, which has been written.

Basic reading:-

Arnold, G. **Modern Nigeria,** (Longman, London 1977).

Nigeria, Federal Republic, **National Policy on Education,** (Federal Ministry of Information, Lagos, 1977).

Crowder, M. **The Story of Nigeria,** (Faber, London, 1978).

Harber, C. 'Schoolchildren and Political Socialisation in Kano State, Northern Nigeria',**Development Research Digest,** No.4 1980.

Further Reading

Blakemore, K. and Cooksey, B. **A Sociology of Education for Africa,** (George Allen and Unwin, London, 1981).

Bray, M. **Universal Education in Nigeria: A Study of Kano State,** (Routledge & Kegan Paul, London, 1981).

Further reading:

Peshkin, A. 'Education and National Integration in Nigeria', **Journal of Modern African Studies,** (Vol.5, No.3, 1967).

Abernethy, D.B. **The Political Dilemma of Popular Education,** (Stanford University Press, 1969).

Peshkin, A. 'Limitations of Education for Planned Political Mobilization: Reflections on Nigeria', **Comparative Education,** (Vol.8, No.2, 1972).

Adesina, S. **Planning and Educational Development in Nigeria,** (Educational Industries, Lagos, 1977).

Foster, P.J. **'Education and Social Differentiation in Africa: What we think we know and what we ought to know'** (IIEP, Paris, 1978).

Marenin, O. 'National Service and National Consciousness in Nigeria', **Journal of Modern African Studies,** (Vol.17, No.4, 1979).

Nigeria, Federal Republic, 'Implementation Committee for the National Policy on Education: Blueprint'; Onabamiro Report, (Federal Ministry of Education, Lagos, 1979).

Taiwo, C.O. **The Nigerian Education System: Past, Present and Future,** (Thomas Nelson, Ikeja, 1980).

Ozigi, Albert and Ocho, L. **Education in Northern Nigeria,** (George Allen & Unwin, London, 1981).

Harber, C. 'Education and Political Socialisation in Nigeria: The Impact of the Federal Government Colleges' **International Journal of Educational Development,** (Vol.2, No.3, 1983).

Chapter 11 **(Comparative Analysis and its Application to Multicultural Education)**

One of the best books on comparative methodology is that by Brian Holmes entitled **Comparative Education: Some Considerations of Method** (Allen & Unwin, London, 1981). This book contains an excellent bibliographic section of up to date sources.

Another excellent bibliographic section is given in Philip E. Jones **Comparative Education: Purpose and Method,** (University of Queensland Press, 1971). This is a most comprehensive listing and classification of all published work on the subject up to 1970.

Race, Migration and Schooling edited by John Tierney, (Holt, Rinehart and Winston, 1982), also contains a very comprehensive list of sources, including a very useful list of organisations and groups concerned with multiculturalism in England.

Graham Allinson in **Essence of Decision: Explaining the Cuban Missile Crisis,** (Little, Brown & Company, Boston, 1971), provides an analysis of decision making processes of national governments using three different frames of reference to study the Cuban missile crisis. His framework distinguishes what he calls a basic unit of analysis, organising concepts, dominant inference patterns and general propositions. These provide the fine tools needed to disect governmental policy decisions in, and between, multicultural societies.

Recent books and pamphlets on education in multicultural societies include the following which are of particular importance to the person interested in comparative studies:

Education for a Multicultural Society, (The Schools Council, London, 1981) includes sections on the way young school children can study other cultures, the Indian sub-continent, Africa and the Caribbean in particular. It also contains a useful section on American practices in the field of cross curriculum policies in multicultural societies.

Education of Children from Ethnic Minority Groups, (The Schools Council Pamphlet 19, London, 1982), presents the evidence from the Schools Council to the Committee of Enquiry established by the Secretary of STate in 1979. In it the Council stresses the role of teachers and the notion of cultural pluralism in the world today.

Policy and Practice in the Multiracial City, by Ken Young and Naomi Connelly (The Policy Studies Institute, London, 1981), offers a series of strategies for action by local government agencies on the question of opportunity for multicultural groups. Essentially a locally based response to multicultural problems in England, this study can stimulate ideas in other societies which face related problems over opportunity for policy development.

Multi-Cultural Education: Views from the Classroom, compiled by John Twitchin and Clare Demuth, (British Broadcasting Corporation, 1981), is a book to accompany a series of films on such subjects as attitudes, language use and specific curriculum areas for primary and secondary school teachers. From the comparative point of view the section on Ourselves and Others in World Perspective provides some useful case studies.

Doing Good by Doing Little: Race and Schooling in Britain, by David L. Kirp (University of California Press, 1979), offers a number of valuable perspectives on the 'British dilemma' of how to deal with racial minorities in schools in England.

West Indian Children in our Schools is the Interim Report of the Committee of Inquiry into the education of children from ethnic minority groups under the chairmanship of Anthony Rampton, H.M.S.O. June 1981, Cmnd 8273. It concerns all teachers and is essential reading for those who would wish to see greater attention paid to programmes of action for underachievers in school.

JAMES A. BANKS is Professor of Education at the University of Washington (Seattle, USA) and Chairman of Curriculum and Instruction. Professor Banks is the Immediate Past President of the National Council for the Social Studies. He is a specialist in social studies education and multiethnic education and has lectured on these topics throughout the United States and in the Netherlands, the United Kingdom, Guam, Canada, and the Virgin Islands. His books include **Teaching Strategies for the Social Studies, Teaching Strategies for Ethnic Studies, Teaching Ethnic Studies: Concepts and Strategies,** and **Multiethnic Education: Theory and Practice.** Professor Banks currently holds a National Fellowship from the Kellogg Foundation to study ethnicity and educational policy.

MARK BRAY graduated in Economics at the University of Newcastle-upon-Tyne. He subsequently took a Masters degree in African Studies and a doctorate in Education at the University of Edinburgh. Between 1970-78 he worked in Kenya and Benue and Kano States in Nigeria and carried out research on the planning and implementation of universal primary education in Nigeria, with particular emphasis on developments in Kano State. After a lecturing post at the Centre of African Studies, University of Edinburgh he moved to the University of Papua New Guinea where he is currently lecturer in Educational Planning. His publications include **Universal Education in Nigeria: A Study of Kano State** by Routledge and Kegan Paul in 1981.

COLIN BROCK is a graduate of the Universities of Durham and Reading where he studied geography and comparative education respectively. Following a decade of secondary school teaching, he lectured at Bulmershe College of Education, and then spent a number of years working in Caribbean countries with the Ministry of Overseas Development. His interest in West Indian education continued whilst attached to the Overseas Education Unit at the University of Leeds, and additionally he gained familiarity with the problems of small Commonwealth countries, obtaining first hand experience of the island systems in the Indian and Pacific Ocean areas. He is the author of several books and articles on comparative and multicultural education. Since 1977 he has been lecturer and Chairman of the International Education Unit at the University of Hull and is currently vice-chairman of the British Comparative Education Society.

285

TREVOR CORNER graduated from Leeds University and lectured in physics at Leeds and Carnegie College of Education. Between 1968-74 he taught in secondary schools in London and worked on teacher education courses with the Nuffield Foundation, and Goldsmith and Chelsea Colleges in the University of London. He moved to Edinburgh to work in comparative and adult education where he lectured in comparative education in the university and Moray House College of Education. He has visited and lectured in a number of European countries including France, Denmark and Hungary, as well asteachers' courses in the U.S.A. His research publications include school and family liaison in E.E.C. countries and minority schools in Ireland and Scotland. Since 1979 he has been lecturer in Education at the University of Glasgow.

ALAN DAVIES is senior lecturer in the Department of Linguistics, University of Edinburgh, and director of the Institute for Applied Language Studies, and has taught applied linguistics at the postgraduate level for many years. Having special interests in the interaction between language and culture he recently edited the special issue of the 'Journal of Multilingual and Multicultural Development' (3/3 1982) on 'Language and Ethnicity' which contains papers from the seminar on that topic which he helped organise at the London Institute of Education in January 1982. He has been chairman of the British Association of Applied Linguistics and secretary general of the International Association of Applied Linguistics. Through work with international organisations he has travelled widely and lived and worked in Kenya and Nepal. Dr. Davies is currently president of TESOL in Scotland.

DAN DOROTICH is a Professor of Education at the University of Saskatchewan. Born in Yugoslavia, he received his post-secondary education in France and Canada. He holds a degree in Theology from France, a B.A. in Arts from Sir George Williams College, as well as an M.A. in Education and a Ph.D. in History from McGill University. Professor Dorotich has taught French in the public schools of Quebec, Russian and Cultural History of the Slavs at the university of British Columbia, and Educational Foundations and Comparative and International Education at the University of Saskatchewan. He has travelled extensively throughout North America and Europe, including Eastern Europe and the U.S.S.R. As a Canada Council Fellow, he spent two sabbatical years in Yugoslavia, doing research on the education of ethnic minorities.

NIGEL GRANT graduated in English at the University of Glagow, returning later to take the M.Ed.and Ph.D.degrees. After military service, he taught in Glasgow secondary schools, was lecturer in Jordanhill College of Education for five years, and moved in 1965 to the University of Edinburgh as lecturer (subsequently reader) in educational studies; he returned to Glasgow as Professor of Education in 1978. He has served as chairman of the British Comparative Education Society, of the Scottish Educational Research Association and the Scottish Universities Council for Studies in Education, and as editor of **Comparative Education.** He has taught and conducted research in the Scottish Gaidhealtachd, Wales, Ireland, England, Canada, the United States, Egypt, Scandinavia, Germany, Italy, the Soviet Union and all the countries of Eastern Europe (except Albania.) Publications cover a range of comparative and multicultural topics, and include **Soviet Education, Society, Schools and Progress in Eastern Europe, A Mythology of British Education** and **Patterns of Education in the British Isles** (both with R. E. Bell), **Education and Nation-Building in the Third World** (with Lowe and Williams) and, most recently, **The Crisis of Scottish Education.** He is currently working on several books in comparative and multicultural topics, with particular reference to small nations and national and linguistic minorities.

CHARLES HOY obtained his first degree in Mathematics and Physics at London University in 1963. He then taught in a number of secondary schools in England and Canada before moving into teacher education; first in Hertfordshire and later in North Staffordshire, where he became coordinator for advanced courses of teacher education. He has graduate qualifications in educational management from the University of British Columbia, and also holds the M.A. and Ph.D. in comparative education from the University of London Institute of Education. His research focussed on the management of multicultural education. He has held appointments at the University of Manchester and Ball State University in Indiana, and has lectured and published on multicultural education. Since 1983 Dr. Hoy has been the education officer responsible for community and continuing education in the London Borough of Barking and Dagenham.

DUDLEY HICK obtained an M.A. in modern languages at the University of Oxford, a Masters degree in the History of Education and Curriculum Studies and a doctorate in Comparative Education at the University of Sydney. He has taught modern languages in schools in England, Germany and Australia and has published various articles and papers in comparative education and modern language teaching. Recent publications include a chapter on Education in Vietnam in **Education in the Third World** (Ed. K. Watson), Croom Helm 1982, and he is currently editing a book on "Schooling in Asia" to be published during 1984. He was President of the Australian Comparative and International Education Society in 1979 and is currently senior lecturer in Education atthe University of Sydney.

JAMES LYNCH has worked in a number of institutes of higher education in the United Kingdom, Australia and North America. He has published widely in British and international journals and he is author and co-author of several books, some of which have been translated into several languages; he has undertaken consultancy work for national and international organisations including UNESCO. His most recent publications in the field of Multi-Cultural Education are **Teaching in the Multi-Cultural School,** Ward Lock, 1981, and **The Multi-Cultural Curriculum,** Batsford, 1983. He is currently Professor and Dean of the Faculty of Education, Sunderland Polytechnic.

WERNER STEPHAN received most of his education in Berlin, Germany. He taught at a high school in East Berlin and later at elementary and high schools in West Germany. After immigrating to Canada, he obtained his M.A. in Comparative Education from the University of Calgary and his Ph.D. in History of Education and Comparative Education from the University of Alberta. He has published articles on multi-cultural education in German educational journals and recently chaired the panel on multicultural education at the Second World Congress on Soviet and East European Studies in Garmisch, Germany. At the present time, he is an Associate Professor in the Department of Educational Foundations, University of Saskatchewan.

KEITH WATSON was educated at Edinburgh, the London University Institute of Education and Reading University, where he completed a doctoral thesis on Educational Development in South-East Asia. He worked for the British Council in Poland, Bangladesh, Thailand and, briefly, Iran. During the mid 1960's he helped to establish a department for teaching English to immigrants at a school in Leeds, when he developed an active interest in multi-cultural education. He has written widely in the multicultural and comparative fields of education; his books include **Educational Development in Thailand, Education in the Third World,** and **Teachers and Community Schools as Agents for Rural Development.** Dr. Watson is currently chairman of the British Comparative Education Society, and (since 1975) Lecturer in Education at Reading University.